Stumbling Over the Cross

LLOYD JOHN OGILVIE INSTITUTE OF PREACHING SERIES

SERIES EDITORS:

Mark Labberton
Clayton J. Schmit

The vision of the Lloyd John Ogilvie Institute of Preaching is to proclaim Jesus Christ and to catalyze a movement of empowered, wise preachers who seek justice, love mercy, and walk humbly with God, leading others to join in God's mission in the world. The books in this series are selected to contribute to the development of such wise and humble preachers. The authors represent both scholars of preaching as well as pastors and preachers whose experiences and insights can contribute to passionate and excellent preaching.

OTHER VOLUMES IN THIS SERIES:

The Eloquence of Grace: Joseph Sittler and the Preaching Life edited by James M. Childs Jr. and Richard Lischer

The Preacher as Liturgical Artist: Metaphor, Identity, and the Vicarious Humanity of Christ by Trygve David Johnson

Ordinary Preacher, Extraordinary Gospel: A Daily Guide for Wise, Empowered Preachers by Chris Neufeld-Erdman

Blessed and Beautiful: Multiethnic Churches and the Preaching that Sustains Them by Lisa Washington Lamb

Bringing Home the Message: How Community Can Multiply the Power of the Preached Word by Robert K. Perkins

Decolonizing Preaching: The Pulpit as Postcolonial Space by Sarah A. N. Travis

Youthful Preaching: Strengthening the Relationship between Youth, Adults, and Preaching by Richard Voelz

Stumbling Over the Cross

Preaching the Cross and Resurrection Today

Joni S. Sancken

FOREWORD BY
Paul Scott Wilson

CASCADE *Books* · Eugene, Oregon

STUMBLING OVER THE CROSS
Preaching the Cross and Resurrection Today

Lloyd John Ogilvie Institute of Preaching Series 8

Cascade Books
An Imprint of Wipf and Stock Publishers
199 W. 8th Ave., Suite 3
Eugene, OR 97401

www.wipfandstock.com

ISBN 13: 978-1-62564-786-3

Cataloging-in-Publication data:

Sancken, Joni S.

Stumbling over the cross : preaching the cross and resurrection today / Joni S. Sancken.

xxvi + 208 p. ; 23 cm. —Includes bibliographical references.

Lloyd John Ogilvie Institute of Preaching Series 8

ISBN 13: 978-1-62564-786-3

1. Jesus Christ—Passion. 2. Jesus Christ—Resurrection. 3. Cross. 4. Preaching. I. Title. II. Series.

BV4211.3 S17 2016

Manufactured in the U.S.A.

For my husband Steve who has modeled Christ's self-giving love in the congregations he has served and in our marriage.

Contents

Acknowledgments

I would like to thank the many people who have supported this venture. Paul Wilson's guidance, mentoring, and suggestions have helped as this project evolved from my doctoral program to the present. Tom Long, Mark Thiessen Nation, and Dick Eslinger have been significant conversation partners at different stages in the project which is stronger for their comments and encouragement. My Deans at Eastern Mennonite Seminary and United Theological Seminary supported my writing by allocating hours and guarding my schedule. My faculty colleagues at United Theological Seminary engaged in critical discussion of chapter 4 and I learned so much from their questions and expertise as I navigated the terrain of interfaith relationships in light of the cross. Students at Candler School of Theology, Eastern Mennonite Seminary, and United Theological Seminary have engaged with much of this material when it was in lecture form and have eagerly experimented with techniques discussed in chapter 5 in their own sermons. Chad Clark's work formatting, proofreading, and conversing about the manuscript has been invaluable. I would not have been able to make my deadline without Chad's help. Finally, my husband Steve and daughter Maggie have patiently supported my writing schedule. Steve, in particular, served as the primary childcare provider in our household for a number of months to facilitate my work on this project for which I am grateful!

Foreword

Perhaps at no time since the Reformation has the church experienced such upheaval and transition as at present. In North America, many churches languish with aging congregants and buildings that are often a burden. Culture itself is changing, truth is challenged (your truth may not be someone else's), and goodness is perceived as relative (what is good for some people might not be good for others). Many people today say they are spiritual but not religious, by which they mean they are open to some notions of the divine but they are uninterested in organized religion. This is not an easy time to be in ordered ministry. Churches try new kinds of music, new technology, and new ways of worshiping to see if that can make a difference. If in the process the church loses its identity and what makes its message distinctive, the path will be more certain to church closures.

Dis-ease about Christian faith is prevalent even within the church. A poll in 2002 indicated that one third of the ten thousand clergy in the Church of England did not believe in the physical resurrection.[1] Another poll in 2014 indicates that 2 percent of Church of England clergy do not believe in God and that 16 percent are agnostic.[2] John Shelby Spong, former Episcopal Bishop of Newark, New Jersey, has recently written an open letter to my own denomination critiquing its decision to challenge Gretta Vosper, a minister who has veered from her ordination vows and now describes herself as "an atheist minister." Her small congregation no longer observes Christmas and Easter and does not pray but rather

1. Petre, "One third."
2. Wynne-Jones, "Two percent."

expresses wishes or affirmations. Spong calls orthodox belief "medieval irrelevance" and writes, "there is no need for a deity, defined theistically, who mounts the rescue operation. So the whole way we tell the Jesus story has got to be rethought and reformulated."[3]

Spong's vision for the future of the church is not everyone's. Many preachers, like Professor Joni Sancken, feel no contradiction between affirming biblical truths and critically engaging faith. Rather than throw out the old, she looks at it anew and discovers a possible route to rejuvenating the church with greater attention to the resurrection.

One of my professors in seminary advocated that preachers rework their Christology each year during Lent. It was wise advice. In rethinking how we speak of Christ, we rethink matters that can help renew our preaching on every Sunday of the year. Sundays are Sabbath for Christians because that is the day of the resurrection, and the church has a long tradition of thinking of Sundays as "little Easters." The cross and resurrection are relevant for our preaching all year, indeed, for all ministry. There may be no better place than the larger Christ event for preachers to find renewed creativity and faith, and the transformational payoff can be large.

However, we speak of matters central to the faith that can be very difficult to wade through. For the sake of one's congregation, a preacher does not want to get bogged down in all the theological complexities of issues around the cross and resurrection—that is why a book such as this one can be such a wonderful resource for preachers. Joni Sancken leads preachers through theological terrain with clarity, insight, and wisdom, reviewing some of the most recent scholarly literature on Christology, identifying the resistance some preachers have to preaching the resurrection, and pointing to fresh opportunities that await preachers if they do. She envisions a hopeful future for a church that proclaims the places of Good Friday and Easter in our contemporary world. Christian identity and the transformative nature of preaching are key to this.

In some ways it is surprising that this volume is needed as much as it is. It might seem that the cross and resurrection are so much a part of Christian understanding that they do not require special focus brought to them here. They are present as concepts and symbols, in the hymns, prayers, sermons, art work, and architecture of worship spaces. In baptism, "we have been buried with him . . . into death, so that, just as Christ

3. Spong, "An Open Letter."

was raised from the dead . . . we too might walk in newness of life." (Rom 6:4).[4] In the Eucharist, the bread is Christ's body "broken for you" (1 Cor 11:22 var.), the wine is "the new covenant in his blood" (11:25), and the future is already present. Preachers are acutely aware of the emphatic claims to the resurrection made by biblical witnesses, of its centrality in the New Testament, and of its importance in communicating faith.

Yet preachers are also aware that accounts of the resurrection are not always straightforward; they may raise as many questions as they answer, as in the disciples not recognizing Jesus on the Road to Emmaus and his sudden disappearance at the meal (Luke 24:13–35). For all of their rich-ness, these accounts will not satisfy those people who feel a choice must be made between science and faith or who deny that both involve reason and revealed knowledge. Arguably the task of preaching is not to prove the resurrection but to be faithful to scriptural testimony, and to leave the final act of persuasion to the Holy Spirit. The primary task of preaching is also not to communicate information, though good teaching is certainly an essential element. The task can be to preach people into a relationship with the living God such that their reliance, trust, and hope rest not on themselves and their own resources, but in the One who saves.

If the ambiguity and poetry of some of the biblical accounts of the resurrection present one set of problems, theories of atonement pose another. Rooted in the Bible, they try to explain, for instance, Christ's death as part of God's plan to restore humanity to be "at one" with God, from whom humans were separated in original sin. In Christ humanity is redeemed from sin and reconciled with God. These theories are rooted in various cultural-historical understandings of sacrifice, debt, ransom, spiritual warfare, or moral development, some of which are not common today. Scholars are divided as to whether these theories of atonement at times conflict with each other. None of the atonement theories is fully adequate on its own to capture the ways in which the Bible speaks of the resurrection, yet each theory offers rich insights, and Christians need a range of differing understandings for greatest clarity and insight.

Preaching the cross and resurrection is problematic. The tempta-tion may be to avoid troubling the waters. Do not raise issues that may cause unnecessary confusion, controversy, or dissent in the congrega-tion. It may seem safer simply to assume the resurrection, rather than speak directly of it. Following this line of thinking, one might preach the

---

4. Bible quotations are NRSV unless indicated otherwise.

resurrection when necessary, like at Easter, when it is admittedly hard to avoid, or at a funeral, when people may be more open to the radical hope it offers. Another tempting strategy might be to avoid the specificity of the Bible. Sensing, as Paul did, that the cross might sound like "foolishness" to some and be a "stumbling block" to others (1 Cor 1:18, 23), one might decide to omit whatever might give offence. Focus instead on resurrection in broad ways, as generic belief in an afterlife, or as what automatically follows this life like the natural cycle of spring. A further strategy can be to treat the biblical accounts as mere metaphor not based in fact, good stories to inspire, but with as much power for transformative living as any other fictional story. None of these routes can be finally satisfying.

Belief in resurrection is not unique to Christian faith. Many people of no religion affirm it, and other religions also affirm it. The Old Testament makes several references, notably: "For I know that my Redeemer lives, and that at the last he will stand upon the earth, after my skin has thus been destroyed, then in my flesh I shall see God" (Job 19:25); "Your dead shall live, their corpses shall rise" (Isa 26:19); the Valley of Dry Bones (Ezek 37); and "Many of those who sleep in the dust of the earth shall awake, some to everlasting life . . ." (Dan 12:2). In each of these it is clear that resurrection is from death, it is not some form of resuscitation from near death, nor is it limited to individuals, nor is it generalized to include all. Jewish understandings were linked to the restoration and justification of Israel. Luke tells us that the Pharisees believe in resurrection while the Sadducees do not (Acts 23:8; see also Matt 22:23). For Muslims, the coming of a Day of Resurrection and Final Judgment is a key belief, mentioned in many places in the Qur'an, for example, "I call to witness the Resurrection Day" (75:1), also known as the Day of Decision (77:38), the Day of Sorting Out (77:134), and other aliases.

Resurrection is nonetheless distinctive in Christian understanding because of its inseparable connection with Jesus Christ. Resurrection is located in the future, after this life, as part of God's final judgment and renewal of creation according to God's numerous promises in scripture to make right what is wrong. Yet resurrection is also located in the past, in the Easter event, and in the present, in as much as Christians participate in new life now through membership in the church, the Body of Christ. Central to all of this is the claim that Jesus Christ is alive now, he is risen from the dead, and in himself he is "the resurrection and the life" (John 11:25). Belief in him is all that is needed to participate in his resurrection (11:26). Resurrection is most commonly understood in individual ways, yet communal understandings are also implied in the notion of the church as Israel, the object of God's redemptive actions, and in Paul's "one has died for all, therefore all have died. . . . So if anyone is in Christ there is a new creation: everything old has passed away; see everything has become new!" (2 Cor 5:14, 17). The entirety of the gospel accounts is written in light of Jesus' resurrection and everything moves to it. For Paul, resurrection is the heart of both preaching and faith, "if Christ has not been raised, then our proclamation has been in vain and your faith has been in vain" (1 Cor 15:14). Rather than avoid the offence that some people find in linking Jesus' crucifixion with resurrection, Paul chose to proclaim it, that the power of gospel on its own might be known. (1:18–25; 2:3–5.)

Other less obvious barriers exist to preaching the cross and resurrection. Here we will name three: current understandings of a biblical "text," lack of clarity about what is "gospel," and failure to link justice and faith:

1) How preachers answer, "What is a biblical text?" has an impact on preaching cross and resurrection. The earliest model for preaching is Neh 8:8, "So they read from the book, the law of God, with interpretation. They gave the sense, so that the people understood the reading." In history at least three practices with regard to texts stand out. In the first 1500 years of the church, preachers commonly understood a text for a sermon to be a few words or a verse, but the sermon was not in any way confined to or limited by the text. The text triggered Christian teachings or doctrine found anywhere in the Bible. This approach continued to be followed by John Wesley and others well into the 1900s, and they might mention the text only in the sermon's introduction. The text was a springboard the preacher used to dive into scripture and freely link with other texts that expressed similar doctrinal teaching, perhaps in the course of developing points derived from the rhetorical division of one's topic into points. The text in this practice, in effect, was without boundary; it was the entire Bible. Whatever may be said against this approach, it helped to sustain the church as the Word of God for several centuries.

A second practice was by notable preachers in history who often were also biblical commentators, like Origin, Augustine, Luther, Calvin, and Barth. They might preach through a text, taking it word by word, or verse by verse, highlighting key thoughts, providing what historical background they had available, and apply it to their day. Both of these approaches, the entire Bible as text and word by word or verse by verse, might easily result in the sermon speaking to core matters of the faith, not least since until recently salvation was understood as the broad subject of preaching. There were always special occasion sermons that might deal with cultural issues like war and coronations, but understanding salvation and care for the soul were central.

A third practice concerning texts for preaching has developed mainly in the last century, under the influence of historical and form criticism. In this time period, the notion of a text has become, in some ways, both smaller and larger. A text is smaller if understood as a pericope or unit of scripture, that is, a proverb or a set of sayings, a parable or portion of a larger story, or a section of an argument that expresses a complete thought. The purpose of preaching has gradually shifted to be to preach a text, in part by recovering the historical context and original form of a text. Hermeneutics has become a popular term to identify the sermon process of fusing two horizons: to explore what the text meant in its own day and what it means today, hence we have current understandings of expository and exegetical sermons.

The notion of a text also became larger: it includes not only what is in the text but also what lies "behind the text" in terms of ancient culture, events, worldviews, and the like. In other words the biblical text does not actually say some things, but the context does, and the context is needed to understand the text. Text now also includes what lies in front of the text, in the responses of readers to it from their own experience, further broadening a text. The reaction to a text is part of its meaning.

The current notion of a text encourages preachers to get as close as possible to the original author or editor's intent (though scholars now question whether the author can actually be arrived at through the text). The purpose of preaching in the last several decades has tended to be to preach a text, and to stick mainly with the text at hand. If one goes beyond it, one goes to another place in the same book, or to another text prescribed in the Sunday lectionary, yet one avoids harmonizing scripture as was popular in previous eras.

For all of the value in giving preachers greater confidence in determining biblical meaning, ironically this approach to text has given preachers less confidence in proclaiming the cross. Preaching may address salvation, but it may equally address a range of legitimate subjects the Bible is seen to address. For all of the value placed on context today, biblical criticism tends to exclude or suppress part of the context of scriptural texts. Each text is part of the larger text that testifies to the gospel, with the cross and resurrection at its core, thus it is arguably part of the meaning of every text. Faith is the context. With the canonical gospels, each individual preaching text is composed in light of the book's ending that proclaims the identity of Jesus as the Christ. Each text contributes to that witness and each text legitimately can be read through the lens of the cross. However, talking about the gospel today can be seen by some scholars to be reading something into a text, or distorting a text in other ways. Even when the legitimacy of this claim is acknowledged, the gospel may still be deemed to be just one of the lenses with which a text may be read of no greater priority than any other.

2) The cross and resurrection tend to be neglected because preachers have not always been clear on their definitions of the good news, at least clear enough to establish it as a standard by which to measure their preaching. Jesus commissions the disciples to "proclaim the gospel to the whole creation" (Mark 16:15), the gospel writers each give their versions of it, arising out of the law and the prophets, and Paul speaks repeatedly in his various letters of his being sent to proclaim the gospel and that as his only message. Some preachers claim the gospel is everything we say, the whole package of worship, prayer, singing, preaching, outreach, and mission. It is the overall message of the church. In some ways this is a good approach. If the message of the church and its actions do not correspond, something is wrong. The gospel ought to be the sum total of what the church says to the world.

On the other hand to define the gospel so broadly does not put any particular responsibility on the preacher to proclaim it, especially if the text does not focus that way. According this understanding, a preacher does not need to be concerned with whether a sermon is heard or received as good news; one preaches a text and lets the pieces fall where they may. A preacher might thus defend not preaching the gospel on the basis that within the context of the entire worship hour, the gospel will be heard, or in the context of the entire years' preaching, the gospel will be made plain. Furthermore, some might say, what one person hears as judgment another might hear as hope. Whether a person hears the gospel is largely up to the Spirit, not the preacher.

Some preachers, particularly those who have emerged out of the "religious wars" in the United States, might define the gospel very narrowly as fundamentalist religion. Gospel in this sense is something negative. These preachers might be intentional in avoiding anything that smacks of narrowness, including mention of the cross and resurrection.

Yet another perspective is to define good news more precisely as the saving actions of God. The good news is this: in spite of human weaknesses and sin, God cares for all creation and intercedes in history. The gospel is found in both Testaments, and for Christians the gospel is most clearly seen in the entire Christ event: the Incarnation, his life, and ministry, his suffering and death, his rising on the third day, his ascension into heaven, his sending his Spirit as a guide and comforter, and his Second Coming to fulfill all of God's promises. In this way of thinking, the whole Bible is needed to communicate the gospel. At the heart of the good news is the cross and resurrection. The gospel is not just content or information, but power, emerging in a life accompanied by the Holy Spirit. As Paul says, "For Christ did not send me to baptize but to proclaim the gospel, and not with eloquent wisdom, so that the cross of Christ might not be emptied of its power." (1 Cor 1:17). The gospel is transforming relationship.

If the gospel is characterized by God's saving actions, then the gospel can become a standard by which we might measure individual sermons. It is reasonable to expect sermons to express good news. This expression happens by intention, not by chance for instance, when a biblical text happens to get to God's saving actions. Most biblical texts/pericopes do not contain the fullness of the gospel yet; they are essential windows to it. The gospel, with the cross and resurrection as its frequent marker, arguably needs to be one of the lenses with which preachers read scripture. In finding it they may proclaim it.

3) A temptation today is to disconnect the gospel from ethics and social justice rather than to keep them linked. The gospel does place demands upon humanity, for instance, to love God and our neighbor as ourselves, yet that is not the fullness of the gospel message. To paraphrase Emil Brunner, Christ meets us in the law but not fully as himself. It is easy for preachers simply to focus on the tasks that fall to humanity and to overlook the manner in which God empowers and equips disciples to do what is required. As Jesus says, "apart from me you can do nothing" (John 15:5). Paul says, "Not that we are competent of ourselves to claim anything as coming from us; our competence is from God who has made us competent . . ." (2 Cor 3:5–6).

When the Bible is read as the church's book, every text implies some change needed in human affairs, continuing evidence of what the early church called the moral sense of scripture that shaped much history. Every text also implies some divine empowerment to make change, continuing evidence of the ancient theological senses of scripture. The good news is not what we do but what God does. God's action empowers us by grace to meet the demands of justice, mercy, righteousness, and peace. When preaching fails to hold ethics and social justice together with the gospel, faith is emptied of power and is traded for instructions, duties, and requirements—musts, shoulds and have-tos. These sermons put a burden on listeners that they may not feel capable of carrying. Such preaching differs little from the world's demands to do better. The message of the church thus becomes largely indistinguishable from a social club like Optimist, or a political party. The demands end up being the standards by which humans measure their failure.

Sermons of this sort offer little to listeners by way of enlisting God's help. They may leave people more burdened than they were when they came to church. Jesus said, "For my yoke is easy and the burden is light" (Matt 11:30). It is light because God does and has done the heavy lifting in raising Christ from death. The question Christians may ask themselves is this: Has the world, and how we view it, fundamentally changed because of the life, death, and resurrection of Jesus Christ, or did these events make no difference?

In the final analysis, the issue of the cross and resurrection for the pulpit is the issue of God's agency. It is possible today for preachers and scholars to value the resurrection accounts for themselves without affirming God's agency. Many people define miracles as that which can be explained in no other ways but by divine action. That approach makes some sense. If doctors have done all they can for a patient deemed incurable, and the patient gets better, the healing is called a miracle. On the other hand, we live in postmodern times and almost anything can be explained in any number of ways. That definition of miracles is not adequate. Further, to restrict God's actions to extraordinary healings or whatever is to limit God. A better definition of a miracle, from a preaching standpoint might be, "any action of God." If James 1:17 is right, "Every good and perfect gift is from above" (NIV). Wherever we see goodness enacted, we see evidence of God's presence in the Holy Spirit. Wherever we see signs of the inbreaking of God's Realm, we see God's action. Our task as preachers is to point to these signs, that other people may see God. Even if we fail to witness, as John the Baptist noted, "God is able from these stones to raise children to Abraham" (Matt 3:9). One could make the case that the extent to which preachers proclaim the good news, every sermon is a miracle. Preachers tacitly acknowledge this in the acclamation of glory that sometimes follows a sermon. They say, "All thanks be to God" and blessedly not "All thanks be to me."

Miracles are possible only if God acts. From a Christian perspective the greatest miracle, apart from creation, is the new creation begun in Jesus Christ, who is raised from the dead. If Christ is alive now, we arrive at that understanding via the cross and resurrection. As Christians, that is our starting place and our ending place.

—Paul Scott Wilson

Introduction

BACKGROUND

This book has been written to help pastors, students, and Christian laity engage with the cross and resurrection and particularly to guide preachers in how to preach sermons with theological depth that explore the cross and resurrection. While in the midst of my doctoral program in Toronto, I began to be bothered by what seemed to be a striking omission in many of the sermons I was hearing and reading. Many sermons lacked theological grounding—I noticed a particular absence when it came to talking about Jesus' death and resurrection. Even during Lent and Easter, these events were not given as much emphasis as I expected. A survey of recent published sermon anthologies backed up my suspicion, as only about 35 percent of the sermons mentioned or addressed the cross in any way. My sense was that preachers weren't denying the cross, but rather the theological heart of Christianity was just assumed. These preachers wanted to preach a fresh word, the cross and resurrection felt stale, and traditional language about the cross didn't connect with modern listeners. For others, the cross and resurrection opened up thorny issues around oppression and suffering that caused them to steer away. Still others may have struggled with how to unpack the challenging doctrines of atonement and salvation in ways that felt authentic to their context that engaged the complexities of being Christian in the twenty-first century.

DEFINITIONS

The cross and resurrection are perhaps best defined in relationship to each other. Christ's death on a cross is a historical and biblical event that functions as a guiding theme for the church, anchoring belief in the resurrection and connecting God with real experiences of suffering today. While it might be tempting for preachers to reduce the cross to a symbol, sign, or theological category, Jesus' resurrection, around which Christian proclamation is based, cannot be understood apart from Jesus' death. The reality of Christ's death grounds belief in the resurrection and our future hope. Because Jesus actually died and is experienced as alive, his resurrection has world-changing power. We have confidence that in Christ we too will be raised from death. As a violent event undertaken by God alone for the salvation of humanity, the cross sounds a note of victory over the powers and principalities, and changes the key of history to that of the new eschatological age.

While I often use the shorthand "preaching the cross" to encompass the cross and resurrection, these events in the life of Christ must be held together. By specifically talking about the cross, I'm making an eschatological statement that acknowledges the promises of God that are still waiting fulfillment. When I write specifically about the cross and resurrection I am emphasizing the unity and the tension of these events. Nevertheless, there may be specific occasions or circumstances that lead preachers to place more accent on either the cross or resurrection. Placing an accent on the cross or resurrection doesn't deny the other or the essential unity of God's actions.

The accent in this book tends to fall more heavily on the cross, in part because this is where I have seen preachers struggle. However, naming signs of resurrection in our world remains one of the most challenging aspects of preaching even though it is also one of the most important. I believe that one of the insidious ways in which sin works in our world is to make us blind to signs of resurrection and God's gifts of new life around us. Part of the calling and one of the joys of preaching is the work of specifically looking for and bearing witness to God's presence among us today.

OUTLINE OF CHAPTERS

When I write about preaching the cross, or preaching the cross and resurrection, I'm encompassing a wide range of approaches which are detailed in the following chapters:

In chapter 1, I discuss some of the reasons why the cross may cause us to stumble, particularly exploring theological challenges, social challenges, and pastoral concerns around suffering. After naming some tensions that are inherent in the event of the cross and resurrection, I show how these same tensions can also provide energy to preaching. To move towards greater freedom in preaching the cross, it can be helpful to break down what happens in a sermon deeply anchored in the cross and resurrection. What does the cross do in the sermon? The following characteristics are theologically related to God's action in Christ in the cross and resurrection and can be found in sermons that deeply attend to the cross:

1. Acknowledge evil

2. Name hope

3. Maintain a sense of tension or contradiction

4. Are grounded in scripture

5. Address personal and social implications of the cross

6. Address the fullness of the Christ event.

After discussing these characteristics, I offer sermons as examples to show the characteristics at work.

In chapter 2, I turn to the challenge of diverse Christological perspectives which may also cause preachers and Christians to stumble when trying to understand Christ's saving work in the cross and resurrection. There are many nuances and ways to describe our experience of salvation brought about through Jesus' death and resurrection. The New Testament offers a range of images and approaches for preachers, including: relational, formational (involving both identity and empowerment), liberating, and healing. Preachers might want to use these images to design a sermon series on salvation or understanding the cross and resurrection, or they may use the images in their own formation as preachers to deepen biblical awareness or vary their theological language around the saving work of Christ.

These approaches are not mutually exclusive. Biblical texts may draw from multiple images and theologically the images support rather than contradict each other. Preaching through different lenses allows pastors a chance to shine light on different aspects of Christ's saving work and address different needs and views within a diverse congregation. In this chapter I have purposely avoided the use of some traditional atonement lingo with the hope that preachers might be able to explore and expand their repertoire beyond the comfortable and familiar.

In chapter 3, I turn to the negative connotations for many inside the church in the context of interfaith relationships. Historically the cross has at times been used in ways that harm or offend our Jewish and Muslim friends and colleagues. This chapter will not seek to explore the common ground between different religions, nor will it prescribe a way of preaching as interreligious dialogue. Rather, I want to continue to address our discomfort in talking about the cross and resurrection—events that lie at the heart of the Christian faith—from the vantage point of interfaith relationships. Many Christians today see value in learning about and engaging in conversation with those who practice other religions and may even find glimpses of the gospel in ways that give greater depth and nuance to our own Christian perspective. However, in order to authentically engage with those who are different than us, it is necessary to have a robust sense of our own Christian beliefs and values. When Christians are not deeply steeped in unique and particular aspects of Christianity, we may not be able to articulate our core beliefs, which can lead to confusion and frustration in interfaith conversation and cross-cultural learning. Understanding the cross and resurrection is necessary for the church's internal formation in order for the church to engage with those from outside Christianity in authentic friendship and witness.

This chapter makes a case that preaching about the cross and resurrection deepens Christian identity and awareness in ways that allow for secure engagement with those of different religions. Given the broadly pluralistic context in North America, I will unpack some of the signs and hallmarks of pluralism to better understand the ways it shapes and challenges the church. I will then turn to specific dynamics of interfaith engagement with some discussion of how Jesus' crucifixion and resurrection are understood within fellow Abrahamic traditions of Judaism and Islam. Next, I will name some of the ways that modern Christians tend to engage with those of other religions. Finally we will explore how the cross can provide a meaningful formative key for deepening Christian identity so that congregations are equipped for authentic witness and relationship in a context of religious pluralism. Part of the process of equipping will include naming specific practices to help preachers grow in interfaith awareness and love of neighbor, while also deepening Christian-cruciform identity from the pulpit.

Chapter 4 explores preaching the cross as a means of formation for Christian witness amidst competing cultural impulses. God engages with humanity in its varied cultures. God means for the good news to exist in human cultures and God's good news both challenges and affirms aspects of every culture. Thinking and writing about culture is challenging because we cannot escape it—even for a moment. To be alive is to be situated in culture or cultures. Culture is the air we breathe—we are so deeply enmeshed that we don't tend to notice unless we encounter a different culture. When it comes to Christianity, David Buttrick aptly notes, that part of how Christians are aware of their faith is "by contrast with the ethos of their culture."[5]

The church today does not need another generation of shallow sermons that reduce the gospel to feel-good platitudes, self-improvement, and individual achievement. We need a renewed sense of preaching that gathers the community around the cross and reorients us for our participation in God's redemption of the world. Set within the context of worship, the sermon has a unique opportunity to offer a transformative tuning note that can help interpret and reorient the congregation's corporate actions and witness as well as guiding individual members in personal discipleship. To this end, I will explore some working definitions of culture and name some aspects of North American consumer-driven culture that are especially seductive for the church, noting how these tendencies sound hollow or dissonant when placed alongside the eschatological crises of the cross and resurrection. Then I will discuss how the cross speaks to our culture before naming ways in which preaching can contribute to counter-cultural Christian formation and renewal that forms preachers and the Christian community according to the cross, equipping members for discipleship amidst the many competing cultural pressures we balance today.

Chapter 5 serves as a hands-on guide for preachers where I explore concrete occasions and methods for preaching the cross and resurrection using sermons from a variety of traditions to illustrate. Using these

5. Buttrick, *A Captive Voice*, 56.

specific methods and occasions to guide our discussion, I will name ways in which we might seek to intentionally engage the cross and resurrection not only during the seasons of Lent and Easter, but throughout the year. Along the way I will note challenges and concerns that may arise, such as designing the sermon to be relevant for listeners across the theological spectrum; balancing the dynamic between teaching and proclamation; and choosing illustrations and examples in light of the concerns raised in previous chapters around awareness of suffering, interfaith concerns, and competing cultural impulses that can foster a consumer-mindset among listeners. I will discuss techniques and circumstances that may allow preachers to choose between starting with a biblical text or from the perspective of a topical sermon.

Preachers can employ the cross and resurrection in a variety of ways, including: in the theologically-oriented rhetorical release of celebration, as a means of validating experiences of suffering, as a specific hermeneutical lens for exploring scripture for preaching, as a means for teaching about church doctrine, as a means of preparation for discipleship, as a means of engaging the liturgical events of Good Friday and Easter, or through the use of narrative sermon forms. Examples from sermons are included throughout as a guide for preachers.

My hope is that this book will help equip pastors to have more tools and less fear as they approach the cross and resurrection. While this book does not prescribe a method or template for every sermon, I would like to encourage more robust theological grounding for all preaching.

1

When Every Day is Good Friday

"Good Friday" dawns in everyone's life. It does not matter what the calendar date is. It might be a Tuesday in November and it might be a Monday in June, but for a good many people, today feels like "Good Friday" and "Good Friday" inevitably can cause even the most faithful and articulate among us to stumble and stammer. Whether you are sixty-eight or twenty-three, "Good Friday" always rolls around and often it lasts far longer than one day. We experience "Good Friday" when we and those we love experience suffering, betrayal, loss, and death as Jesus experienced in the events surrounding his crucifixion. Every congregation has experts on "Good Friday," those who have experienced tremendous suffering and loss. Walking with a congregation through "Good Friday" rightly brings wise preachers to a posture of silence before the mystery of God.

As a student, I worked as a part-time youth pastor for a congregation in Indiana. This small congregation was rocked by some unusually challenging events affecting children and youth in the church. I participated in an intervention with the lead pastor for a teenage addict whose church-member parents could not keep him from getting high from sniffing common household products like nail polish and cooking spray while on house arrest. A junior high student suddenly contracted Guillain-Barre Syndrome and we watched an active boy transform into a weak shell on life support in the local hospital. Two sisters in the youth group lost a favorite uncle in a hunting accident and were held-up at gun point with their mom in a local supermarket. A final blow came when a vital and beloved science teacher, just a few years out of college, caught a virus that attacked his heart and died despite doctors' best efforts. As we waded our way through this local experience of "Good Friday," it became clear that the leadership of the church could not stay silent. These teenagers, most of them raised in Christian homes, were asking the kind of tough questions that teens have the courage to voice (questions that scare the rest of us), and feeling the full weight of pastoral responsibility I offered to step in to help them sort things out. Ten years later, I still don't have "answers" for why so many bad things happened to one small circle of families, but I remember what I told the eleven to twelve-year-olds seated in a circle on the floor of the fellowship hall, "Some of us have had some pretty terrible things happen to us or to people we know and love in the past few weeks. Some of us haven't been as closely affected, but all of us will experience hard things and terrible things, things that we struggle to explain and understand sometime in our lives. So it is important that we find ways to talk about it." "Good Friday" dawns in everyone's life.

I've been evoking a metaphorical sense of "Good Friday" but the real Good Friday, the one that falls during Holy Week, can be just as challenging for pastors and preachers. When Holy Week rolls around, preachers are faced with the privilege of rehearsing again the "old, old story" that lies at the heart of our faith. Unfortunately, the drama of the cross and resurrection looms as burden more than joy for many pastors. Part of the problem with the liturgical experience of Good Friday is our inescapable connection with the other "Good Fridays." We struggle to give voice to the hope engendered by Christ's crucifixion and resurrection. They seem more like remote, abstract, and unreachable doctrines than life-giving, faith-nourishing living muscles that can propel, transform, and add theological depth to preaching. Preachers who feel called to turn to the Bible week after week to offer moral guidance, serve those in need, and inspire faith often find themselves stumbling when it comes to allowing their sermons to be shaped by these crucial events that lie at the heart of Christianity. As Good Friday approaches, preachers find themselves trying to navigate Christ's journey from death to resurrection, seeking vital and fresh revelation for a world caught between the agony of the cross and the promise of resurrection. Preachers want to proclaim a word of hope enshrouded in the mystery of atonement, but we struggle to know how to engage with the cross and resurrection in our sermons. For the liturgical observance of Good Friday and for all the other "Good

Fridays" we need a way to engage head-on with the cross and resurrection in our preaching that takes human experience and the core of the gospel seriously.

The struggle to address the cross and resurrection truthfully in our context can lead congregations to take bold and drastic steps. Several years ago a Toronto-area congregation of the United Church of Canada— the largest protestant denomination in Canada—removed all reference to Christ from their Easter liturgy. In a bold move they retreated from the cross and resurrection to focus instead on the actual lives of the people in the congregation. They celebrated, sang, and proclaimed the rebirth of hope, of new faith in the human spirit, of the chance to end pain and misery on earth, all without any reference to Jesus Christ, crucified and risen—God among us.[1] Why, on Easter Sunday of all days, would a Christian congregation leave this important affirmation on the cutting room floor? This is an extreme example that does not reflect the stance of the United Church of Canada as a whole, but it does offer us a window into the struggles that we all experience around Good Friday and Easter. Although few of us would modify our Easter liturgies by cutting out Christ, we can understand the circumstances that may have motivated West Hill United Church. Those present may have even experienced this service as providing a breath of fresh air and a relief from orthodox Christian dogma that clings heavily around Good Friday and Easter.

STUMBLING OVER THE CROSS

There are many reasons why preachers and Christians at large stumble over the constellation of events surrounding the crucifixion and resurrection of Jesus. While there are other resources that explore these reasons at depth, I will briefly name some top reasons here as a way of bringing them out in the open. However, our purpose here is not to get hung up on the reasons but to uncover the underlying tensions that can make preaching the cross and resurrection feel so thorny.

Theological Difficulties

First, the difficult theology surrounding the suffering, death, and resurrection of Jesus is extremely challenging to unpack and understand. We

1. Globe and Mail, "Taking Christ out of Christianity."

are uncomfortable with Jesus' death. It is terrible, even unthinkable regardless of our Christological slant. If we hold a Christology that stresses the divinity of Christ, it is difficult to imagine how God could die, how God could allow Jesus Christ as a member of the Trinity to die. If we hold a Christology that stresses Jesus' humanity, it is still unbearable that Jesus as the embodiment of love and peace who offered grace and healing to suffering people should die in such a terrible way. All the theology that has been heaped upon it in the millennia since Christ's death and resurrection should not ease the horror and finality of the nails that held Jesus to the rough wood of the cross, exposing him to the elements and a violent agonizing death. Christ's death on a cross is a historical and biblical event that also functions as a theological cipher for the church, anchoring belief in the resurrection and connecting God with real experiences of suffering today. While it might be tempting to collapse the cross into serving as merely a symbol, sign, or theological category, such a stance could lead us toward a path of cutting Christ from our Easter services. The good news around which Christian proclamation is based cannot be understood apart from the particularity of Jesus Christ and the cross. It is necessary to navigate the space between the function of cross in its historical context and the ways the cross functions in broader salvation history.

At best, the cross can help to clarify our theology. The reality of Christ's death grounds belief in the resurrection and our future hope. Because Jesus actually died and is experienced as alive, his resurrection has world-changing power and we have confidence that in Christ we too will be raised from death. At its most challenging, the cross obscures. The cross will not be easily categorized, it is a violent event undertaken by God alone for the salvation of humanity that also announces victory over the powers and principalities, and reframes all of history within a new eschatological age.

Language Difficulties

A second difficulty surrounding the cross has to do with the language we use to talk about the saving significance of Christ's death. If we learned about atonement in seminary primarily through memorizing a set of theories in a classroom, moving into a congregational context becomes very difficult. Atonement theology is tricky in the pulpit because the language can be abstract and feel distant from both the text and the contexts from which we preach. For example, Anselm's satisfaction theory of atonement is rooted in his own medieval feudal society, which reflected different social constructs having to do with honor and rank than we hold today. It is difficult to bring a disembodied theory into a sermon and have it connect to congregational life in a meaningful way.

Good preaching attends deeply to the context of the preacher and listeners while also bearing witness to God's inspiration, the Spirit's movement in Scripture, and the tradition of the Church. The interface between context and the language of atonement can cause us to stumble. Phrases like "Jesus died for my sin" reflects a shorthand that is deeply meaningful to some church members but likely confusing to others. As preachers in some traditions struggle to bring every sermon "to the cross" it is easy to rely on theological shorthand that doesn't exactly bear witness to the complexities that uphold the mysteries of atonement. The complexity of Jesus dying for our sins means that that our implicit and explicit participation as part of fallen creation still contributes to God's suffering and the suffering of creation this side of the Eschaton, but ultimately Jesus Christ has faced all this brokenness and evil head on, has taken it into the very being of God, and overturned it, de-activated it, made it powerless, and inert so that ultimately sin, brokenness, sickness, estrangement, and death no longer have a hold on us. How to apply this and other nuances of atonement in a sermon depends on the preaching text, the perspective of the biblical author, and the particularities of the context of the sermon. There is no easy formula, only the call to boldly face the cross anew from the perspective of the biblical text and the pressing contextual realities at hand in a given time and place.

Resurrection Difficulties

Recent preaching trends have rightly encouraged more engagement with congregational context and realities of cross and resurrection can be difficult to square with day-to-day life. The visceral experience of suffering and death is common to all humans and God's choice not to escape this destiny tells us that God can profoundly understand human suffering today.[2] Yet, the resurrection itself can cause us to stumble. We know and

2. Among others, LeRoy H. Aden and Robert G. Hughes assert that Christ's suffering gives weight to, and acknowledges, the reality and importance of our own

deeply believe that the event of Christ's death on the cross and resurrection demonstrates that God cares about humanity and that good news is relevant for people today. But while we have many points of contact with death, resurrection is a much harder point of identification. Indeed, my preaching students rarely have trouble finding concrete ways to bear witness to brokenness in the world and routinely struggle to name signs of good news and resurrection in concrete ways. For most if not all of us, helping the congregation to see and experience God's presence in our world today is simultaneously the most important and most challenging task of preaching.

Homiletical Shifts

Nevertheless, a focus on relevance and points of theological contact with human experience is important for recognizing the sermon as more than an opportunity for teaching about the cross and resurrection, but as a deeply formative event, which can help to bring about the formation and reformation of believers and the church as a whole. A focus on the sermon as event is not a new development but the world of preaching is still exploring the implications of this shift from the sermon as a vehicle for information to the sermon as a means of formation.[3] An early leader in this movement, David James Randolph, defines preaching as "the event in which the biblical text is interpreted in order that its meaning will come to expression in the concrete situation of the hearers."[4] While Randolph does not discuss the cross specifically, preaching that emphasizes the crucifixion as both a historical and present event, rather than mainly a theological concept, gives weight both to biblical testimony and real human experiences through history and today. Randolph views the sermon as

---

suffering. Aden and Hughes, *Preaching,* 7.

3. See Randolph, *Renewal of Preaching.* For a concise historical overview of the theological development of the shift from information to event, James F. Kay traces understandings about the eventfulness of preaching to the influence of the "New Hermeneutic," a paradigm shift that changed the idea of preaching from models of rhetorical preaching that focused on communicating information to communicative action " . . . from 'exposition' of a text to its 'execution,'" Kay, *Preaching and Theology,* 77.

4. Randolph, *Renewal of Preaching,* 1. Craddock joins Randolph in helping to articulate the sense that, "The method is the message . . . *how* one preaches is to a large extent *what* one preaches." Craddock, *As One without Authority,* 52. See also Kay, *Preaching and Theology,* 78.

an instrument for working and expressing the formative impact of close engagement with the Bible and with deep theologically significant events such as the cross and resurrection.[5] The cross as a biblical event serves the purpose of exposing human reality in new ways that offer hope.

While the cross and resurrection are an experience in the life of God, they also have echoing effects on humanity both as a paradigmatic example of God's relationship to humanity that is recapitulated in individual and communal experiences of salvation and as a once and for all event that has radically changed the pitch of human relationships with God and each other. Following this shift from information to formation and a renewed focus on the eventfulness of language, preaching takes on new meaning as a "Word-event," through the work of scholars who emphasize the "performative" or active quality of language itself, which functions in time and cannot be abstracted from the context and the relationships in which it is spoken. Through language, preachers have the potential to participate and invite listeners to participate in a new reality where our theology truly lives and breathes. For example, Ernst Fuchs sees in the parables of Jesus a situation in which God truly becomes incarnate and creates a new reality through language.[6] Fuchs writes, "Jesus' preaching is exactly like his conduct, his whole appearance: it is quite simply *the announcement of the time itself,* the *new* time of the kingdom of God."[7]

While the historical reality of the cross is a connecting point with human experience, the cross also represents a unique act done by God in Christ alone, an act that ultimately ends futile human attempts to save themselves. Only Christ could choose the cross and only God can turn crucifixion into resurrection. Preachers may be tempted to allow human experience to drive the sermon whether through the lens of present day people or biblical figures. However, in attempting to bridge the text and the present world, preachers can risk bypassing the gospel. The cross offers a corrective as its particularity and confounding logic both stabilize and de-stabilize us, humbling and empowering human actions and true

5. Randolph also suggests that the subject matter of preaching will be historical (*Renewal of Preaching,* 19–20).

6. Kay expounds on the transforming power of the Word of God proclaimed through "'Word-event,' in which the God, who came into expression in the teaching and preaching of the historical Jesus, again comes into expression in our teaching and preaching." Kay, *Preaching and Theology,* 80, 82, 84. See also Ebeling, *God and Word,* 16–22, 30.

7. Fuchs, "New Testament," 128–29. See also Kay, *Preaching and Theology,* 84.

discipleship that focus on the uniqueness of Christ rather than only on human responsiveness or formation itself. James Kay helpfully brings the legacy of the shift from language aimed toward information to language as event to the "word of the cross." He writes,

> The language-history of Jesus or the Word-event of Jesus of Nazareth thus continues today as the language of Jesus' cross is re-released in the sermon. . . . The word of the cross thus poses to us the same decision for our existence that was posed to the historical Jesus. Will we live for ourselves or for God? Jesus, too, had to decide for faith. Jesus, too, had to decide for a self-hood free from self-assertion—even if it led to death. That death could not overcome the Word-event, which came to expression in Jesus, means that it can yet come to expression for us and in us. Jesus is thus not only the witness to faith, he is the basis for our own faith. . . . [8]

Difficulties with Sacrifice and Oppression

Another significant stumbling block for preachers is the terrible legacy of twisting language about the cross in ways that bear witness to human brokenness rather than God's saving intentions. Many liberationist theologians have critiqued atonement language and theology that has the effect of lifting up sacrifice in general as somehow noble. Following the counsel of well-meaning pastors and preachers, victims of domestic abuse have tried to rejoice in their suffering and bear a cross of exploitation and victimhood as something potentially redemptive. This twisting rewards the powerful and punishes the weak, becoming a most insidious distortion of cruciform power-in-weakness.

It is extremely challenging to separate the cross and Christ's sacrifice from sacrifices that people make, either by choice or through coercion. Sally Brown rightly points out that preachers "are ethically obligated to attend to the ways our theological language can be misconstrued and misapplied."[9] Scholars and liberationist theologians in particular have addressed some of the ways in which the victimization associated with Christ's death has been harmful for marginalized hearers who need liberation. Clearly, the idea and language of "sacrifice" needs rehabilitation

8. Kay, *Preaching and Theology*, 85–86.
9. Brown, *Cross Talk*, 17.

beyond those who have been encouraged to embrace sacrifice as an un-ambiguous good in ways that can lead to needless oppression.

Even those of us who are not caught in cycles of abuse are guilty of bringing unhelpful freight to the concept of sacrifice. While sacrificial language in the New Testament likely carried a widely understood comprehensive set of understandings, focused more on God's giving life rather than death and the loss of life, today both liturgical emphasis and the broader use of sacrificial language often glorifies sacrifice. Such language can portray even relatively small sacrifices as abnormal losses rather than as an acceptable part of being in relationship with God or other people. Walter Brueggemann writes of the dangers of preaching "gospel without demand."[10] Brueggemann links our present avoidance of sacrifice in "works" created by some readings of the role of the cross in the writings of the Apostle Paul as being concerned with relieving existential guilt coupled with Modernity's lifting up of "freedom" as an ultimate good.[11] Of course, to live an engaged life, one must "sacrifice" a certain amount of freedom, and moreover, these sacrifices themselves can be a source of joy when experienced in the context of relationship. In both the Hebrew Scriptures and the New Testament, sacrifice was and is a natural part of covenant with God, whose love of us is both conditional and unconditional. It comes to us freely while simultaneously demanding everything.[12] Brueggemann lights on an appropriately biblical example of a marriage or parent-child relationship where spouses and parents regularly make sacrifices along the scale of taking out trash to quitting work to care for children joyfully out of love for the other.[13]

In addition to consigning acts of sacrifice to the realm of heroes, the concept of sacrifice can also take on controversial or trite connotations when people use the same language of "sacrifice" to talk about Christ's work on the cross and a person giving up a morning latte habit, when the cross is worn primarily as "bling" around the neck of an athlete, or when news analysts speak of soldiers making "the ultimate sacrifice."[14] Sally

10. Brueggemann, "Duty as Delight," 2.

11. Ibid.

12. Ibid., 3.

13. Ibid., 3–6.

14. Brown, "Negotiating," 279–81. Robert Dykstra notes some similar dangers in using the cross itself in preaching. He echoes Sally Brown's concerns about triteness, noting that the cross as a symbol is "numbingly familiar" and its use makes the "sermon's trajectory too clichéd." Dykstra, *Discovering*, 112. On the other hand, Richard

Brown addresses these concerns by calling preachers to envision sacrifice "as creative self-giving" in the direction of God towards humans rather than humans toward God, so that life is respected and offered as gift from God and is experienced as a type of "communion" with God.[15] Brown traces this understanding back to Judaism and Luke's Gospel where Jesus speaks of his own death "as an act of giving."[16] This self-giving respects and offers life, leading to "communion" with God.[17]

Thus, Christ's sacrifice highlights the inadequacy of our own often trite understanding and practices around sacrifice while also making possible the kind of necessary substantive sacrifices associated with discipleship and relationship with God encouraged by Brueggemann.

Besides concern over the language of sacrifice, in her recent book, *Cross Talk: Preaching Redemption Here and Now,* Brown names four concerns with traditional atonement theology that can cause us to stumble when preaching the cross:

1) separating the actions of God from those of Christ within the Trinity;

2) focusing too much on human sin rather than on God's love and redemptive purposes;

3) holding Jesus' suffering up as a model to follow; and

4) "envisioning divine justice as retributive rather than reparative. . . . "[18]

Eslinger discusses the importance of narrative to frame even a familiar image in a new way. He describes numerous possibilities for the image of the cross, including: connections with human sacrifice in war, the cross on a crusader's banner, a cross hung on the wall of a hospice patient, a cross worn by a punk-looking teen, and a cross worn by a young person being confirmed. He writes, "Homiletically, this deciphering of the language or languages of an image can provide for some of the richest irony within a sermon." Eslinger, *Web,* 261–62.

15. Ibid., 285–86.

16. Ibid. "This is my body, which is given for you" (Luke 22:19).

17. Ibid.

18. Brown, *Cross Talk,* 50–55. Brown helpfully offers four criteria by which to analyze different atonement metaphors to help preachers find useful metaphors for their own contexts: 1) how it characterizes the "human predicament"; 2) what it says about the "nature of God"; 3) "what it looks like to be redeemed"; and 4) what happens— what is done to bring about redemption. Brown, *Cross Talk,* 43–44, 46–47).

Difficulties with the Relatively Small Space in Scripture Devoted to the Cross

Another reason why some preachers are uncomfortable with preaching about the cross is that they would rather focus on Jesus' life and teachings. For these preachers, the cross represents a small part of the total Jesus event and they would rather make connections between Jesus' life and our call to discipleship today.

Lastly, some preachers struggle to engage with the cross because it is not specifically mentioned in so much of the Bible. These preachers strive to be responsible exegetes and don't want to import the cross into a text where it is not mentioned. This can especially be a concern with preaching from the Old Testament.

NAMING THE TENSIONS OF THE CROSS: CAUGHT BETWEEN GOOD FRIDAY AND EASTER

These reasons and others can help explain why we are often tongue-tied when it comes to preaching on Good Friday and Easter Sunday in the face of human suffering in general and Christ's own suffering, death, and resurrection specifically. However, these reasons serve as husks for deeper tensions that both engage and repel. One of the most significant challenges of preaching the cross is the tension or sense of contradiction raised for preachers who feel caught or stuck between seemingly irreconcilable realities. We have one foot in Good Friday and one foot in Easter Sunday, we live by the light of Christ's resurrection and God's inbreaking realm in a world where crucifixion, suffering, and death appear to mark human existence fully and finally. Caught in the middle of salvation history, preachers have to choose between being culturally astute and pastorally sensitive realists and expressing deeply held theological convictions. When it comes to the sermon, the theology we profess in the creeds may feel more appropriate to a seminary classroom than to people's lives. It is easy to forget that our present understandings of atonement theology have their origins in the messiness of controversy and conflict, in the real life experiences of early Christian pastors and preachers who prayerfully hammered out doctrines over centuries of conversation. The resulting doctrines are like living and breathing garden containers for what we believe. They can grow and expand to hold our shifts and the evolution that occurs as we continue the hard work of faithfully cultivating a system of beliefs that support and build up the church. Doctrines can become problematic when we forget that they are containers and believe that they are solid impenetrable blocks. When we look inside the containers, the doctrines no longer feel alien or impenetrable; the contents are familiar as the touch of God's hand in our own lives. Scripture is a primary source for Christian theology, one of the first familiar things we see when we explore the container for a doctrine like atonement. Here we see again God at work in the lives of people and people bearing faithful witness to God's activity in the world.

Many pastors experience a deep tension or even a separation between theological convictions and congregational reality. At best this separation remains a manageable ditch that we can nimbly jump but at times it spreads to an unbridgeable chasm.

"You think it, but you cannot say it," the pastor commented during a discussion about how the cross and resurrection might factor in a sermon preached to a congregation dealing with a crisis. This fifty-something clergywoman had just finished preaching to our class a self-revelatory sermon about failure that she was also planning to preach to her congregation. She had made a calculated decision that highlighting her own shortcomings might make people in her declining rural congregation feel better about some recent setbacks they had experienced as a congregation. This clergywoman deeply believed in the promises of the gospel that God can bring life from death, but she could not preach those words at this time when arguably they might be most needed, because the familiar words of good news felt hollow in her mouth, insensitive or dishonest in some way. She continued, "You cannot say it because they cannot hear it right then." "You always think it, but you just cannot say it."

In addition to the existential promise of resurrection in a world still marked by the cross and the chasm between convictions and reality, the following are some of the most challenging areas of tension created in the event of the cross.

The cross addresses both individual and societal implications of reconciliation and forgiveness. Christ's death and resurrection affect us personally and at a social level, God promises healing and reconciliation not just within ourselves and between God and us, but also between groups of people, within communities, and in larger societal changes. In fact many critiques of atonement theology accurately highlight how we have too often ignored relational ramifications for tightly held religious beliefs.[19] Much preaching that addresses the cross is rightly criticized as being too personal or individualistic, that is, mainly concerned with restoring a relationship between God and me. On the other hand, preachers that tend to emphasize the social or community-minded thrust of the gospel tend to find it challenging to incorporate the cross into their sermons. Yet the sense that God loves individuals, that Christ died "for me," may still be an important part of piety and faith formation in these same congregations. Naturally, sermons may tend toward one or the other of these areas: the individual or the social. They do not need to be in tension with each other when embraced as different aspects or arenas of the same experience of gospel.

Nevertheless, a lack of intentional balance can deeply affect a congregation's view of God over time. For example, a personal approach rightly illustrates that no one, no matter how lowly, is outside of God's care. However, without any social emphasis, silence inadvertently shrinks the scope of God's care. If we are not regularly reminded of God's engagement with the world and the larger network of social relationships within salvation history, it becomes easier to forget that God's redemptive vision encompasses all of creation and involves every area of life. On the other hand, we should take care that we don't cast our sermons so broadly that we only explore social implications of the gospel. Several members of one congregation were uncomfortable mentioning any personal concerns for prayer in public worship. The focus on social aspects of the gospel had made God so large and global that they felt it was inappropriate to bring their personal cares or troubles before God in public worship.

Further, our affiliations and conversation partners might not be helping us with this balance. While we fully understand the breadth of the gospel, as preachers, we tend to fall into patterns so that most sermons that attend seriously to the cross tend to focus on individual rather than community or social aspects of the gospel and when sermons do express the social aspects of the gospel, we resist mentioning the cross. Regrettably, these trends often fall along divisions already present in the church between ethnic groups, socio-economic strata, and between congregations that self-identify as evangelical or more socially liberal.

---

19. Feminist and womanist critiques of theologies of the cross illustrate how an emphasis on the passive suffering of Christ has caused women and others to justify their experiences of passive suffering at the hands of abusers. For concise discussion, see Trelstad, *Cross Examinations*, 6–7.

A more holistic and balanced approach to the cross and resurrection is challenging but necessary to address both reconciliation that is between "God and me," and socially oriented reconciliation, that is between me and my neighbors, between groups of neighbors, and between people and the created world. The truth of the gospel is that God's new covenant established through Christ for me must affect my relationships with others.[20] The truth is that Christ has ultimately overcome evils like racism and classism. Paul's words to the Galatians are a good reminder for us, "There is no longer Jew or Greek, there is no longer slave or free, there is no longer male and female; for all of you are one in Christ Jesus."[21] Salvation and new life are like the ever-expanding rings that form when a stone is thrown into a smooth lake. The ripples grow until they reach the shore even though they can all be traced back to just one stone. While concerns for time limitations and sermon unity might mean that not every sermon can address both individual and social implications of the gospel, preachers may find it helpful to keep track of where they cast the wide nets of God's saving graces from week to week and make a conscious effort to balance personal and social implications of the cross.

The cross effects our struggle of when and how to ascribe meaning to human suffering. An unforeseen early summer flash-flood has drowned children sleeping in their campers in a remote Arkansas campground. A massive tornado strikes a Midwestern town with little warning, scattering bodies and intimate possessions for miles. At the time of this writing, the news screams of atrocities of all kinds from local tragedy, to war, to environmental disasters, and economic fears. Yet, in the face of unquantifiable suffering, the situations that strike our own lives and congregations often loom the largest. A wanted pregnancy ends in miscarriage, a man is diagnosed with prostate cancer, a woman loses her job, and a long marriage ends in divorce. The tensions held together in the event of the cross and resurrection largely stem from complications related to this existential tension that holds us taut: between the hope-filled destiny of our fate already decided by Jesus Christ and the way things are right now. Suffering in the light of the resurrection is maddening, we do not understand it. Yet suffering Christians have often voiced a special connection to the cross that is ripe for proclamation.

20. Paul Wilson addresses one approach to preaching in this way, "It is spoken to the individual, but it is also spoken to the entire community. In fact, one could argue that these words form the community . . ." Wilson, *Practice of Preaching*, 257–59.

21. Gal 3:28.

While Christ's own suffering and death lead ultimately to redemption, can we find any meaning in the suffering people experience this side of the Eschaton? Christian thinkers have been struggling with this back to the Apostle Paul's own time. Present-day feminist, womanist, and liberationist critiques of atonement theology have pulled back the veil, exposing how some have twisted the cross to encourage oppressed people to accept suffering as "their cross," as a mark of faithful discipleship. This use of the cross runs counter to life and liberation from the powers of sin brought about through Christ's own death and resurrection. We cannot turn away from the importance of this critique. We cannot lift up involuntary suffering as redemptive. However, we also cannot avoid grappling with the persistent presence of suffering. This concern too emerges frequently in Paul's writings. Until God's work is completed we live in a world of both good news and suffering.

Christians past and present have sought to make sense of random suffering by enfolding their present suffering in the suffering of Christ on the cross. Where pain and suffering take place in the world today, Christ continues to suffer crucifixion. Yet, grace also accompanies suffering and loss; families and friends tell of faith and hope being strengthened while accompanying loved ones through illness and death. While Christians are not to seek out suffering as a good in itself, it is an unavoidable addition to life in a broken world. Suffering may offer gifts as it rides as a backseat passenger to the over-riding Spirit of God-given joy that drives us on in discipleship.[22] While the relationship is mysterious and not easily grasped as causal, suffering and sanctification often go together, although sanctification is a gift from God while suffering pains God.

The cross stands between God's judgment and the limits of humanity and between God's grace and human potential. The cross simultaneously lays bare human brokenness and the disastrous outcome of fallen human behavior that has strayed from God's good intentions along with God's supreme love and grace and the future hope that Jesus' death and resurrection have broken open for us. Through Jesus, we are offered new lives as we allow old harmful patterns and experiences to die with Christ. This new life in Christ is a restoration of life and a liberating promise in the midst of a world that is still longing for the redemption of all of creation.

The cross stands in a holy space that affirms the deep value of humanity so much that Christ is willing to die for us while also showing the

22. Jervis, *At the Heart*, 26–27.

limitations of what people can do. In Paul's words, "Indeed, rarely will anyone die for a righteous person—though perhaps for a good person someone might actually dare to die. But God proves his love for us in that while we still were sinners Christ died for us."[23] Christ displays a divine act of love in giving himself up for fallen humanity. Jesus is like a hound with his nose to the heels of humanity, who doggedly sticks to us no matter how far off the path we stray—willing to do whatever it takes to get us back to a state of authenticity—to living as the people God created us to be. The ability to bring new life out of death is God's work alone. We cannot do it. So while humans have God-granted potential, the cross and resurrection ground human potential in God's work rather than our own work. For preachers who long to inspire "yes we can!" congregations to action, to living into the future God in Christ has opened, the cross offers the most honest route that casts light on our humanity, also helping to stave off the danger of burn-out when we place the burden of restoration, peace, and hope completely on ourselves. Only God can bring life out of death. In the events of Good Friday and Easter, all human efforts reach their end, meaning both our limit and our future. It is only through Christ's power that we are empowered to be the people God created us to be.

The cross holds together the costs and the benefits of discipleship. The dividing line between costs and benefits is not clearly defined. Costs are not necessarily negative. Everything costs something and often we are happy to bear the costs of things that we value. In a similar vein, benefits often come with responsibilities. Dangers arise when the tension is lost. Splitting costs and benefits causes some of us to focus mainly on the gifts that flow from commitment to God, that is, what God promises to do for us, while others focus mainly on the costs, what faith requires us to do. The New Testament is clear that on this side of the Eschaton following Jesus Christ leads to suffering, but Jesus also promises and offers benefits of faith that are witnessed to in passages such as the Beatitudes in Matthew 5, numerous passages where the recipient's faith is mentioned as a reason for healing, and often in the letters of Paul where suffering here and now is seen as a precursor to eschatological glory.

For those of us who tend to mainly see benefits, the cross reminds us that the good news cost Jesus Christ his life. Splitting costs and benefits has allowed some believers to assent to a suffering servile existence where

23. Rom 5:7–8.

WHEN EVERY DAY IS GOOD FRIDAY 17

hope, freedom, and prosperity are envisioned as a future reality unattainable here and now. The other side of that split is prosperity preaching, which in its simplest forms teaches that God wants to reward us with prosperity here and now. Insofar as this is empowering for those who have traditionally been victimized, this is not a harmful message. However, it becomes troubling when it focuses exclusively on material benefits of discipleship and forgets that grace is not cheap—it costs God deeply.

Focusing on the benefits of the gospel and losing sight of the cross is more insidious than simple prosperity preaching. Sociologist Christian Smith, who conducted extensive interviews with American teens, describes a religious impulse that has formed a pervasive and deep-seated belief system that exists alongside and interacts with orthodox belief that is held by teens as well as parents and caregivers within every Christian denomination to some degree.[24] He identifies this impulse as "Moralistic Therapeutic Deism."[25] While not a separate religion, the god of Moralistic Therapeutic Deism is not particularly engaged in human affairs but generally promotes happiness and feeling good about oneself.[26] Smith enumerates five articles which he identifies as comprising a "creed":

1) A God exists who created and orders the world and watches over human life on earth.

2) God wants people to be good, nice, and fair to each other, as taught in the Bible and by most world religions.

3) The central goal of life is to be happy and feel good about oneself.

4) God does not need to be particularly involved in one's life except when God is needed to solve a problem.

5) Good people go to heaven when they die.[27]

Moralistic Therapeutic Deism skews Christianity away from the physicality, sacrifice, and personal engagement of the cross.

For those of us who tilt to the side of focusing on the costs and responsibilities of discipleship, the cross reminds us that Jesus Christ has

24. Smith and Denton, *Soul Searching*, 163, 165–66. Smith found moralistic therapeutic deism to be *especially* prevalent among mainline Protestant and Catholic youth but was also evidenced in black, conservative Protestant, Jewish, and non-religious teens.

25. Ibid., 162.

26. Ibid., 162–63.

27. Ibid.

ultimately taken care of the costs; we proceed as disciples only because Jesus Christ has made a way for us out of no way.

While Christ has ultimately redeemed the world this side of the Eschaton, we live both within the light of the resurrection and the shadow of the cross. A life of discipleship still means accepting the way of the cross, but we can accept it with the sure knowledge that Christ has gone ahead and walks this way with us.

These tensions illustrate some of the potential directions a preacher can take when approaching the cross and resurrection, and the acts of naming and holding these areas together in sermons preached over time offer a way through the theological and pastoral minefields that many preachers face each Holy Week.

Within the Bible, the experiences of the earliest Christian communities can serve as resources for how to preach the cross in the midst of a difficult and challenging pastoral context. We are called to preach into the tensions of life, in the tensions created by our situation in salvation history, between the advents of Christ when we experience simultaneously the redemptive realities of hope and new life inaugurated by Christ in the cross and resurrection and the agony of a world where crucifixion, suffering, and death are all too real. Rather than serving as harmful to preaching, these tensions can be harnessed to give energy and theological depth to the sermon, addressing the complexities of what it means to be human.

TENSIONS ENERGIZE PREACHING

While it may be easier to seek to bypass or resolve the tensions that cause us to stumble over the cross in our preaching, when they are allowed to co-exist, these same tensions can be vital sources of energy for preaching. Allowing tensions to exist side by side expands our ability to address our contexts in ways that resonate as true with diverse listeners. Working the tensions of atonement have helped to fuel theologians throughout the history of the church and may have sparked deeply rooted theologies of atonement past and present.

We can thank Gustav Aulen, author of the influential classic *Christus Victor,* for the concise understanding of three main atonement theologies (Christus Victor, Satisfaction, and Moral Influence) that many learned in seminary. The Christus Victor theory addresses among other things, the tension between the real presence of evil and the sovereignty of God. This theory, with roots in the early church, employs a "ransom" analogy where humanity was held by Satan and God offers Christ as ransom, tricking Satan with Christ's own innocence, in a sense defeating Satan with his own greediness. Christus Victor is also understood to have a larger cosmic sense to it; initially in the crucifixion it seems that evil has won, but the resurrection demonstrates God's power and final victory.

The Satisfaction theory, linked to Anselm of Canterbury's writing in the medieval period, addresses the tension between God's righteousness and good promises to humanity and human fallenness. Such a holy God cannot engage with such broken and sinful people. To resolve this concern, Jesus, the "God man" dies as a perfect sacrifice maintaining God's honor in a way that no ordinary human sacrifice ever could and closes the chasm between God and people in an ultimate way. The satisfaction theory later went on to take forensic or judicial tones where Jesus Christ pays the price for guilty humanity's sin. A favorite example of forensic atonement lies in Karl Barth's mid-twentieth century understanding of Jesus Christ as the "judge judged in our place."[28] While the satisfaction theory has deeply taken root in Christianity, Anselm's contemporary Peter Abelard did not follow Anselm's logic, believing that God as all powerful did not need Jesus' sacrifice to span the chasm between God's holiness and human fallenness. He sought to address what he saw as a tension between Anselm's theory and God's power and past acts with humanity attested to in scripture. The Bible illustrates a long history of God's enduring commitment to fallen people. Abelard resolves this tension by viewing Christ's death on a cross as showing God's depth of love for humanity. This loving sacrifice is so great that humanity is changed by it—Christ's death initiates faith and transforms lives where Christians bear witness to this same love.

The desire to address tensions and resolve questions continues to this day. Many present-day theologians work to address tensions and name problematic impulses or trajectories in these classic understandings of atonement theology. For example, J. Denny Weaver wonders who requires Christ's death: God, Satan, or people.[29] He has written concerning violence in atonement theology and is concerned that satisfaction atonement requires that God be an initiator of violence or that God

28. Barth, Church Dogmatics, IV.1.
29. Weaver, "Violence," 228.

requires violence, something that seems clearly at odds with non-violence demonstrated in the life and teachings of Jesus Christ as God incarnate. Weaver sees this violent intention as having taken hold of Christian theology in such a way that it threatens what he sees as the non-violent core of Christian ethics.

Delores Williams joins other feminist and womanist voices in addressing the tension between individual and social concerns surrounding the cross. Williams discusses African-American women's social experiences of "coerced and voluntary surrogacy" before and after the Civil War.[30] Enslaved African-American women "mammies" served as surrogate mothers to slave holder's children, as field workers substituting their hard physical labor for that of men, and as sexual objects used by white male slave holders to satisfy their desires in place of white women.[31] Following the Civil War, fewer African-American women were forced to serve as sexual surrogates, but societal limitations continued to force them to work jobs that involved strenuous physical labor or surrogate mothering "mammy" roles.[32] These surrogate roles continue to affect how African-American women are perceived today. In terms of atonement, interpretations that view Christ as an "ultimate surrogate figure" who hung on the cross in the place of humanity, taking on sin that was not rightly his, have the effect of sacralizing surrogacy itself, even in insidious forms that encourage racism and sexism.[33] Ultimately, Williams finds Jesus' life a more potent source for liberation than his death, which primarily bears witness to the power of human sin.[34] Many other voices join Weaver and Williams in navigating tensions found in the historical development of atonement theology or in the cross itself.

While preachers are indeed theologians in the congregation and have a responsibility to unpack and explore biblical and theological angles of the cross, the unique relationship between a preacher and congregation means that preaching unfolds as a conversation over time, allowing the preacher to stand in the midst of the tensions of the cross, addressing different aspects and angles on different occasions. Preachers must be aware of recent theological literature, especially the work of authors who

30. Williams, "Black Women's Surrogacy Experiences," 20.

31. Ibid., 20–23.

32. Ibid., 24–25.

33. Ibid., 27–28.

34. Ibid., 30–31.

enlighten us to diverse expressions of human experience. Preachers are called to attend deeply to God's action both in the biblical world and in our world today. Nevertheless, the main job of a sermon is not to justify or rationalize theology, but to preach good news in all its many complex facets. When it comes to the sermon, as Tom Long puts it, "the *poetry of proclamation is to be preferred* over the hydraulics of explanation."[35] Choosing proclamation over explanation is not an excuse to let preachers off the hook theologically. We are still called to do careful theological work, but this work can unfold over time and can work multiple angles of complex theological issues as our preaching texts change and contexts shift from week to week.

Preachers have the unique privilege of being able to hold together critique and affirmation, historical perspective and present-day experience. In fact, the very tensions that drive theologians to create new language to talk about atonement theology offer fresh and fertile soil for cultivating sermons for Good Friday, Easter, and every other Sunday of the year. Sermons deeply marked by the cross are not formulaic; they honor the ruptures in our lives and the continuity of a God who abides with us in the midst of death, creating new life out of ashes. Preaching the cross is not for the faint of heart, these sermons challenge closely held beliefs even as they attend to the needs of the community of faith.

CHARACTERISTICS OF SERMONS MARKED BY THE CROSS

To move towards greater freedom in preaching the cross, it can be helpful to break down what happens in a sermon deeply anchored in the cross and resurrection. What does the cross do in the sermon? The following characteristics are theologically related to God's action in Christ in the cross and resurrection and can be found in sermons that deeply attend to the cross:

1) Acknowledge evil.

2) Name hope.

3) Maintain a sense of tension or contradiction.

4) Are grounded in scripture.

5) Address personal and social implications of the cross.

35. Long, "Presence of God," 66.

6) Address the fullness of the Christ event.

1) Sermons marked by the cross and resurrection are not afraid to name and face evil and trouble head-on in real and palpable ways because evil, trouble, and death itself are radically taken into God's own being and defeated through the cross and resurrection. While some argue that the cross bears stronger witness to human sin than to God's redemptive intentions for the world, Jesus death on the cross shows us that God is willing to engage with evil and brokenness—even death itself. Indeed, the cross is a witness to the power of evil and the real consequences of its presence in the world. People going through their own "Good Friday" experiences need to know that "Good Friday" is an event in the life of God. In the sermon itself, evil and trouble do not have to be of the most dire and huge types to cast a sermon into the presence of the cross. In fact, preachers should be careful not to allow evil a toehold in their congregations by providing salacious stories and troubling details that captivate the imaginations and can hijack listeners from redemptive aspects of the sermon. Ordinary trouble and brokenness are relatable to everyone.

2) Sermons attuned to the cross and resurrection speak boldly of hope, offering a balance of obvious signs and less obvious signs so that listeners will be able to recognize hope in their own lives. As any working preacher can testify, arguably this is often the hardest and yet most important task for preachers. Christ's resurrection means that death is not the last word. Because we have been given the possibility of new life in Christ, we have hope that death is not the last word for us either.[36] Yet the pervasive brokenness of creation and our own limited vision means that even the most hopeful preachers can get stuck in the quagmires of the "Good Fridays" in our lives. Real-life examples of resurrection hope do not need to be explicitly Christian; as long as they tell stories respectfully, preachers have permission to name and claim God's action everywhere in the world from a reading program at the public library, to an explicitly Christian feeding program, and even to legislation passed by civil governing bodies. When these events are named in a sermon, they become Christian witness.

3) Sermons anchored in the tensions of the cross and resurrection also have a sense of tension—a pushing and pulling, lively quality that keeps listeners on the edge of the pew—communicating God's unexpected

36. "He who rescued us from so deadly a peril will continue to rescue us; on him we have set our hope that he will rescue us again . . . (2 Cor 1:10)."

and contradictory action of choosing the cross and ultimately bringing life out of death. Preachers can proclaim the gospel without needing to resolve every tension or iron out every mystery. For example, allowing that the cross testifies to both human sin and God's power in weakness maintains an important tension that acknowledges diverse present-day theological discussions about the cross.

4) Sermons rooted in the cross and resurrection are biblical. The scriptures are where we learn about the life, death, and resurrection of Jesus, although they clearly do not take the form of systematic Christology or atonement theories. To say that sermons deeply attuned to the cross are biblical means that scripture serves as a foundation for the content and guide for the ways we talk about the cross. Sally Brown emphasizes the metaphorical and particular nature of New Testament images for atonement: "Talk about the cross in the New Testament is not abstract and general, it is local and specific, crafted to interpret the saving significance of Jesus death for a time and place."[37] A particular Scripture text does not necessarily need to mention the cross in order to be affected by the cross. The trajectory of God's revelation moves towards the cross and resurrection, meaning that the event of the cross as an event in the life of God allows us to look towards the cross while also attending thoroughly to texts from the Hebrew Scriptures.

5) Sermons attuned to the cross and resurrection are both personal and social. Many preachers shy away from preaching the cross because they have experienced cross-oriented preaching as overly personal and individualistic. The lack of explicit linking between God's intentions for individuals and God's intentions for the world lies at the root of disordered and harmful misuses of the cross in the lives of many. Recovering a robust eschatological sense of the scope of the cross in relationship to deeply broken institutions and behaviors may helpfully rehabilitate the cross for those who have suffered victimization of twisted theology. While we may not see the full expression of how the cross has overcome racism and sexism in the world, we can highlight fragmentary expressions of God's intentions for individuals, institutions, and society at large.

6) Finally, sermons oriented by the cross and resurrection acknowledge the fullness of the Christ event and its implications in some manner. The sermon does not necessarily have to mention the cross and resurrection explicitly if many of the above characteristics are present and

---

37. Brown, *Cross Talk,* 30–31.

if reflection on the cross was a part of the sermon-creation process in some way. However, as the death and resurrection are important aspects of Jesus Christ's identity and have affected human destiny, sermons cannot fully focus on the person of Jesus or on God's abiding promises to humanity without dealing with the cross along the way.

CHARACTERISTICS OF THE CROSS IN ACTION: EXAMPLES FROM SERMONS

Looking at actual sermon examples can help put some "flesh" on the bones of theory. So while it can be hard for sermons to fit a set of criteria applied after the fact, the following sermons serve as excellent examples of preaching that uses the cross and resurrection as significant anchors. I've selected published sermons from relatively well known and accessible preachers. Each sermon example is discussed using the previous characteristics. While none of these sermons were written for Good Friday, their deep sense of connection to the cross means that they do attend to the human experience of "Good Friday" wherever it falls in the church year. These characteristics illustrate significant theological aspects of the cross and resurrection, that can come to the fore in preaching, but they are not meant to be exhaustive as there are aspects and trajectories of preaching and the cross that are not addressed by these criteria.[38] Nevertheless, they are broad enough to allow a wide variety in sermon styles. The following examples are illustrations of what sermons can look like when they are connected deeply to the cross. None of these preachers have done anything particularly fancy, nor have they gone out on any shaky theological limbs. At best, they serve as concrete possibilities for how a preacher might use the preceding characteristics of the cross and resurrection to contribute to teaching or proclaiming the gospel during Holy Week or any other Sunday.

38. For example, I have not included direct address as a necessary criteria of preaching that is anchored to the cross. While I do see direct address in the sermon as contributing to an experience of the gospel, in the interest of allowing broadness of styles and approaches, my criteria encompass direct address but do not require it, at minimum, my criteria would help to foster "teaching" the gospel. See Wilson, *Setting Words*, 78–80.

"The Magnificent Defeat"

The cross can be preached from the Old or New Testament and for any occasion. Frederick Buechner's "The Magnificent Defeat" and "A Sprig of Hope" fit nearly all of the previous characteristics and are good examples of how Old Testament texts, part of the story of Jacob (Gen 32:22–31) and the story of Noah (Gen 6:11—8:11), can be interpreted and preached with a heightened awareness of the cross.[39]

Evil: Buechner names evil in the story in easily understood ways that can connect to the lives of hearers. He addresses lying, opportunism, blind ambition, and manipulation that trumps relationships, and favoritism in families among other issues. He notes that Jacob's somewhat immoral methods continue to be well-rewarded in the world. He writes,

> There is no law against taking advantage of somebody else's stupidity, for instance. The world is full of Esaus, of suckers, and there is no need to worry about giving a sucker an even break because the chances are that he will never know what hit him anyway. . . . And the world is full of Isaacs, of people who cannot help loving us no matter what we do, and whose love we are free to use pretty much as we please. . . . [40]

Hope: In spite of the ways in which Jacob's scheming has resulted in advantages at the expense of others, he has hope of redemption through the gift of a blessing, not given because of his own "strength of cunning" but as a gift.[41] The ending of the sermon also shows that through God, blessing can emerge from defeat.[42]

Contradiction: The title of the sermon addresses a gospel-sense of contradiction, like that of the cross, where "defeat" is "magnificent." There is also contradiction in that the shady character of Jacob is the one chosen by God. Buechner also contrasts the gifts of the world: "power, success, and happiness" with God's gifts of "peace, love, and joy."[43] He calls God, "the beloved enemy," who " . . . before giving us everything, he

---

39. Buechner, "Magnificent Defeat," 3–11; and "Sprig of Hope," 225–33.

40. Buechner, "Magnificent Defeat," 9.

41. Ibid., 10–11.

42. Ibid.

43. Ibid.

demands of us everything; before giving us life, he demands our lives—
our selves, our wills, our treasure."[44]

Bible: Buechner's sermon is thoroughly biblical. He uses the Genesis
text as an episode in a larger biblical story and as part of God's ongoing
involvement with people.

Personal and Social: As in many other sermons that attend to the
cross, Buechner tends more towards the personal than the social. Although he views the world as a broken social entity where our actions
may not always have immediate consequences, he does not illustrate
hope for the world as a collective but more for the individual who can
experience transformation through God.[45]

Christ: Much of the sermon prefigures the contradiction of the
cross, but the very end specifically moves from Jacob's experience to
Jesus Christ and the cross and resurrection as the ultimate example of
"magnificent defeat." Buechner writes, "Only remember the last glimpse
that we have of Jacob, limping home against the great conflagration of the
dawn. Remember Jesus of Nazareth, staggering on broken feet out of the
tomb towards the Resurrection, bearing on his body the proud insignia
of the defeat that is victory. . . . "[46]

"A Sprig of Hope"

In "A Sprig of Hope," Buechner offers a relatively rare example of social
benefits of the good news.

Evil: Biblically, evil is present in the wickedness of humanity that
moved God to take such drastic action as well as the sense that God views
creation as beyond redemption.[47] In the present world, Buechner men-
tions, "murder and lust" and "the nightmares of our age, the sinister, bru-
tal forces that dwell in the human heart threatening always to overwhelm
us," which we cannot face for all their horror so we trivialize things ". . . so
that we can laugh instead of weep. . . . "[48] It is a manifestation of brokenness that people turn away from hard things rather than face them and

---

44. Ibid., 11.
45. Ibid., 8–9.
46. Ibid., 11.
47. Buechner, "Sprig of Hope," 227, 230.
48. Ibid., 227–28.

WHEN EVERY DAY IS GOOD FRIDAY 27

acknowledge them—ignoring them gives them more power than they deserve.

Hope: God speaks to Noah and he cannot turn away from the horrors of the world. God upholds the ark amidst the suffering and drowning of the world, and when the dove returns with a branch, Noah has hope that the world will be given a fresh start.[49] Just as the ark brought a remnant of creation together, the ark exists today "wherever people come together," and Jesus saves us from drowning with the promise that there is " . . . a reality beyond the storm more precious that the likes of us can imagine."[50]

Contradiction: Buechner contrasts Noah's seeming clown-like foolishness with the gravity of his role. He later speaks of Christ in a similar manner. Contradiction is also present in the clumsy weakness of the ark and of human connections today—yet much rides on these tenuous vessels.

Bible: The bible story gives structure and plot to the sermon as well as an angle for helping present-day hearers understand the gospel.

Personal and Social: This sermon addresses personal and social benefits of the gospel, offering comfort and grace to individuals as well as hope that war and racism are also meeting their end through Christ.

Christ: Christ is only mentioned at the very end of the sermon and not even by name but through his actions. He writes,

> . . . we must not forget the one whom Noah foreshadows and who also looked like a fool spread-eagled up there, cross-eyed with pain but who also saved the world from drowning. We must not forget him because he saves the world still, and wherever the ark is, wherever we meet and touch in something like love, it is because he also is there, brother and father of us all.[51]

However, because he uses Noah as a kind of type of Christ, when he becomes explicit, his images and language are so powerful that it affects the sense of the sermon as a whole.

49. Ibid., 228–31.
50. Ibid., 232–33.
51. Ibid.

"Beginning at the End"

Sometimes a sermon bears many of the characteristics of preaching the cross and clearly communicates gospel, but stops short of explicitly mentioning the Christ event. An example is Barbara Brown Taylor's sermon, "Beginning at the End."[52] In this sermon, Christ's actions on the cross are mentioned briefly near the beginning but are implicitly present throughout the sermon as foundational undertones. Arguably, the sermon might have been strengthened with more of an explicit connection to the cross, but as the cross is not mentioned in her particular pericope, Taylor's method effectively communicates the gospel in Matt 20:1–16.

Evil: Taylor's simple statement, "Life is so often not fair," could encompass a variety of human experiences from the not so serious to matters of life and death.[53] In this sermon, she applies it to the behavior of the householder from Jesus' parable and to every day experiences of people not being rewarded proportionally for good works done. In both instances, the evil is not so much the lack of fairness in reward, but the perception of not getting the good things we think we deserve. This perception can fester into self-righteous superiority that creates divisions and hostility among people—certainly a manifestation of brokenness in the world.

Hope: Taylor relocates us as listeners so that rather than only seeing ourselves as laborers deserving a higher wage, we also acknowledge the places where we have fallen short but not received what we deserve and instead been graciously and generously rewarded. She emphasizes, "God is not fair; God is *generous*. . . ."[54] This time a lack of fairness is received as hope rather than trouble.

Contradiction: Taylor's sermon is full of contradiction, from the title, "Beginning at the End," to the main premise, that we desire fairness or generosity depending upon where we "stand in line" on any given day.[55] Our "place in line" is a dynamic and contradictory concept, as there are times when we are better or worse comparatively to those around us. God does not give to us what we deserve and that is ultimately a good thing.

Bible: The sermon is biblical in content and form. It addresses both the parable and the narrative context that surrounds it. The parable's

52. Taylor, "Beginning," 12–20.
53. Ibid., 17–18.
54. Ibid., 20.
55. Ibid., 18–19.

placement between situations in which the disciples are competing for the best rewards, for what they think they deserve for following Jesus, strengthens Taylor's point. Her form is also informed by her text in that, like the parable itself, she surprises the listeners with a twist that relocates them in the story and causes them to experience something of the nature of God.

Personal and Social: Like Buechner, Taylor's sermon engages both personal and social experiences of the gospel. Her use of the pronoun "we" throughout the sermon encourages a sense of community amongst hearers and between preacher and hearers. While she views it from a personal perspective, the primary trouble in the sermon is of a social nature—it concerns relationships between people and social stratification.

Christ: Taylor's text is a parable of Jesus but throughout the sermon she speaks more generally about God rather than the specifics of Jesus. The life-from-death sense of the gospel is present as an undercurrent for the whole sermon but the cross is only made explicit near the beginning where she contrasts the glorious "thrones" James and John's mother desires for her sons, with Jesus' throne, which is not " . . . made out of gold and jewels but out of wood and nails, in the shape of a cross." While brief, putting this explicit reference to the cross at the beginning of the sermon lets the listeners know where this story is ultimately heading.

"Raging Faith"

Douglas E. Nelson's sermon, "Raging Faith," drawn from 2 Kgs 5:12, is an example of a sermon that draws near but ultimately stops short of the cross.[56] It bears most of the characteristics listed above, but ultimately sounds different notes when it comes to connecting the sermon to the work of Christ.

Evil: In "Raging Faith," brokenness is represented by Naaman's leprosy, with its physical and social ramifications. It is this illness that drives him to step out in faith, but it is a faith borne from having no other options other than a slow and agonizing death.[57] While not every listener may be able to immediately relate to debilitating illness, Naaman's anger at being out of options and being forced to stoop in "humility" for what

56. Nelson, "Raging Faith," 44–47.
57. Ibid., 46.

appears to be a "trivial little prescription" in the face of a big problem is a common symptom of life in a fallen world.[58]

Hope: The sermon does not delve into it in detail but from the outset, Nelson establishes that Naaman is cured of leprosy so that amidst all the actions and hesitation in the story, the listeners know that his frustrated faith is rewarded. Naaman's hope is fulfilled.

Contradiction: Nelson's sermon does use contradiction: Naaman is an angry anti-hero who is held up as an example of faith by Jesus himself. We see that through God, limited human action can yield big results in that little is asked of Naaman but his healing is great.[59] Even the title, "Raging Faith" seems to be a contradiction; listeners may think of faith only as submissive or passive, not "raging." Nelson writes, "We touch God where we had not dreamed he would be. We meet him in some utterly unplanned event—perhaps not on our knees but at a lunch counter, possibly not in some thrill of reverence but in a crisis of emptiness."[60]

Bible: Nelson vividly retells the story around his text, he also shows the connection between this story and later New Testament Scripture. He paints a clear and relatable picture of Naaman that connects present-day experiences with the text.

Personal and Social: Nelson too stays with a more individualistic understanding of the gospel. He focuses on one individual's struggle and tends to focus inward on the individual Christian's struggle of faith.

Christ: God is only a supporting player in this sermon. Christ does not have an active part. The sermon could have been more clearly connected to the cross by comparing Naaman's faith to Christ's perfect faith displayed through the cross, or by explicitly talking about the God who meets us in the most desperate situations and answers our small steps with great love, a love so great that God in Christ would give up everything, even life itself for us.

"The Only Question"

Joanna Adams' funeral sermon, "The Only Question," written for a family and a community in the throes of "Good Friday" draws near the cross.[61]

---

58. Ibid., 47.
59. Ibid.
60. Ibid.
61. Adams, "Only Question," 267–70.

Her sermon might more closely fit the characteristics if the sermon was more closely anchored in Scripture, but a sense of Scripture's promises is present throughout. Adams' context of a funeral service has also necessarily contributed to less of a social focus.

Evil: The context for the sermon provides the sense of evil and trouble as those attending the funeral service struggle with the deaths of a father who killed his schizophrenic son and himself after the son's illness had worsened.[62] Adams uses this one awful situation as proof for the kind of situations that seem to accompany human existence in a fallen world, saying, "In a world that fell from grace a long time ago, brokenness, illness, tragic endings are facts of life—inevitable, universal, unavoidable."[63]

Hope: Adams quickly and confidently answers "The Only Question" that matters under such terrible circumstances, "God says, 'Yes it is true.' Christ died and was raised so that Jim and Mark could live again. Eternal life is true. Even when fear and sorrow beat their restless wings close around us, it is true. It is true that God will lead us through the worst life can do."[64] Adams also expresses hope through the words and faith of the widow and mother of the victims and through the budding faith of the widow's granddaughter.[65]

Contradiction: Contradiction is present between the preacher's words and the circumstances of the sermon as she proclaims life and hope in the face of death. She describes God's work amidst pain and suffering, "God is so relentlessly committed to being the God of life that God can use even the worst that can happen, in ways we cannot fathom, for God's good purposes."[66] Here is the power of tensive preaching at its best—it speaks complicated truth into painful situations, reminding us that the pain that threatens to smother us is not our ultimate destiny.

Bible: The sermon is relatively weak in connection to the Bible. Adams offers scriptural paraphrases and uses the phrase, "what the Scripture promises" as a way to back up the reality of God's good intentions for the world, but she does not anchor the sermon with any specific Scripture

---

62. The context is explained in a forward to the sermon and only hinted at in the message itself as those attending the funeral are well aware of the circumstances. Ibid., 267.

63. Ibid., 268.

64. Ibid., 268–69.

65. Ibid., 269–70.

66. Ibid., 269.

text.[67] There are many reasons why she may not have used a particular text, including a context where many might not be familiar with the Bible. However, using a particular passage could have arguably strengthened the sermon by providing examples for her theological claims and actual biblical "promises" that listeners could turn to and read again as comfort.

Personal and Social: The sermon's purpose is to use the gospel as a means of comfort to a specific community, which accounts for an individualistic slant to the promises of the gospel. It was not necessary in this circumstance to broaden the scope; this is a situation where depth of the gospel is probably more important than breadth.

Christ: God's actions in Christ through the cross and resurrection are central to the theme of this sermon. Adams names them specifically and uses the cross and resurrection as a way to understand the nature of God.

"When the Wine Gives Out"

In "When the Wine Gives Out," William J. Ireland, Jr. succeeds in preaching the essence of the cross without actually mentioning the cross in the sermon.[68] While his focus is more individual than social, the trajectory is set for a broad social understanding of the gospel.

Evil: Ireland deals with commonplace troubles. The textual issue from John 2:1–11, of running out of wine at a wedding is turned into a metaphor for the common human experience of "the wine giving out" in life.[69] His examples include: a family with a "loved one" in the hospital, a young person who cannot find meaningful employment, and a middle-aged person who is depressed with life.[70] He writes, "It happens to all of us. The wine gives out, and what is meant to be a joyous celebration soon turns quiet, anxious, and empty."[71]

Hope: Jesus' miracle of turning water into wine is an example and metaphor of the kind of transformation Jesus can bring to people today. "Jesus took what is and said it has the possibility to become something else. . . . What is—whatever is tired, worn-out, devoid of joy, empty and

67. Ibid., 270.
68. Ireland, "When the Wine," 280–84.
69. Ibid., 282–83.
70. Ibid.
71. Ibid., 283.

lacking purpose—can be turned into something else. Something rich, fragrant, and ripe with the fullness of joy."[72]

Contradiction: The biblical miracle exemplifies the contradiction of the gospel; in the hands of Jesus, water can become wine. "Jesus can bring new life. He can take whatever is stagnant and stale in your life, whatever has failed to live up to its potential, and renew it."

Bible: Ireland uses John 2:1–11 as an example and window into human experiences today of desperation and despair and the power of Jesus to transform.

Individual and Social: Ireland too focuses more on individual than social experiences of the gospel. His examples focus on the experience of individuals or family units rather than social groups. He could have offered broader examples of how "the wine runs out" in society as well. Another way to have broadened the scope of the gospel is to include more of a missional thrust that shows how Christ's transforming power moves from individuals to broader societal changes. God has promised that the whole world will be changed.

Christ: While he does not bring the text to the cross, the work of Jesus and the sense of God bringing life out of death play a significant part in the sermon. Thus, Ireland's sermon stays anchored to the cross even without specifically mentioning it. Arguably, he could have deepened the experience of the gospel by bringing in the cross and resurrection—the supreme example of the kind of transforming power also displayed in the miracle of turning water into wine.

CONCLUSION

While the cross and resurrection are fruitful and necessary theological themes for preaching, particularly during Holy Week, and for addressing the realities of life in a broken world from the pulpit, many preachers struggle to give voice to the complex issues and tensions that spur theological debate in seminaries and in the pews. We can easily get tripped up navigating the tensions between God's eschatological promises to us and the persistent shadow of the cross that falls across every life. We also struggle to balance individual and social implications with how and if to ascribe meaning to suffering, with human potential and human limitations, and with how to express the costs and the benefits of the gospel.

72. Ibid.

While these tensions can be treacherous, they can also be extremely en-
ergizing for preaching—maintaining these tensions can help us to preach
sermons deeply anchored to the cross and resurrection. Exploring characteristics of sermons anchored to the cross helps us see what the cross
actually "does" in a sermon. Sermons that are deeply rooted in the cross
and resurrection seek to acknowledge evil, name hope, maintain a sense
of tension or contradiction, are grounded in scripture, address personal
and social implications of the cross, and address the fullness of the Christ
event. We saw how some present-day Christian preachers encompass the
cross and resurrection through these characteristics.

2

Conflicting Christologies

The woman looks out from the window of her second-story bedroom in a residential-care facility for those struggling with mental illness. She entered the facility after experiencing a breakdown brought on by recovered memories of horrific childhood abuse. It is winter and the gently rolling landscape is covered with a thick layer of white snow when she sees a vision that later comes to mark a turning point in her journey to wholeness and healing. A wounded lamb is sitting beneath her window, its blood slowly staining the white snow red. The woman experiences the presence of Jesus Christ with her in the midst of her pain, taking on her suffering so that she might be free to live.

Whether this vision was a manifestation of her illness or a gift of the Holy Spirit, when the woman recounted her vision to her pastor by phone several days later, the pastor was given a gift of seeing into another person's understanding of the saving power of Jesus' crucifixion and resurrection. Without realizing it, many of us have a composite picture of Jesus drawn from sources across scripture, our denominational traditions, and our own experiences. This is particularly true when it comes to understanding the cross and resurrection. Our composite images of Jesus become most important to us when we draw upon our deepest faith convictions or experience Jesus in times of crisis. When people face trouble they need to be able to count on Jesus in familiar language and images; we need to know how Jesus will save us and we don't have the resources in

35

the midst of crisis to stretch our minds around something new. Beyond the stress of crisis, congregational conflict can arise in ordinary circumstances when composite understandings of Jesus clash or contradict each other. Every Sunday, the challenge looms for preachers to be aware of the needs of those in their congregation. Along with this they must be in tune with the theology and worldviews that are central to their denomination or tradition and those that have shaped their own experience of salvation, while also fully attending to and acknowledging the diverse perspectives represented by scripture and within the congregation. When it comes to preaching that addresses such a central and deep theological theme as the cross and resurrection, the blessing for preachers is that they do not need to limit themselves to just one narrow way of understanding the person and work of Jesus. Scripture is a multifaceted jewel offering many dimensions and vantage points on this central event in the identity of the church. We must surrender our composite image to gain access to many diverse and expanding windows into Jesus' identity and saving work in the world.

Movie archives are littered with cinematic attempts to shine new light on the life, teaching, and personhood of Jesus, from "The Greatest Story Ever Told" to "Godspell," the "Life of Brian," "The Last Temptation of Christ," and "The Passion of the Christ." Movie portrayals of the life of Jesus are fraught with challenge and often controversy for Christians, in part because the sense of consensus that believers have around Jesus is limited to the creedal statements created at ecumenical councils over fifteen hundred years ago. Understanding the identity of Jesus, his teaching, and his saving work is not a new challenge, but one that is chronicled even within gospel accounts of Jesus' life. "Now when Jesus came into the district of Caesarea Philippi, he asked his disciples, 'Who do people say that the Son of Man is?' And they said, 'Some say John the Baptist, but others Elijah, and still others Jeremiah or one of the prophets.' He said to them, 'But who do you say that I am?'"[1] The members of our congregations would likely answer this question in a range of ways, some speaking with passion from the trenches of aching need, some from a safe distance echoing deep doctrinal truths remembered from long-ago catechesis, others speaking from the slow formation of relationship with the living Christ hammered out over time, while others may cite popular works or current theological conversations. Our answers to this question

1. Matt 16:13–16.

depend on our own identity and experiences as individuals and communities, and women and men, representing diverse generational, racial, and cultural traditions. The way we understand Jesus' identity and saving work depends on our present situations—where do we need saving? Are we financially stable, just getting by, or struggling? Are we healthy or suffering from illness?

While faithful biblical preaching invites the pastor to stand in the midst of a chorus of scriptural voices attempting to answer questions of Jesus' identity and saving work, pastoral and contextual awareness demands that we also listen and respond to the voices coming from our congregation and the surrounding culture. Faithful Christian proclamation requires more than unpacking narratives, biblical nuances, and historical ideas about Jesus; we must push ourselves beyond comfortable formulas and images to show the diverse members of our congregations the span and depth of salvation offered by Jesus Christ. As we straddle Scripture and our world, preachers have an opportunity to grow in *christological* awareness. Christology involves close biblical engagement and study about the historical figure of Jesus but also represents a sense of practical integrated gospel lenses that links the saving work and person of the crucified and risen Christ to human existence unfolding here and now. In the words of Tyron Inbody, "Christology is about *why* and *what* one recalls about Jesus for the life of faith . . ."[2] In short, it is what aspects of Jesus' life and teaching are experienced as "saving" for us when we are caught up and need saving!

Fortunately the Bible is not uniform in how it talks about salvation. Instead we have what Brenda Colijn describes as "a variety of pictures taken from different perspectives," rooted in the diverse experiences of New Testament authors and audiences.[3] Being clear about particular aspects or angles of Jesus' saving work can guide preachers as they make biblical and contextual choices to address pastoral concerns as well as attend to and lead to balanced formation in a congregation over time. After all, "no single picture is adequate to express the whole."[4] In an age marked by "selfies," we want to take care that we are experiencing the gospel in a range of ways rather than hammering every text to fit what *we want* from God *right now*. Experiences of the good news are complex.

2. Inbody, *Many Faces*, 10.

3. Colijn, *Images of Salvation*, 14.

4. Ibid.

While the gospel will sometimes directly address a concern in the ways we want, often the gospel surprises us with something fresh and we leave an encounter with the crucified and risen Christ convicted rather than simply placated.

There are many nuances and ways to describe our experience of salvation brought about through Jesus' death and resurrection. The New Testament offers a range of approaches for preachers, including: relational, formational (involving both identity and empowerment), liberating, and healing. These approaches are not mutually exclusive. Biblical texts may draw from multiple images and theologically the images support rather than contradict each other. Preaching through different lenses allows pastors a chance to shine light on different aspects of Christ's saving work and address different needs and views within a diverse congregation. I have purposely avoided the use of some traditional atonement lingo with the hope that preachers might be able to explore and expand their repertoire beyond the comfortable and familiar. Preachers may use the following images to design a sermon series on salvation or understanding the cross and resurrection or may use the images in their own formation as preachers to deepen biblical awareness or vary their theological language around the saving work of Christ.

PREACHING THE CROSS AND RESURRECTION AS RELATIONAL

Humans need relationship as much as we need other necessities like food and water. While the detrimental effects of isolation and loneliness might take longer to show up, scientific studies have shown that lack of social relationships can lead to significant decline in mental and physical health.[5] Our congregations can be potentially life-saving places of connection for those who are lonely and struggling with broken relationships. The relational love of God can bring salvific healing and hope to those who have experienced trauma or horrific breaches in human relationships. Often lurking quietly in the lives of those in our congregations, loneliness can take many forms: those who have lost a spouse through death or divorce, people who have recently moved, those who are single, college students or young adults living away from home for the first time, people with a variety of disabilities or chronic illness, immigrants and international

5. Marano, "Dangers of Loneliness."

students, people who are estranged from family members, or people in the midst of a transition that has affected their social identity. Jesus' saving work through the cross and resurrection offers a theologically significant and biblical way for the church to speak uniquely and authentically to these pressing concerns and experiences with more depth than can be offered by secular therapeutic approaches alone.

Often preaching about Jesus' saving work through the cross and resurrection takes on a very personal tone, but preaching relational understandings of the cross and resurrection also allow us to lift up a communal sense of salvation.[6] Relationship necessarily involves more than one individual. Whether we acknowledge it or not, our commitments and behaviors affect others around us. When one member of a family, congregation, or community hurts, all other members suffer as well. This is part of the present-day embodiment of Jesus' solidarity with us as we wait for complete redemption and healing when God's reign is enacted on earth. Positively our acts of witness and faith, including public worship are events that impact others even beyond our local faith community. Preaching that addresses social or public issues as arenas for God's salvation and that pulls examples from personal, local, and global relational networks speaks to relational Christology.

Exploring the cross and resurrection through the lens of relationship takes several forms that are reflected across New Testament literature. Jesus' life, death, and resurrection inaugurate a new covenant that transforms our relationship with God. Jesus' life, death, and resurrection repair broken relationships between people and between God and people through the tools of reconciliation and forgiveness. Finally, Jesus' own human experiences bring the joys and challenges of human existence into the life of God, deepening attachment and sympathy—God understands our experiences and acts accordingly. Relational understandings of Jesus are drawn in part from an emphasis on Jesus' incarnate presence—Emanuel, "God with us." People who are concerned about or struggle with separation or estrangement from God and other people are drawn to relational impulses in Christology. Preaching that addresses the relational angle of Jesus' saving work can actually enact healing for those who have experienced trauma and suffering in the course of broken human relationships.

6. Ibid.

New Testament texts that draw from the images of new covenant, forgiveness and reconciliation, and Emmanuel companion offer pathways for preachers to establish or nurture relational experiences of salvation in their congregations.

New Covenant

Biblically, the concept of covenant is an important relational impulse and is less frequently used in preaching about the cross and resurrection. Yet this is the way that Jesus talks about his own sacrifice in the meal he shares with his disciples; we remember the "new covenant in his blood" each time we share the cup during communion. In this act, Jesus reinterprets the covenant that God keeps with Israel in the Exodus. Jesus himself becomes the cleansing blood sacrifice that offers forgiveness and a new start in their relationship with God.[7] The understanding of covenant between God and people is deeply rooted in the Old Testament but is also threaded throughout the New Testament and is part of how the church continues to understand Jesus' identity and saving work.

In the Old Testament, the covenant with God is marked by the understanding, "I will be your God, and you will be my people."[8] The possibility of being God's people springs forth from God's love for Israel as experienced in God's promises and blessings of abundant life, God's abiding presence with Israel, and God's deliverance through the Exodus. Israel's response is also motivated by loving relationship, laid out in the Law that calls Israel to holiness, requiring that absolute allegiance, obedience, and worship be given to Yahweh.[9] The covenantal history present in the Old Testament lifts up aspects of how we experience the gospel. Of course, the drama of Scripture reveals that humanity is unable to fulfill its side of this intimate relationship with God, leading the prophet Jeremiah to name God's desire and promise, "I will put my law within them, and I will write it on their hearts; and I will be their God, and they shall be my people. No longer shall they teach one another, or say to each other, 'Know the Lord,' for they shall all know me, from the least of them to the

7. Colijn, *Images of Salvation*, 52.

8. Ibid., 46. Gen 17:7–8; Exod 6:7; Jer 31:33.

9. Colijn, *Images of Salvation*, 46–47.

greatest, says the Lord; for I will forgive their iniquity, and remember their sin no more."[10]

Covenant in the New Testament is transformed into the new covenant made possible by Jesus. In the New Testament, the idea of covenant is at work behind the scenes, shaping interpretation of the entire Christ event that is an important part of numerous theologies of atonement. New Testament authors draw from God's covenants with Abraham, Moses and Israel, David, and the new covenant prophesied by Jeremiah to help us understand Jesus' identity and saving work.[11] The gospel writers identify Jesus, in part through continuity with the Davidic covenant. God's covenant with Moses and Israel is directly paralleled in Jesus' life, teaching, and liberating "exodus" as well as in the book of Hebrews.[12] Paul's unpacking of the complex relationship between Jews and Gentiles within God's unfolding plan of salvation draws heavily from God's covenant with Abraham.[13] The covenant brought about through Jesus also brings something new for God's people. Jesus' blood cleanses humanity and makes us holy and set apart for service to God.[14] All of God's eschatological promises will be brought about through Jesus Christ. The new covenant in Jesus will surpass the old covenant and everyone under the new covenant will become citizens and have a share in God's kingdom.[15]

Preaching about the cross and resurrection in covenantal terms can make an important connection with listeners, particularly in an age that is marked by relational commitments that fall short of our expectations—let alone God's intentions. While Jesus models self-sacrificing love where parties desire to engage in mutual service out of love for the other, our lives are too often marked by broken marriage vows and broken promises of all kinds, relationships torn asunder by careless actions and words, hurt feelings, and failed communication. The lens of covenant across scripture provides key insights for preaching relational impulses within Jesus' death and resurrection that can speak to those struggling in the midst of broken relationships. The practice of covenant shows that God is relational and desires connection with people. God is not a

10. Jer 31:33–34.

11. Colijn, *Images of Salvation*, 50.

12. Ibid.

13. Ibid.

14. Ibid., 52.

15. Ibid., 53–54.

distant, abstract being who created the world in order to abandon it to its own struggles; rather God chooses to engage with people through history in a real relationship where God takes risks and experiences loss. God's faithfulness provides a strong anchor in the midst of the broken relationships that too often cause pain and suffering.

Texts that speak about this new covenant provide opportunities for preachers who want to invoke aspects of a relational Christology. Galatians, Romans, and the book of Hebrews provide specific preaching texts that use the lens of new covenant. In Galatians 3–4, Paul argues for a way for Gentiles to become Christian without first becoming Jewish. Yet he also affirms God's prior covenant with Israel by drawing from God's covenant with Abraham and shows how the new covenant in Christ is the fulfillment of God's earlier covenant.[16] Paul describes the covenant with Abraham in the form of promise accepted in faith and the covenant with Israel as law. Jesus is the true inheritor of God's promise. Thus Gentile believers in Christ who have faith are heirs of Abraham and inheritors of the covenant ultimately fulfilled by Christ.[17] Those under the old (Mosaic) covenant were subject to the law and when they could not obey, they broke covenant. Brenda Colijn describes Paul's use of Jesus' death to build his understanding of salvation through a new covenantal relationship, "He suffered as a covenant breaker in solidarity with unfaithful Israelites and godless Gentiles, so that both might receive the blessing of the promised Spirit."[18] In Christ, Jews and Gentiles, slaves and free persons, and men and women are all united in Christ. Paul writes, " . . . if you belong to Christ, then you are Abraham's offspring, heirs according to the promise."[19] In Galatians 4, Paul goes on to explain that prior to Jesus, they were considered minors and under the discipline of the law. Now that Christ has come and fulfilled God's promises, they have been made heirs and are no longer slaves to the mediating discipline of the law.[20] Thus the new covenant is seen as growing from and completing God's covenant with Abraham that preceded the covenant with Moses and the Law.[21] For

16. Ibid., 55–56.
17. Ibid., 56.
18. Ibid.
19. Gal 3:29.
20. Ibid., 56–57.
21. Ibid., 57.

those who are united in Christ the fruit of death and resurrection is new life under the new covenant in the Kingdom of God.

Paul's discussion of the new covenant in Romans also seeks to defend mission among Gentiles who do not keep the Law while also maintaining God's faithfulness in covenant with Israel. His argument in Romans 4 is similar to his argument in Galatians in that it looks to God's covenant with Abraham that predates the Mosaic covenant. However, rather than drawing a sharp distinction between the old and new covenants, Paul focuses on continuity with Israel through their common "spiritual ances-tor" Abraham.[22] In Christ, both roots and branches, whether grafted in or natural, are made holy and all may share in the promise of life from death.[23]

Paul's discussions in Galatians and Romans may feel complex at times because they are rooted not only in the context of his recipients but also situated within the context of the whole letter. Preachers will want to allot time to read the whole letter as part of their preparation although they will likely only be preaching from shorter passages. Through the relational lens of new covenant, Jesus' death and resurrection show the depth of God's self-sacrificing love and commitment to humanity, that God is willing to do whatever it takes to keep relationship—even fulfill-ing both sides of covenant, initiating a new covenant that is open to ev-eryone, and becoming the cleansing sacrifice that seals the new covenant made possible through Jesus Christ.

New covenant is just one theme in Galatians and Romans but it becomes a major motif in the book of Hebrews. Hebrews is more of an essay or even a sermon than a traditional epistle and is full of relational connections to the cross and resurrection. In our exploration of covenant as a lens for preaching, the author is using persuasive techniques to convince recipients not to return to the old covenant.[24] In chapter 8, the author posits that not only is the new covenant through Jesus a superior covenant than the first covenant, it is also the only covenant as the old covenant is now obsolete.

In exploring relational impulses within the cross and resurrection, preachers should remember that covenants are not one-sided relation-ships. Relational ways of understanding Jesus' saving work lead directly

22. Ibid.

23. Rom 11:16–24.

24. Colijn, *Images of Salvation*, 58–59.

into discipleship or mission because being in relationship with Jesus asks something of us.[25] Yes, in some ways Jesus' death and resurrection satisfy and complete aspects of the Old Testament law and covenant that created barriers for Israel, but the new covenant also requires a response from us. God's saving love as expressed in Jesus' death and resurrection is not an "unconditional love." Relationships with lopsided investment are not lasting or fulfilling—the same is true in our relationship with God. God's love and investment in us invites us to commit to covenant with God. This means that preaching the saving aspects of relationship should lead directly to a sense of mission in the sermon. Relationship with God calls us to faithful discipleship in the world.

Forgiveness/Reconciliation

A recent article described divisions between rich and poor who live in the same building in New York City. In order to get tax credits for providing low-income housing, exclusive condos reserve a few spaces for those who make $50,000 a year or less (this is Manhattan!).[26] The Department of Housing Preservation and Development approved a request from an upscale building to create a separate entrance for low-income residents.[27] The lower-income tenants must enter the building through doors in the rear of the building, while wealthy tenants are permitted to enter through the front.[28] The use of so-called "poor doors" is only the most recent example of concrete means of separating rich from poor, even within the same building. The article notes, "Some buildings offer amenities such as gyms, playgrounds and pools to only their higher-paying tenants."[29] While the politics of housing in Manhattan may not be relatable to all of us, the article reveals yet another concrete example of the deep divisions that increasingly separate people in North America. People do not associate with those who are different from them. People choose to live, work, shop, and worship with those who are similar. Meanwhile, the gap between rich and poor expands and our national government grows

25. Ibid., 48.
26. Fox, "Poor Door."
27. Ibid.
28. Ibid.
29. Ibid.

more divided and gridlocked as political parties refuse to work together for the common good.

The images to express forgiveness and reconciliation are common and comfortable themes when preaching the cross and resurrection. Jesus' self-giving and voluntary suffering on the cross heals human relationships, by undermining and overcoming violent systems that seek out and destroy those who are different or weaker, and heals divine-human relationships by removing very real systemic barriers that come between God and people. By offering forgiveness from the midst of his suffering on the cross Jesus helps to heal these broken relationships. In the New Testament, the language used has a root that can also mean loosed or released and is at times expressed with the concept of binding and loosing.[30] Jesus' followers are given the authority through the Spirit to administer church discipline by releasing or freeing a person from his or her transgression and restoring that person to full relationship with the community.[31] True forgiveness can only come from God, which is why Jesus' acts of forgiving were considered blasphemy by religious authorities.[32] Whether forgiveness is granted by other people with God's authority or directly by God, it is experienced as a gift from God and comes with a sense of freedom from compulsion or duty.[33]

The gospels offer accounts of Jesus forgiving sins in his earthly ministry but his death on the cross expands the possibilities for forgiveness for everyone. Gregory Jones describes Jesus' forgiveness on and through the cross as building throughout his ministry.[34] For example, in Luke's gospel we see Jesus acting both in continuity with God's forgiving nature as seen in the Old Testament and also showing signs that in Jesus, God is doing something new. Jesus claims the divine authority of granting forgiveness, even at times when the recipient has not yet repented.[35] In Luke 5, Jesus grants forgiveness to a paralytic and when questioned by present officials about his authority to grant forgiveness, he heals him. The man goes forth glorifying God.[36] Later Jesus teaches about forgiveness using

---

30. Colijn, *Images of Salvation*, 162.

31. Ibid., 163.

32. Ibid.

33. Ibid., 162–63.

34. Jones, *Embodying Forgiveness*, 102.

35. Ibid.

36. Luke 5:17–26. See also Jones, *Embodying Forgiveness*, 102.

the parable of the prodigal son and his brother and publically commends and extends forgiveness to Zacchaeus by proclaiming him restored to the community as a "Son of Abraham."[37] Jesus' behavior leads to his eventual crucifixion and proclamation of forgiveness from the cross, "Father forgive them; for they do not know what they are doing."[38] Jesus' death and resurrection serve as a seal for our forgiveness, and following the resurrection, Jesus instructs his disciples to continue this work.[39]

The work of forgiveness today has a therapeutic and personal edge to it that was likely not part of the first century consciousness reflected in the New Testament. As Christian preachers, we need to take care that the forgiveness we profess is anchored theologically in the life, death, and resurrection of Jesus rather than representing just another version of therapeutic understandings of forgiveness that our congregations could gather from a counselor or self-help website. Gregory Jones warns us of four issues surrounding forgiveness that are of special interest to preachers who are committed to Christian character formation. First is our broader culture's preoccupation with individual achievement, which devalues acts that are oriented towards building community.[40] This means that forgiveness will be "deployed" as a particular action or set of actions only if it is deemed beneficial in a quantifiable way.[41] Jones also critiques the church's trivialized and scattered rhetoric around forgiveness that is not typically anchored in concrete practices. Jones' criticism of the church is sharp. As the church moved through history and became distanced from Jewish and early Christian practices " . . . Christian piety turned increasingly inward; God's forgiveness became principally an individual transaction between God and a particular person, largely devoid of its eschatological context and with virtually no consequences for either Christian community or social and political life."[42] This is an especially apt warning for preachers who need to take care to avoid words that have become churchy jargon or placeholders in our sermons. Transactional words in particular are hard to understand in the context of a living relationship; similarly, language that borrows from the medieval feudal system is rarely heard outside of

---

37. Luke 15:11–32; 19:1–10. See also Jones, *Embodying Forgiveness*, 102.

38. Luke 23:34. See also Jones, *Embodying Forgiveness*, 102.

39. Luke 24:47. See also Jones, *Embodying Forgiveness*, 103.

40. Jones, *Embodying Forgiveness*, 37.

41. Ibid.

42. Ibid., 38.

church. Such words can become stumbling blocks to listeners who aren't sure precisely what we mean. If traditional theologically-laden "church" words have become hard to understand or imprecise, the words we often substitute are also not helpful. Jones holds that the church has allowed secular therapeutic language to replace theological terms and as a result we run the risk of God being drained from of our language and witness. He writes, "Instead of baptism, we talk of 'getting the baby done.' Instead of sin and grace, we talk about 'accepting that you are accepted.' And instead of practices of reconciliation, we talk about 'managing conflict' or 'coping with difficult people.'"[43] Finally, Jones claims that therapeutic approaches have slowly encroached upon and "co-opted" the church. Indeed, these models are not only popular and powerful in the broader cultural zeitgeist; Jones claims, "Psychological language and practices have become more powerful than the language and practices of the gospel."[44] While psychology and therapeutic training have brought great gifts to the church we must be nuanced in noting the differences between therapeutic and theological accounts of forgiveness in our preaching. The years since Jones' biting critique have not softened his claims. If anything, as North America becomes increasingly post-Christian, it has grown more crucial for the church to recover and claim its own unique voice in contrast to broader culture.

Purely therapeutic approaches to understanding forgiveness deny our congregations the opportunity to experience the richness and healing found in theologically-rooted forgiveness connected to God in Jesus Christ. One area of healing that is possible through Christ is forgiveness when the one who has been wronged is no longer available to grant it, most extremely in the case of murder. While our culture tends to focus on the individual, we do not live isolated lives. We are connected to others who help to shape our identity. Some of these identities are self-selected, for example, joining a book club or fantasy football league. Some are givens such as our ethnic identity or family. Sometimes when a member of a group is wronged the whole group experiences that pain and if the wronged member is no longer available to offer forgiveness, then a family member or other member of a close group might be able to extend forgiveness. Lewis Smedes suggests that for human-to-human forgiveness, our ability to extend forgiveness when we were not directly

43. Ibid., 38.
44. Ibid., 39.

wronged may extend only to the limits of our own deep empathy.[45] One example is the deep connection between a parent and child.[46] The good news of uniquely Christian forgiveness is that because we have been made brothers and sisters to Christ, we are deeply connected to God as God's children and because of that connection God is always able to extend forgiveness on behalf of another—even one who is no longer able to offer direct forgiveness. This is a source of great hope because it means that no one is beyond the possibility of forgiveness and that healing is always possible—even if it must have eschatological dimensions within the Realm of God.

It is clear that preaching forgiveness as part of the relational motif of the cross and resurrection is not for the faint of heart. Yet, it is very important for many believers' experience of salvation and has nurtured the life of the church. Tapping into this experience of forgiveness has long been key for revival preachers and others who end sermons with an invitation.[47] In a sense, Jesus' proclamation from the cross shows us that forgiveness is extended even without awareness and recognition of our need for it. This puts an important accent on forgiveness as Christ's unique and gracious act. We do not deserve it and it is extended to us independently from our behavior. Of course this does not mean that the gift comes without a reciprocal claim on us; the reception of forgiving grace is morally charged. Our faithful response of repentance and changed behavior is part of being in a reciprocal relationship with God—even if God is the one doing all the heavy lifting in the relationship.

In order for people to experience forgiveness, they need to be aware of shortcomings, sin, and brokenness in their lives. Homiletics Professor Paul Wilson groups this experience under the rubric of "trouble" and describes three possibilities: "God judging/commanding us; the human condition after the fall/the old order; and God suffering (that is, Christ's ongoing crucifixion in the world)."[48] Herman Stuempfle offers two additional deeply related and connected images, Luther's "hammer of judgment" and Tillich's "mirror of existence."[49] The "hammer" is a vertical

45. Smedes, "From Forgiveness," 348.

46. Ibid.

47. Krister Stendahl cautions readers concerning the reading of Paul's letters through the lens of Luther's "introspective conscience" in "Paul and the Introspective Conscience of the West." Stendahl, *Paul among Jews*, 79–83.

48. Wilson, *Practice of Preaching*, 161.

49. Stuempfle, *Preaching Law*, 20–21. Stuempfle's language and understanding of

understanding of brokenness, where God exists as "demand" or "threat" that acts upon the conscience of the hearer invoking guilt at the unrighteous state of being human.[50] The concern is to repair the relationship between people and God. Often this approach invokes personal culpability in sin and can be more personal in tone. The "mirror" is a horizontal metaphor, which focuses on the existential human experiences of "alienation, meaninglessness, brokenness, finitude, anxiety and despair," and on a cursory level, remains "morally neutral" in terms of personal accountability.[51] The mirror image speaks to brokenness in relationships among humans and can be effective for addressing systemic, societal, and communal concerns. This angle is a good approach for educating and mobilizing the congregation to act in response to a pressing public issue and for helping them to see connections between the mission and ministry of the church and brokenness and suffering in the world.

Preaching about sin is necessary to preach forgiveness within the relational approach to the cross and resurrection. Fortunately sermons don't have to involve fire and brimstone, finger-wagging, or accusations. When sin, brokenness, and trouble are communicated in new and modern ways that surprise hearers with their depth and relevancy, the reality of the cross and the need for new life can become more than just a topic for the sermon and encompasses the movement or form of the sermon itself as the preacher concretely names aspects of brokenness as well as concrete signs and fruit of God's forgiveness and new life in Christ. Preachers can use both "vertical" (oriented toward rifts in relationship with God) and "horizontal" (oriented toward rifts in relationship with creation) approaches effectively in their sermons. However as Wilson notes, listeners tend to respond better to horizontal understandings that encourage a realistic description of life rather than accusation.[52] Preachers on this horizontal axis lay bare the human situation; "they seek first to open our eyes rather than to bring us to our knees."[53]

Forgiveness is one part of the mending and restoration of relationship brought about by Jesus' life, death, and resurrection. We talk about this experience using words such as reconciliation and peace; in a sense

these two types of law are informed, in part, by Martin Luther, *Lectures on Galatians*, 310, and Paul Tillich, "Christian Message," 203–4.

50. Stuempfle, *Preaching Law*, 23.

51. Ibid., 24.

52. Ibid., 25, see also Wilson, *Practice of Preaching*.

53. Stuempfle, *Preaching Law*, 25.

these are the fruits of God's forgiveness and they have major implications for relationships not only between people and God but also between and among people at all levels, from broken familial relationships to healing across racial boundaries or in the aftermath of war. Reconciliation represents a countercultural ideal in an age where bullying invades households through the internet and revenge is normalized in interpersonal and political arenas. Still most people have experienced the pain of a broken relationship in some area of their lives and those in the midst of relational breech easily agree that this is an area of concern that longs to be addressed and healed.

In the New Testament, only Paul talks specifically about reconciliation, although the idea is theologically important and undergirds our reading and understanding of other New Testament texts.[54] Reconciliation and peace are closely related and express a kind of holistic sense of salvation that connotes wholeness, inclusion, well-being, and flourishing that is also expressed by the Hebrew term, "shalom."[55] For reconciliation to occur, the starting state must be one characterized by estrangement, separation, and hurtful conflict.[56] Such enmity certainly existed despite the infamous Pax Romana, where Rome's military might was used to dominate other cultural aspects of belief and behavior that conflicted with the Empire. Jesus brings reconciliation to Jews and Gentiles, clean and unclean, men and women, Jews and Samaritans, slaves and free persons so that these diverse people can work together in mission as witness to Christ's saving work. Lest we imagine a kind of cosmic "hand-holding Kumbaya experience" it is helpful to acknowledge that biblically, reconciliation is likely less about emotional experience than about a change in relational status.[57] However, as relational behaviors change, our emotions are formed and changed as well. In Romans 5, Paul writes about Jesus' death and resurrection as reconciling actions that restore our relationship with God.

> But God proves his love for us in that while we still were sinners Christ died for us. Much more surely then, now that we have been justified by his blood, will we be saved through him from the wrath of God. For if while we were enemies, we were

54. Colijn, *Images of Salvation*, 177.

55. Ibid.

56. Ibid., 179.

57. Ibid., 181. See also Fitzmeyer, "Reconciliation," 165–66, 170.

reconciled to God through the death of his Son, much more surely, having been reconciled, will we be saved by his life. But more than that, we even boast in God through our Lord Jesus Christ, through whom we have now received reconciliation.[58]

Reconciliation with God is mostly about Jesus' death and resurrection creating the possibility for reconciling transformation rather than appeasing God's "wrath."[59] God's righteousness is real, but to think of God's wrath as analogous to human anger is misleading. God's love is stronger than God's wrath and God's love moves God in Jesus to the cross. Brenda Colijn puts it succinctly, "God is always the reconciler, never the reconciled."[60] It is God's action that reconciles us to God and to each other. When we are enfolded into the life of Christ we too undergo the process of death and resurrection. Those things that separate us from God die with Christ and we are raised as new people, brothers and sisters to Christ, joint-heirs/children of God, and members of Christ's own body. Through the power of the Holy Spirit we are able to live a life of peace that is opened up for us by Christ.

The work of reconciliation is ongoing in our lives, part of the continuing impact of the cross and resurrection that affects all that came before and all that follows it chronologically.[61] This relational aspect of the cross and resurrection continue in the Spirit's work of sanctification as we conform ourselves to Christ over time. Jesus' saving work becomes our work as we are his disciples or "ambassadors." Paul puts it this way,

> So if anyone is in Christ, there is a new creation: everything old has passed away; see, everything has become new! All this is from God, who reconciled us to himself through Christ, and has given us the ministry of reconciliation; That is, in Christ God was reconciling the world to himself, not counting their trespasses against them, and entrusting the message of reconciliation to us. So we are ambassadors for Christ, since God is making his appeal through us; we entreat you on behalf of Christ, be reconciled to God. For our sake he made him to be sin who knew no sin, so that in him we might become the righteousness of God.[62]

58. Rom 5:8–11.

59. Colijn, *Images of Salvation*, 180–81.

60. Ibid., 181.

61. Ibid., 184–85.

62. 2 Cor 5:17–21.

The work of reconciliation is also challenging. Just as Jesus Christ suffered in securing our reconciliation, so too acts of Christian reconciliation today come with a cost. Reconciliation was arguably one of Paul's chief pastoral concerns in his letters.[63] He calls on Christian communities to engage in acts of reconciliation and peacemaking within and even beyond the boundaries of the community.[64] In Philippians 2, Paul invites the congregation to imitate Christ's humility by showing deference to one another.[65] In Romans 12 he encourages reconciliation with even unbelievers, writing, "Live in harmony with one another; do not be haughty, but associate with the lowly; do not claim to be wiser than you are. Do not repay anyone evil for evil, but take thought for what is noble in the sight of all. If it is possible, so far as it depends on you, live peaceably with all."[66] The early church endured persecution and martyrdom in following Christ. While the costs are great, the cost of reconciliatory work is more than covered by the abundance of God's love and grace, which nurtures and fuels our actions.

In light of all this, it is challenging but crucial for preachers to name concrete ways that Jesus' death and resurrection are making reconciliation possible through the Spirit's work here and now as a foretaste of the complete peace that will mark the Reign of God. If we truly believe that Jesus' death and resurrection have made the church one and have overcome harmful divisions between people then we need to show what this looks like in our world. One profound example is the ministry of Coming to the Table, a program that brings together descendants of former enslaved African Americans and descendants of former owners. Phoebe and Betty Kilby are linked by history but their lives unfolded quite differently because of racism.[67] Betty Kilby was one of the pioneering African American students who helped to desegregate her Warren County Virginia school. Her family's bravery made them a target for those who felt threatened by change. People regularly fired gunshots at their home and even poisoned the family dog.[68] As a descendant of former slave owners, Phoebe contacted Betty and her family to see how she could make

---

63. Colijn, *Images of Salvation*, 188.

64. Ibid. See also Rom 14:9; 15:5–13; Phil 2:1–2; 4:2–3.

65. See also Colijn, *Images of Salvation*, 188.

66. Rom 12:16–18

67. Drash, "When Kin."

68. Ibid.

amends. Betty invited Phoebe to join her for a family dinner so that they could meet and talk. Betty's action and desire to engage helped to heal divisions. Not only is it rare for descendants of enslaved and owners to meet, people struggle to meet and talk frankly across racial lines. Moved by Betty's story and inspired by an idea from Betty's brother James, Phoebe applied for and received a grant to hold a "community conversation on race" in Warren County.[69] It was an important event for people on all sides and began to bring healing within that community. The initial conversation inspired the community to place a historical marker at the school to commemorate desegregation and to host a celebratory dedication ceremony to bring diverse people together.[70]

Emmanuel Companion

When God became human in Jesus Christ, God demonstrated the value of humanity and God's deep investment in us. We are worth so much to God that God is willing to die for us. Through Jesus, God becomes flesh and dwells among us, taking a share in the full spectrum of life, from birth to death. This means that Jesus can understand isolation and loneliness along with many other challenging and common relational experiences. That God in Jesus has experienced the full spectrum of human experience and can relate to what we experience can also be greatly comforting to people in the midst of a variety of relational experiences. For example, early in his ministry he experiences a sense of estrangement and disconnection from people in his hometown of Nazareth, after preaching a message that challenged their expectations, while offering liberation to others.[71] He also gives voice to changes in his relationship to his family in light of his unfolding ministry, divine identity, and commitment to his new family of disciples, when he asked "Who is my mother and who are my brothers?"[72] His comments may have caused some sense of grief and challenge for his family, an experience that may be relatable in many families to some degree. Jesus also experiences the fickle limitations of friendship. Shortly before his arrest, he invited his disciples to pray with

69. Kilby, "Crossing the Line."

70. Ibid.

71. Luke 4:16–30.

72. Matt 12:46–50; Mark 3:31–35; Luke 8:19–21.

him and they could not stay awake to give him support.[73] Peter, one of the most prominent and active disciples in the gospels denies even knowing him.[74] Yet, according to John's account, in the midst of his suffering on the cross, Jesus still attends to the social and relational needs of his mother, affirming the importance of family and relationship.[75] This is especially interesting since God, like Mary, is on the verge of losing a beloved son. On the cross not only does God lose his son, Jesus apparently loses his Father and experiences even God's absence as he cries out, "My God My God, why have you forsaken me?"[76]

The horror of the cross as "an instrument of execution" may feel remote to present-day congregations, but we should not fall into a trap of cleaning up the cross. Suffering believers across the centuries have felt a deep connection with Jesus because of his suffering and death.[77] Romanticizing or domesticating the cross paints a weak and ineffectual portrait of the Savior of the world and risks not only trivializing the very real human life of Jesus Christ in living, suffering, and dying but also trivializing the suffering that people continue to experience today.

Certainly the suffering associated with Christ on the cross, as well as any human suffering, exposes a "stumbling block" for many as it raises questions about God's faithfulness. But Jesus' suffering also opens up an opportunity for preachers to make important links between our experiences and the life of God in ways that can defy ordinary language.[78] Mary Catherine Hilkert, Luke Powery, and other scholars suggest using the sermon as a kind of lament.[79] Hilkert writes, "In Christian faith the last word about the cross may be that it is indeed a mystery of divine love, fidelity, and solidarity, but in the context of global suffering the first word that must be spoken is of its scandal, injustice, and absurdity."[80]

73. Matt 26:36–46; Mark 14:32–42; Luke 22:39–46.

74. Matt 26:69–75; Mark 14:66–72; Luke 22:54–62; John 18:15–18, 25–27.

75. John 19:25–27.

76. Matt 27:46; Mark 15:34. See also Schweitzer, *Contemporary Christologies*, 78; Moltmann, *Crucified God*, 204–6. The fact that Jesus cries out to God shows that even in the midst of this experience, Jesus uses the tools of the psalmist to continue to engage with God and bring his anguish before a God who cares.

77. Hilkert, "Preaching the Folly," 40.

78. Ibid., 42; 1 Cor 1:23.

79. Hilkert, *Naming Grace*, 119.

80. Hilkert, "Preaching the Folly," 40. Aden and Hughes also view the sermon as an outlet for human lament, although instead of the cross they turn primarily to Old Testament texts for scriptural grounding. Aden and Hughes, *Preaching*, 52.

Jesus lived in ways that challenged authorities and morays of his time and brought him into relationship with those on the fringe of society.[81] As God incarnate, his "entire life proclaimed "God's 'no' to human suffering," but Jesus suffered a terrible death on a cross, betrayed and abandoned by friends, victimized by an unfair legal system, and apparently abandoned by God as he cried out, "My God, my God why have you forsaken me?"[82] Hilkert cautions preachers against "moving too quickly to the good news of the resurrection without honoring the depths of the anguish of the crucified and human process of grieving."[83] Preaching "the saving power of the cross" does not focus on God's vengeance or role as judge against sinful humanity, but proclaims "God's unlimited mercy and forgiveness," and ultimate defeat of death in Christ.[84] There are times when faithful preaching involves holding up traumatic and terrible human experiences before our God and reminding God and God's people of God's good promises for us.

It follows that the cross can be a potent vehicle for validation and healing in those who are struggling with grief and despair.[85] Preaching can take the form of biblical psalms that lament the present state of affairs and call God into account. Luke Powery envisions lament in preaching (among other practices) as evidence of the Holy Spirit's presence in worship.[86] The experiences of forced enslavement and deep pervasive racism have made lament and a sense of connection with Christ's suffering an important part of the African American Christian experience. But the spirit of lament is held together with the spirit of celebration, which gives voice to the power and experience of resurrection life.[87] Indeed, the pattern of a psalm such as Psalm 22, whose language provided words for Jesus' own anguish on the cross, shows us how lament and celebration can be held together in ways that authentically bear witness to human experience and our encounters with the Spirit. Writing specifically for

81. Hilkert, "Preaching the Folly," 41.

82. Ibid., 41–42.

83. Ibid., 42–43.

84. Ibid.

85. Hughes, *Trumpet*, 48–50. Scott M. Gibson cautions that the preacher should note the difference between a funeral sermon and a eulogy and not confuse the eulogy with the gospel. Gibson, *Preaching for Special Services*, 48–50.

86. Powery also names celebration, grace, unity, and fellowship as "manifestations" of the Spirit. Powery, *Spirit Speech*, xv.

87. Ibid., 28–30.

contexts of mourning and grief, Robert Hughes especially connects human suffering with suffering in the life of God, writing, "God suffers when people suffer, because God shares everything with them.[88] "The gospel declares God with us—Emmanuel. . . . The cross and resurrection of Jesus are testimony to God's deep and unwavering love for us."[89] Trust in God's loving presence and sovereign power can be a huge relief for mourners who may feel guilt surrounding a death. Mourners can "let God be God."[90] Thus, "Like the weak and dying Christ, the bereaved can be invited to commend themselves to God's care."[91]

Jesus' death caused a time of separation between Jesus and his disciples. We too experience the separation of death; however, in the resurrection Jesus returns to fellowship with his beloved followers and through the presence of the Holy Spirit we are assured that Jesus will be with us always, "to the end of the age."[92] While the resurrection is assured, on this side of God's Kingdom we still experience suffering and death and the risen Christ accompanies us and continues to suffer alongside us. In his life and death, Jesus chose to experience dark and painful aspects of human life including betrayal, suffering, and death. The Christ who is our brother takes our experiences into the life of God. Using the psalms as a model, preaching in a lament style is one possibility for bringing our personal and corporate complaints before a God who cares and can effectively speak to those who hold a more relational Christology. While preaching lament can be an appropriate response to suffering in the human experience, our identity in Christ does not end at the cross but in the resurrection. In the act of baptism we proclaim that our relational link with Jesus in suffering and death means that we are also linked to his resurrection and new life. The resurrected life shows us that suffering and death do not have the final say in our existence.

88. Hughes, *Trumpet*, 49.

89. Ibid., 53.

90. Ibid., 59.

91. Ibid.; Luke 23:46.

92. Matt 28:20.

PREACHING THE CROSS AND RESURRECTION
AS FORMATIONAL

A recent news broadcast cited a Harvard University study surveying ten thousand middle school and high school students in thirty-three different schools around the nation about what they thought was most important to their parents for their future: " . . . that they achieve at a high level, that they are happy (defined as "feeling good most of the time"), or that they care for others." Around 80 percent of the young people surveyed picked success/achievement or happiness as their top choice, while only around 20 percent picked care for others. The survey further revealed that about 80 percent of the kids also ranked achievement or happiness as most important for their future, reflecting what they think is most important to their parents.[93] The study discussed what the researchers called a "rhetoric/reality gap" because most parents voiced that caring for others was their top priority for their children's development.[94] Despite claims and common clichés of children rebelling against parents, studies consistently show that the formation that children experience in their homes from parental actions and behaviors effects them at a deep level and that their own values tend to reflect the values of their parents. Many of these well-meaning parents and teens are sitting in our churches on Sunday morning. Preaching can be part of a program of Christian character formation that reorients us towards the cross and resurrection and helps us to deepen our commitment to following Jesus in speech and behaviors whether at home, at work, at school, or in a social setting.

In many ways, understanding Jesus as an example for us is linked to relational understandings of the cross and resurrection. In the case of viewing Jesus as our example or role model, the accent falls on our response to Jesus' tremendous love, a love so deep that he is willing to die for us, which inspires and transforms us so that we can love and live more like Jesus. In Luther's classic description of people as both justified by Christ and yet still sinners, this understanding puts the accent on our redemption and the potential and promise we have in Christ of being able to live as new people in Jesus' image. In classic atonement theologies, this impulse is voiced by Peter Abelard.[95] Sometimes called the "moral influence" model, the primary "evil" overcome by Jesus is humanity's failure to

---

93. Weber, "Children." See also Smith, "For Most Kids."

94. Weber, "Children."

95. Abelard, "Solution," 283; Schweitzer, *Contemporary Christologies*, 33.

love and pursue good.[96] Jesus saves us by kindling within us a longing to love as Jesus loved.[97] This love can drive followers to engage in costly acts of discipleship and inspire tireless efforts in overcoming systemic evils such as racism, sexism, and environmental destruction.

Preaching a formational understanding of the cross requires more than inspiration to love as Jesus loves. It necessitates eschatological awareness. The victory of the cross redefines human reality and marks a turn to a new age in history. Because of Christ's activity on the cross, humans are no longer defined by their old lives but have new lives defined by the righteousness of Christ. These new lives bear witness to a new age, which is no longer oriented towards sin and death but by God's good and healing intentions for creation. Therefore, the historical event of the cross moves beyond human understanding of linear history to define the inbreaking of eschatological reality. One could say that the cross strikes a decisive tuning note for all of history, changing the sound of all that came before and all that comes after it.

Professor of Homiletics and Liturgics James F. Kay envisions the cross as the apocalyptic turning point for history, which initiates a new reality that has implications for preaching.[98] The new reality brought forth through the cross recasts human life and relationships. Kay reads the words of the apostle Paul concerning the cross in 1 Corinthians as meaning that "the apocalyptic event of the cross—God's power in weakness—continues in the present proclamation and proclaimers of that event."[99] He elaborates, " . . . the word of the cross effects the same death to the construals and patterns of the old age and the resultant awakening to those of the new as the original cross-event itself. . . . Preaching the cross brings to its hearers the death and the life that stand at the juncture

96. Schweitzer, *Contemporary Christologies*, 52.

97. Ibid., 53.

98. Kay, "Word," 46. David Buttrick asserts that "apocalyptic consciousness" is key to understanding " . . . the significance of Christ's death and resurrection. . . . " Later he adds, "So though we cannot reinstate an apocalyptic mindset, we can grasp a narrative metaphor and insist that in Jesus Christ there has been a change in the plot line of the human story." Buttrick, *Preaching Jesus, 20*, 67. See also Kay, "Word," 49–50.

99. Kay, "Word," 47. Nancy Lammers Gross describes Paul as a "practical theologian," building on Kay's work as she calls preachers to reclaim Paul. She encourages preachers to "Do what Paul did; don't just say what Paul said," by viewing and proclaiming the world according to the eschatological reality ushered in by Christ on the cross. Gross, *If You Cannot Preach*, 12–20, 37.

of the ages."[100] Kay stresses that the old way of knowing, "by the norm of the flesh" ends with Christ's death on the cross and now the cross defines human knowing.[101] He writes,

> At the juncture of the ages we do not yet see God "face to face," and death remains the last enemy even for the Christian. The test, therefore, of all our earthly God-talk is not whether it demonstrates itself in ecstatic spirituality, but whether, by passing through the cross, it proclaims God's power to extinguish in us all that prevents us from discerning and serving "the neighbor who is in need."[102]

Life at the "juncture of the ages" means "the word of the cross always retains a human form," important for how we understand ourselves as "works-in-progress" and how we understand our calling as the church.[103] This is also important for preachers because it means that our words matter to a world still caught between crucifixion and resurrection, a world that needs the healing and hope that only God in Christ can bring. However, God's action in Christ, which "deconstructs" the old "fleshly" ways of knowing " . . . means that rhetoric (and poetics) cannot be unquestionably baptized for Christian use. . . . Rather, the word of the cross overturns reigning rhetorical strategies, 'taking them captive' (2 Cor 10:5) in the service of its message."[104] This is especially important as preachers discern the use of illustrations, examples, and technology in their sermons. When a preacher utilizes a video clip, the worldview and perspective of the film enter the sermon. In selecting illustrative material, the preacher must reflect on how things look from the vantage point of the cross and resurrection. Does this illustration reflect life under the shadow of the cross, or does it show us a glimpse of resurrection life? Several years ago, students in my preaching class reflected on a sermon preached in a local congregation during the season of Advent. The preacher used a clip from the film *Iron Man 2* to contrast Iron Man's entrance with Jesus' entrance. Iron Man entered with fireworks and fanfare to a tremendous

---

100. Kay, "Word," 47. Buttrick links the end of the old age and the beginning of the new with Jesus' proclamation itself and suggests that Jesus was crucified in part because he threatened the old structures and systems. Buttrick, *Preaching Jesus Christ*, 40–41.

101. Kay, "Word," 46–47.

102. Ibid., 47.

103. Ibid., 48.

104. Ibid.

crowd gathered in an arena, accompanied by the music of *AC/DC* and celebrated by his own scantily clad "Iron Man cheerleaders." In contrast, Jesus entered the world quietly as a helpless infant, born to a poor and obscure unwed teenager. The contrast is key and set the preacher up for sharing something important about God's ways in the world, but the students raised concerns that the sexy cheerleaders in the clip reflected values that demeaned and objectified women. Women receive these messages everyday through ever-present advertising and popular culture. They felt that it was irresponsible of the preacher to have invited these images to invade worship. The church and its preachers stand at a crossroads where they see the passing away of the present world and proclaim the coming reality of God's kingdom.[105] In light of this, Kay writes, ". . . what is required of preachers are not simply illustrations from history and nature, but illustrations that place history and nature, indeed all of life, into the crisis of the cross."[106] Because these two distinct realities exist "simultaneously," the metaphor of a polyphonic piece of music with more than one melody sounding at once is helpful as it alludes to the "layered" rather than "sequential" quality of the old and new ages.[107] Preaching accurately about the cross requires that we honestly show our congregation evidence of both realities: the old that is passing away and especially the new reality of the resurrection. However, we should also remember with humility that it is not human words but "the power of God at work in the cross and its word," that ultimately communicates God's message to the world.[108]

Besides impacting the way that we make decisions as preachers, preaching about the cross is generative and deeply formational for the church. "The proclamation of the cross has produced something new in the world: a cruciform community," which "is not of the world but lives in the world at the juncture of the ages."[109] This sense of transformation through the inbreaking Realm of God is visible in our New Testament, particularly through the actions of Jesus in his life of healing and teaching as well as his death and resurrection. Professor of Homiletics and Liturgics Emeritus David Buttrick understands the person of Jesus Christ

105. See also Buttrick, *Preaching Jesus,* 44.

106. Kay, "Word," 50.

107. Ibid., 51. The preacher must see with what Kay refers to as "stereoscopic vision."

108. Ibid., 49.

109. Ibid.

as inaugurating God's Kingdom in the "now" as his parables and teaching are in "present tense."[110] He calls upon preachers to proclaim God's reign now by understanding our present social reality as being "a world framed in creation and eschaton, a world in which God is redemptively active. . . . So we live in God's social order now, and watch on tiptoe a coming fullness."[111] Buttrick notes, "Preaching participates in the shaping of our consciousness and thus in the reconstruction of a social world."[112] Yet in the midst of a broken world, he acknowledges, "We preach a gospel we cannot live."[113] Thus, the church, though sinful, is called to live as a sign of God's "Kingdom-intentions," which is only possible because by God's grace the future of human history has already been decided by Christ on the cross.[114] It follows that Buttrick encourages preachers to allow the cross and resurrection to be definitive of the nature of God so that when the cross and resurrection are added to eschatological visions of judgment, "The one who will judge is the one who died for us in heartbreaking love and who lifted up the condemned Jesus, condemned as a sinner, to glory."[115]

Indeed, our new identity in Jesus Christ is the truth, but there is some lag time in the "already, but not yet" experience of life this side of God's Kingdom. Willard Swartley puts it this way, " . . . we learn to be what we have become in Jesus Christ, a participant in God's great shalom vision and purpose. The "in Christ" identity shapes our ethics, as both gift and task."[116] Following Jesus asks something of us, and Jesus does serve as an important model, yet our humanity also places a limit on us. We will always be disciples not teacher, creatures not creator. When we preach about discipleship and following Jesus in our sermons, it needs to be balanced by the uniqueness of Christ and of what Christ does for us. The cross exposes humanity at its most broken and sinful; it arrests us. The resurrection shows us who God is. Only God can bring life out of death! Recognizing the gap between humanity and God and our constant need for grace is key to preventing burnout for congregations and

---

110. Buttrick, *Preaching the New,* 69.

111. Ibid., 81.

112. Ibid., 82.

113. Ibid., 110.

114. Ibid., 110–11, 118.

115. Ibid., 59, 61–62.

116. Swartley, *Covenant of Peace,* 383.

pastors. My own experience growing up in a Mennonite congregation may be instructive; I remember the importance placed on living a life of service to God, of going on service trips, and being called upon to act as Christ would act in this world. As a dutiful child, I was aware of the many problems in the world. Although I strived to make the world a better place and my confession of faith upon baptism stressed my desire to live as a disciple, I always fell short, frustrated, and burdened by the weight of the world's many problems and my own human inadequacy. The hands laid on my shoulders when I was licensed for a youth ministry position felt like heavy weights and burdens that were drilling me into the ground as I knelt. Later as a seminary student, John Calvin's description of humanity's sinfulness reminded me of the distance between God and people and how human activity on its own can often contribute to brokenness. These new insights allowed me to experience grace, which made ministry a joyful possibility rather than an impossible duty. At my ordination service, the hands of the congregation instead felt supportive and uplifting.

Attending to the specifics of context is crucial to any preaching, particularly when attending to congregational formation. While it is important to acknowledge the limits of human potential in some settings, in other contexts people need to hear about the promise of redeemed living and the hope of transformation. In this vein, understanding Jesus' work as an example for us is particularly effective in preaching to people who are part of oppressed and marginalized groups or people with low self-esteem who have not experienced their ability to make a change in their environment or lives. Understanding Jesus' saving work as example for us can be empowering for people who have traditionally been on the receiving end of abusive power in the past or who contend daily with experiences of powerlessness.

One summer I had the opportunity to worship with a congregation in Kansas City, mostly consisting of people without addresses who lived in the urban core. Preferring the name, "urban sojourners" to the pejorative "homeless," the participants in worship were well aware of their fallenness, they were reminded daily by passersby who either ignored them or treated them as less than human. Rather than the limitations of humanity, sermons in this congregations needed to focus on God's love, God's power, and the possibility of redeemed existence and human transformation brought about through the cross and resurrection.

Liberationist theologians have rightly critiqued some formational approaches to the cross as harmful to women and other oppressed persons who are instructed to submit to suffering as a way of imitating Jesus. This formation has brought devastation rather than salvation. Rebecca Parker's and Rita Nakashima Brock's powerful and self-revelatory book, *Proverbs of Ashes,* names at least one instance where a woman's faith and view of sacrifice as part of following Jesus led to her death at the hands of her abusive husband in the presence of her young children.[117] Reading this and other painful stories help us understand how high the stakes are in careful preaching about the cross and resurrection. Approaches to atonement that continue to crucify the fragile sense of self and self-preservation of oppressed persons have understandably turned some away from God and the church.

While we are called to follow the way of Jesus, our sermons should reinforce the unique character of Jesus' story. We should not encourage listeners to try to find their own story in the story of Christ but to claim Christ's story, the gospel story, which moves from death to life as their own story.[118] As believers who are truly in Christ, our life stories and destinies are ultimately merged with his, which should lead oppressed persons to claim the triumph of the resurrection rather than remain trapped in situations of abuse. We can only follow Jesus as fully actualized human beings. Theology that robs someone of his or her personhood no longer bears witness to God, who created us. It is a sign of the still fallen nature of the world that words intended to bring life are misunderstood so as to give a sense of separation from the church or cause hearers to turn away from God's embrace. Preachers can remedy this misinterpretation by stressing Jesus' actions alone as salvific. Human suffering should never be portrayed as good or part of God's saving intentions. Present-day pastors have a long way to go in helping to heal past damage caused by well-meaning but misguided clergy. Fortunately, preaching offers a way of allowing the Bible and theology to have an ongoing conversation with God's people in changing times and cultures; it makes sense that language surrounding the atonement will need to change in order to better communicate Christ's gracious self-offer for the reconciliation of God and the world.[119]

117. Parker and Brock, *Proverbs of Ashes,* 19.

118. Campbell, *Preaching Jesus,* 197. Campbell cites Lindbeck, *Nature of Doctrine,* 118. See also Kay, *Preaching and Theology,* 117.

119. Kay, *Preaching and Theology,* 20–22.

In contrast to preaching that focuses narrowly upon the formative importance of self-sacrifice, preaching that reminds us of our baptismal identity can provide a more balanced avenue for drawing out formational understandings of the cross and resurrection. Because we are redeemed or purchased by God through Jesus' costly death on the cross, our identity is marked by the one who now claims us—we are God's and deeply valuable to God.[120] Strengthening this sense of identity can provide a sense of worth for those who have suffered from mistreatment and oppression. This kind of deep baptismal formation can also serve as a powerful remedy for a lack of connection between the values we espouse and the values we live. Reminding congregants of *who they are* and *to whom they belong* can be significant, particularly for youth and others who are in the midst of discerning identity, navigating relationships with parents and peers, and making significant life choices.

PREACHING THE CROSS AND RESURRECTION AS LIBERATION

Today we tend to think of freedoms as rights guaranteed by political documents, laws, and government officials or as liberties that are threatened by the same documents, laws, and officials. While slavery is very much a real issue both globally and in North America, it is a concept that feels distant from many in our congregation. Theologically, true freedom comes not from governments but from Christ who sets us free from tenuous tethers that keep us anchored to our passions, fear, money, powers, and principalities, or other substances that hold significant sway over our lives and decision-making. While many of us deny our enslavement, those in recovery from addictions readily name their power. Many churches host twelve-step programs such as Alcoholics Anonymous or Overeaters Anonymous in their buildings but the liberating power of Jesus Christ who decisively overcame the powers that bind us is a powerful New Testament image and relevant approach to preaching the cross and resurrection that can connect to many in our congregations.

In the biblical world, freedom for enslaved persons almost always bears a cost.[121] In the Old Testament, this process is encompassed by the term redemption and is applied to numerous recipients including prop-

120. Colijn, *Images of Salvation*, 147.
121. Ibid., 145.

erty, such as slaves and dwellings, as well as family members, like the firstborn.[122] However, the primary Old Testament model for redemption, the Exodus is not brought about by monetary payment but by God's sovereign action.[123] Liberation from slavery in Egypt is a free gift from God, reciprocated through Israel's covenant with God and faithful obedience to the Law. As with our other images, Old Testament understandings and practices undergird the New Testament. For example, the Exodus is a deeply engrained image and motif that spans both Old and New Testaments.

As in the Old Testament, redemption in the New Testament is described with language that speaks both of purchase and release.[124] The image of purchase is used by Paul as he calls the congregation at Corinth to holy living, "Do you not know that your body is a temple of the Holy Spirit within you, which you have from God, and that you are not your own? For you were bought with a price; therefore glorify God in your body."[125] More important than the price itself is the identity of those who have been purchased—they belong to the one who has redeemed them. In Israel's case and ours, we belong to God.[126] The language of release or ransom is more common, in the gospels of Matthew and Mark, Jesus describes his work and calling using language of ransom, "to give his life as a ransom for many."[127] For most of us the idea of "ransom" may call to mind crime dramas or action movies but biblically this idea is linked to the idea of freedom. When connected to the cross, ransom is more than just paying someone off. Jesus serving as ransom means that he puts himself in our place.[128] He dies so that we can live. In other texts, biblical authors talk explicitly about freedom. In the eighth chapter of the Gospel of John, Jesus links truth and his saving action with freedom and in Romans 8 Paul writes of creation's longing for the "freedom of the children of God."[129]

122. Ibid.

123. Ibid., 145–46.

124. Ibid., 147.

125. 1 Cor 6:19–20.

126. Colijn, *Images of Salvation*, 147.

127. Matt 20:28; Mark 10:45.

128. Colijn, *Images of Salvation*, 149.

129. John 8:32–36; Rom 8:21.

The freedom granted to us by Jesus' death on the cross is challenging to understand for many of us who feel that we are "free." For many first-century Jews, the idea of freedom was tied to political hopes. They longed for God to free them from oppression through a powerful Messiah.[130] This impulse is present throughout Luke's gospel. Well before Jesus' earthly ministry began, Zechariah and Anna link Jesus with the promised Messiah who will bring redemption and freedom and following Jesus' death when he appears to two disciples on the road to Emmaus, they confess that they had hoped that Jesus might be the one to redeem Israel.[131] Even into Luke's second volume of Acts, just before the ascension, the disciples still connect the freedom Jesus offers to Israel's political situation.[132] Yet Jesus resists giving answers concerning Israel's political situation and instead calls his disciples to look outward, their spiritual freedom will lead them to mission and service towards the world.

Freedom may indeed have political overtones, but it is not limited to the political. Jesus did not start a violent political revolution but he did challenge the systems and structures that oppressed or trapped people. Jesus shows us that freedom can be personal and social, spiritual, emotional, relational, and/or physical. He ate and socialized with people from diverse social strata. He healed those suffering with physical and mental illness. He forgave sins and restored isolated people to community. He fed hungry crowds and challenged unjust leadership practices. By going to the cross without resisting or retaliating he undermined the violent use of power and fear tactics. In the resurrection he ultimately put an end to the power of those tactics and freed all of humanity from fear and enslavement to the power of death itself. The liberation granted in Jesus' ministry directly foreshadowed his liberating action through the cross and resurrection. Preachers may use any passage with overtones of liberation as an opportunity to also preach and teach about the cross and resurrection.

Following Jesus, Paul also challenged oppressive systems. His letters to Corinth bring liberation by encouraging peace, mutuality, and sharing diverse gifts rather than creating a hierarchy. In 1 Corinthians, the apostle Paul offers pastoral care and instruction for specific issues

---

130. Colijn, *Images of Salvation*, 152.

131. Luke 1:68; 2:38; 24:21. See also Colijn, *Images of Salvation*, 152.

132. Acts 1:6. See also Colijn, *Images of Salvation*, 152.

at work in the newly formed Christian assembly at Corinth.[133] Among other things, Paul seeks to shift the people's worldview from that of focusing on their former lives, which emphasized the scattered diversity of heritage, socio-economic status, religious beliefs, and leadership views toward their new lives as members of a new eschatological reality unified in Christ. In light of what Paul saw as the imminently impending advent of the Kingdom of God (1 Cor 7:26–31), his principle lens for shifting the worldview and practices of the congregation come not from exercising political influence through overt authority but through proclaiming the cross—the gospel of Jesus Christ crucified. Through a pattern that can be adapted for present-day preachers, in his letter to Corinth, Paul uses the cross to remind the Corinthians of his earlier proclamation and to shape his present preaching (in the letter), which pastorally addresses current issues and concerns of the congregation that are keeping them bound and unable to fully witness to the freedom offered by Christ.

In the face of an impending schism within the Corinthian community, Paul uses the cross as the lens through which the life and the calling of the congregation at Corinth are radically reoriented. This means that for Paul, while the complete fulfillment of God's salvific will for the world has not fully been realized, even in the midst of imperial Rome, the cross offers a new way forward by ultimately redefining Israel's religious traditions, the shape and witness of the Corinthian community, and the use of authority or power within the assembly according to the ultimate purpose to which they are called. Christ's actions on the cross allow them to live as new people freed from bondage to their former lives, enjoying unity and mutuality—self-sacrifice, love, and harmony—where there were divisions and hierarchies.

As an example for preachers today, Paul's rhetoric in the written proclamation of his letter to the Corinthians displays both "countercultural" patterns, along with popular slogans, language, and patterns of discourse that would be familiar to his audience. While the message of the gospel is often out of tune with the messages congregants might hear throughout the week, sometimes sermons can be "stumbling blocks" or create barriers for listeners when preachers use abstract theological or scholarly language or ramble without a clear sermon structure. A sermon can be both theologically rich and concretely relevant by employing illustrations, words, and tools that are part of people's everyday lives. Further,

133. The congregation may have only been about five years old as Richard B. Hays notes. Hays, *First Corinthians*, 6.

use of a clear sense of structure or direction will help both preacher and listeners stay with the sermon. Jesus served not only as the content of Paul's proclamation but also as the means of effective communication through his Spirit. Thus, regardless of sermon structure or technique, neither Paul's proclamation nor ours depends on "eloquent wisdom" or "lofty words" but upon the Spirit and power of God—displayed subversively through the cross—in order that the attention of the Corinthians and present believers would be drawn to God rather than to Paul or modern-day preachers who act as servants of God.[134]

To help listeners experience freedom, it is important for preachers to call attention to the many ways in which we are not free. Possibilities can range from examples of financial debt and payday lenders, to cultural morays that are bound by racism, sexism, and classism, or concrete addictions, like alcoholism that slowly take hold of lives and families until everything revolves around managing the addiction. Once listeners begin to recognize their own bondage, they can more fully understand Jesus' action on the cross that breaks the power of the things that control our lives. The more concrete preachers can be in describing present-day bondage in ways that will be relevant to listeners, the more concrete the experience and understanding of Jesus' liberating action in the cross and resurrection.

Those who grew up in a church or who have read books about the cross will be familiar with ransom and substitutionary atonement models that are built upon Jesus' suffering and death to repay humanity's debt. These are among the most common and familiar ways that preachers tend to preach about the cross and resurrection. There is relational warmth in a God who loves us so much that he is willing to take on suffering that is meant for us, but unless preachers are careful to unpack the thorny questions veiled by comfortable but abstract language these images may derail present-day listeners, including those who are turned off by violence and "churchy" language that lacks a foothold in real life and those whose questions mirror those found in scholarly debates about the cross. Many scholars and Christians struggle with the origins of the violent punishment that Jesus suffered. While it is readily accepted in popular culture and foreign policy, many struggle with Jesus' violent death. In movies and T.V. shows, when a ransom is required, it generally is paid to someone. The hostage's family is seen leaving a duffel bag of cash in a Central

134. 1 Cor 1:17; 2:1–5.

Park garbage can to be picked up by the kidnapper. So who demands Jesus' suffering and death? Early Christian theologians posited that Satan demanded the price, but other critics felt that this gave Satan too much power. Assertions that God demands a price and that Jesus' suffering and punishment were truly substitutionary in our relationship with God, in that Jesus received punishment from God that was meant for us, have come under critique in recent decades. Some have labeled Jesus' death as the outcome of divine child-abuse. Depending on how one understands the Trinity, holding that God demands this price runs the risk of God seeming to be either a sadist who harms another or a masochist who harms himself. An alternate view is that Jesus' suffering and punishment came from a sinful and violent world, broken human systems demanding a scapegoat. In this vein, Jesus' death breaks the power of systems that bind outsiders, marginalize persons, and alienate those who are different than the mainstream—good news indeed for any who have been bullied or live in fear because of minority status. The debate over violence and the relationship between the first and second members of the Trinity in the crucifixion can stymie even the most seasoned preacher. However, in the midst of this debate, reaching for scripture is instructive for preachers.

Brenda Colijn helpfully points out that the New Testament does not actually engage in this debate. While texts speak of ransom and cost, they do not say that a ransom is demanded by or paid to anyone.[135] In God's paradigmatic action in the Exodus, God's cost is God's power exerted on Israel's behalf, similarly Jesus freely chose to give his life to set us free.[136] Perhaps a slightly more apt analogy is giving one's life to charitable service rather than purchasing an item or paying off a debt. This debate is just one example of where refocusing our preaching on what the Bible actually says can be helpful for preaching and teaching about a challenging and theologically rich topic such as Jesus' death and resurrection.

PREACHING THE CROSS AND RESURRECTION AS HEALING

If we understand healing in a holistic way—it necessarily affects our relationship and communities and can best be understood in conjunction with relational approaches to the cross and resurrection. Healing can

135. Colijn, *Images of Salvation*, 150.
136. Ibid.

be physical, emotional, spiritual, relational, systemic, or environmental. In the New Testament the term for salvation often coincides with this broader understanding of healing. The salvation brought about through Jesus' death and resurrection is meant to touch every part of our lives that has been affected by sin and brokenness.[137] The Greek terms *sōzō* and *sōtēria* mean "deliverance" or "preservation" but in the Greco-Roman context of the first century these terms were mainly understood in a medical sense.[138] The New Testament expands the understanding by including deliverance from sin.[139]

The gospels offer a range of links between healing and salvation; the writers use Jesus' healing actions as evidence both that Jesus is the promised Messiah who will save God's people and that God's Kingdom is emerging.[140] Jesus tells the hemorrhaging woman that she is healed/saved by her faith after touching him.[141] The question surrounding Jesus healing the man with a withered hand on the Sabbath concerns whether Sabbath laws "save life or destroy it."[142] Jesus saves/heals a man possessed by demons and even saves/heals Jarius' daughter by raising her from death.[143] Brenda Colijn argues that the New Testament writers portray Jesus' healings as allowing people to fully participate in the inbreaking Realm of God.[144] God's plan of salvation, brought about by Jesus' death and resurrection, involves complete and all-encompassing human health and wholeness.[145] Unlike present-day mindsets where people may compartmentalize different aliments and not always recognize the social dimensions of physical and mental illness, disability, or addictions, New Testament writers envisioned every hurt or broken arena of existence as an opportunity to experience the healing salvation of Jesus.[146] People may be isolated from others and marginalized due to physical or spiritual causes, but Jesus' healing allows those who have been suffering in

137. Ibid., 122.

138. Ibid.

139. Ibid., 122–23.

140. Ibid., 126.

141. Ibid., 125; Matt 9:22.

142. Colijn, *Images of Salvation*, 126; Luke 6:9.

143. Colijn, *Images of Salvation*, 126.; Luke 8:36; 8:50.

144. Colijn, *Images of Salvation*, 126.

145. Ibid., 126–27.

146. Ibid., 129.

isolation to return to community.[147] Jesus' saving acts are arguably more strongly evidenced by Jesus' actions during his life and ministry rather than isolated in the event of his death and resurrection. However the movement from brokenness to wholeness mirrors the move from cross to resurrection and those who experience healing in any area of their lives certainly experience a foretaste of resurrection life.

Preaching the cross and resurrection as a means to healing doesn't mean glossing over the hurt and pain that people have experienced. Indeed, the risen Christ's body had scars and holes marking his ordeal on the cross. Jesus' willingness to allow Thomas to probe these healed wounds affirms our own storytelling and acknowledgement of pain and suffering experienced.[148] Further, because of our eschatological context in which we experience both aspects of the cross and resurrection, it is important to acknowledge the layers of human existence and our experiences of brokenness and healing. We should avoid neat and tidy examples and stories that don't ring true to the complexities of human existence this side of God's Kingdom. We want to tell the truth. That does not mean dialing back the miraculous but it does mean acknowledging a diversity of experiences from the pulpit.

While testimonies and stories of personal physical healing can be important to include in a sermon, examples of environmental, social, or familial healing can be just as powerful and more relatable for some in the congregation.[149] For example, a family suffering the effects of alcoholism moves to honesty in their relationships and freedom from addictions and codependent behaviors. A congregation shrinking in size and threatened with closing has a broken-down building. The building and congregation experience healing and new life when they embark on a new ministry that connects to their neighborhood and allows their building to be used in a new way as a community-gathering place. A woman experiences a calling to ministry that heals past experiences with patriarchy. A congregation turns part of its land into a community garden in an urban neighborhood, which creates an opportunity for relationships, much needed green space, and healthy vegetables. Using social examples

---

147. Ibid., 127.

148. John 20:26–28.

149. In Rom 8:18–23, Paul's writing evokes a sense of the environment also longing for healing. Such an image is particularly appropriate in the wake of human-caused environmental disasters such as oil spills, strip-mining, and use of fossil fuels that have caused climate changes that threaten many species of plants and animals.

broadens the possibilities for healing for many who may have limited their understanding to the healing of a physical ailment.

CONCLUSION

Amidst a North American context where our churches are experiencing a decline in membership and cultural marginalization, preachers today struggle to find relevant ways to talk about matters that lie at the heart of our faith. Further, core convictions around the identity and work of Jesus Christ linked to the cross and resurrection can often feel thorny since there is a lack of consensus among Christians. We are fearful of alienating or offending our listeners, of turning off newcomers, or driving away the faithful. The good news is that preachers have a wide range of language, images, and biblical and theological motifs to anchor faith to the core of Christian theology. There are many nuances and ways to describe our experience of salvation brought about through Jesus' death and resurrection. The New Testament serves as our primary model. In our Bible, we find a range of approaches for preachers, including relational, formational, liberating, and healing. These images provide a starting place for preachers to do their own constructive work of preaching about the life and saving work of Jesus Christ.

3

Formation for Interfaith Relationships

The cross has negative connotations for many inside the church in the context of interfaith relationships and historically the cross has at times been used in ways that harm or offend our Jewish and Muslim friends and colleagues. This chapter will not seek to explore the common ground between different religions, nor will it prescribe a way of preaching as interreligious dialogue. Rather, I want to continue to address our discomfort in talking about the cross and resurrection—events that lie at the heart of the Christian faith from the vantage point of interfaith relationships. Many Christians today see value in learning about and engaging in conversation with those who practice other religions and may even find glimpses of the gospel in ways that give greater depth and nuance to our own Christian perspective. However, in order to authentically engage with those who are different than us, it is necessary to have a robust sense of our own Christian beliefs and values. When Christians are not deeply steeped in unique and particular aspects of Christianity, we may not be able to articulate our core beliefs, which can lead to confusion and frustration in interfaith conversation and cross-cultural learning. Understanding the cross and resurrection is necessary for the church's internal formation in order for the church to engage with those from outside Christianity in authentic friendship and witness.

Preaching can play a significant role in this process of internal formation as the preacher takes a confessional posture, providing language,

73

knowledge, and experiential engagement with the narrative death-to-life thrust of Christian theology that moves us through the cross to resurrection Sunday by Sunday through the interplay of scripture and the particular dynamics of context. My own Mennonite tradition's long-held skeptical resistance to many aspects of broader culture may be instructive for preachers from diverse traditions. This chapter will argue that deepening Christian identity with preaching that engages the death-to-life movement of the cross and resurrection, with a cruciform sense of openness and love towards others, will help equip our congregations for honest and dynamic interfaith encounters and relationships.

My own journey with this challenging dynamic draws from the experience of one of my former preaching students, a Muslim seeking to learn about Christianity by actively engaging ordinary Christian believers and pastors. Rasoul was an unusual student in my advanced preaching class. While the others represented North American Mainline Protestant traditions either as working pastors taking the course for continuing education credit or seminary students, Rasoul was an Iranian Muslim who served as an imam in his home context and was nearing the end of a master's program in another department at the university. One of Rasoul's stated reasons for coming to study in the United States was his passion for learning about Christianity. His thesis involved a comparison between Muslim and Christian theologies of peace building. For the eighteen months Rasoul and his family had been living in the U.S., first in a smaller university town and later in suburban Washington, D.C., he had been diligently visiting churches, Christian congregations representing a wide range of denominations. His goal was to learn more about Christianity and he would seek out conversation with pastors and church members after worship. Unfortunately, he was unable to accomplish his aim by visiting churches. Week after week, worship would yield few details about Christianity. He explained that the sermons and prayers often sounded similar to what he would hear in a mosque and that in conversations afterwards the pastors and church members would go out of their way to stress continuity and similarities between Christianity and Islam. In his frustration, he petitioned his program and got special permission to take a seminary preaching class to learn what Christians believe! Concerned with being sensitive and hospitable, even some Christian seminary students struggled with talking about key elements of the faith in sermons and class conversations. "Every time I say, 'Jesus' around him, I feel so bad!" quipped one student after class. Nevertheless, we embarked on a fascinating semester of interfaith engagement around preaching.

Working with Rasoul was a joy and privilege, but the truth is that the church let Rasoul down. Rasoul did not necessarily encounter bad pastors or believers who were not engaged in discipleship; rather, the churches he visited likely assumed a sense of familiarity with the complex identity and work of Jesus. Preachers used to preaching to "insiders" were not speaking explicitly about the core of the Christian faith and the result was that Rasoul encountered what seemed to be a "cross-less Christianity," which made it easier for well-meaning and friendly pastors and church members to focus on areas of commonality with Rasoul rather than noting the particularities of the cross and resurrection that undergird the heart of Christianity. Preachers and church leaders today need to take seriously the reality that Christendom is over. We cannot assume a general understanding of the identity and work of Jesus Christ—even among insiders. We cannot assume that those who show up to hear us preach already have some experience with the cross and resurrection. Unless we re-center preaching and worship around Jesus Christ, we are not only letting down those from outside our congregations who want to learn about Christianity, but also our own committed members who are missing the deep formation that will equip them for discipleship in an increasingly pluralistic world. In an age of religious tolerance where many sermons are readily available online, people who are interested in understanding what makes Christianity unique should not have to enroll in a seminary class.

The challenge of learning to live with authenticity amidst diverse cultural and religious expressions is not a new one for Christians. In fact Christianity was born in a pluralistic context and has had to navigate dynamics with other religions throughout history, but after centuries of Christendom many of us struggle with demonstrating hospitality while also bearing witness to our deepest Christian beliefs. This is a challenge we ignore at our peril. As Christian pastors, many of us interact mainly with those who are already Christians from our congregations, interested visitors who have come to our churches with some past church exposure, or seekers with no religious affiliation who may become Christian. However, our sermons are not limited by the walls of our churches. Many congregations post sermons online, which expands potential listeners. Even more significantly, our listeners give our sermons legs. In a sense, our sermons go wherever the church goes, which means that engaging with other faith traditions is a growing reality. Some of us may already have interfaith families in our congregations and members of our congregations are living and working in diverse contexts and have relationships that extend beyond the church. People in our congregations are counting on strong and relevant Christian preaching to form their character and aid their own actions and relationships amidst competing options.

Pluralism is a growing cultural reality that provides an opportunity for discernment for the church around identity and mission. Without discernment, clergy and laity alike may be anxious when talking about the particularities of Christianity. In some settings, preachers may feel apologetic and almost ashamed to talk of Jesus and the cross, for fear that this will be received as being inhospitable to those who hold different beliefs. In other settings, pastors feel that they must defensively express their faith much like a cornered cat chased under a sofa by a curious child. Some of the most challenging interfaith contexts involve other "people of the book." Muslims and Jewish believers share some of our scriptural ancestors and commitments but we also have fundamental differences that must be openly named in order for all parties to be faithful.

In the midst of all these challenges, the cross emerges as a key element—both in the content of our beliefs and sermons as well as in our formation as preachers and as Christians in dialogue with others. The cross itself is a source of difference and separation for Christians. It helps us recognize the boundaries of our beliefs, yet it also provides a model and a means for us to extend ourselves in self-giving hospitality towards "the others" we encounter—even towards our enemies. This chapter makes a case that preaching about the cross and resurrection deepens Christian identity and awareness in ways that allow for secure engagement with those of different religions. Given the broadly pluralistic context in North America, I will unpack some of the signs and hallmarks of pluralism to better understand the ways it shapes and challenges the church. I will then turn to specific dynamics of interfaith engagement with some discussion of how Jesus' crucifixion and resurrection are understood within fellow Abrahamic traditions of Judaism and Islam. Next, I will name some of the ways that modern Christians tend to engage with those of other religions. Finally we will explore how the cross can provide a meaningful formative key for deepening Christian identity so that congregations are equipped for authentic witness and relationship in a context of religious pluralism. Part of the process of equipping will include naming specific practices to help preachers grow in interfaith awareness and love of neighbor, while also deepening Christian-cruciform identity from the pulpit.

PLURALISM AND INTERFAITH RELATIONSHIPS

In 1937 Yale theologian H. Richard Niebuhr described liberal faith "as being about a God without wrath [who] brought men without sin into a kingdom without judgment through the ministrations of a Christ without a cross."[1] Decades later, Liberal Protestantism has gone into decline and mainline congregations across the evangelical-liberal spectrum are struggling. If this is a hard truth for us to hear, then part of the challenge according to sociologist Christian Smith is that Liberal Protestantism has "won." The dominant values of American Liberal Protestantism named by Smith, following sociologist N. Jay Demerath, are "individualism, pluralism, emancipation, tolerance, free critical inquiry, and the authority of personal experience"; the same as the common cultural values of North America.[2] There is nothing inherently wrong with these cultural values. In many ways pluralism is a blessing in that practitioners from different religions and those who claim no religion can live and work together peacefully. However, a pluralistic context can also be challenging in that it invites us to actively discern and engage in particularly Christian beliefs and behaviors. Many of the practices and values that we see reflected more broadly are not explicitly Christian and may be attached to narratives that compete with the gospel or biblical narratives, which guide us towards loving our enemies, service, and placing the needs of others above our own interests. In addition to this melding of cultural and religious values, some scholars and practitioners have also moved towards a synthesized view of different religions, seeking peace and cooperation by naming what different religions hold in common rather than where they differ in their views and practices.[3] This search for commonalities has an echo in the faith of emerging adults who also express a sense of relativism when it comes to faith that seems to iron out the distinctions that give structures, shape, and boundaries to our core religious convictions.

1. Niebuhr, *Kingdom*, 193.

2. Dean, "Review of Souls," 34.

3. An example is the late philosopher John Hick who sees all religions as quests for an ultimate reality, "the Real," that transcends any particular religion. See Hick, *An Interpretation.*.

In his study of the religious lives of young adults, Christian Smith notes tendencies that reflect our cultural context of pluralism. Unlike previous generations who would steer clear of religion in polite casual conversation settings in order to avoid getting into intense debates, emerging adults today do not view faith as something worth getting worked up about so the stakes in conversation are relatively low.[4] Young adults tend to be fairly indifferent, viewing their religious beliefs as something that goes on in the background.[5] Further, young people today tend to see all religions as benignly beneficial, sharing common convictions at their core, which makes any particularities merely dross.[6] This certainly includes the specifics of the life and work of Jesus Christ including the complexities of the cross and resurrection. This relativism is not surprising to sociologist Peter Berger who writes about pluralism in late modernity.

Berger and fellow-researcher Anton Zijderveld describe pluralism as one of the fruits of Modernity, born from urbanization, more transitory lifestyles, mass education, and the explosion of data and knowledge available through diverse media resources and the internet.[7] Berger views pluralism, as an ideology that "welcomes" the social reality of "plurality," which describes our twenty-first-century context, " . . . in which diverse human groups (ethnic, religious, or however differentiated) live together under conditions of civic peace and in social interaction with each other."[8] One of the hallmarks of plurality is cross-pollination or "cognitive contamination" as members of diverse groups interact with each other, which can eventually lead to "group norms" and religious syncretism or homogenization.[9]

In addition to blurring the lines between different groups, modernity has also drastically expanded the choices many people have in their lives—both material choices such as the cars we drive and the coffee we drink, as well as identity and relational choices.[10] Berger and Zijderveld note that many people can choose a career/calling/profession, if and when to marry, choose how to set up relational behavior patterns, if, when,

---

4. Smith and Snell, *Souls in Transition*, 144.

5. Ibid., 145.

6. Ibid., 145–46.

7. Berger and Zijderveld, *In Praise of Doubt*, 9.

8. Ibid., 7.

9. Ibid., 11.

10. Ibid., 12–13.

and how many children one will have, and how to raise those children.[11] We can choose how to self-identify in a range of areas from politics to religion, to lifestyle and even ethnicity.[12] For example, as seminary students my husband and I met with a group of people who self-identified as Mennonite for a monthly social gathering around a potluck meal. My husband and I grew up in Mennonite families and congregations and attended a Mennonite church. These relationships and commitments led us to claim and profess a Christian Mennonite identity, but others in the group had seemingly no connection to the Mennonite church and some were not even Christian, yet they had chosen to describe themselves as "Mennonite." Our fellowship group suffered because of our deep differences. Some of us wanted to include prayer and worship together as part of our meetings while others strongly resisted anything beyond simply sharing a meal and light conversation. The wane of institutions has further contributed to a sharp increase in the amount and number of choices that many people can make in their lives. While choice marks the lives of many of us and those we serve, the poor, including the working poor, who struggle to make ends meet or who have not had extensive education, those with mental and physical disabilities, the very young, and older persons have far fewer choices although this does nothing to lessen the power of choice. The possibility or expectation of choice is a privilege and source of hope that is increasingly linked to what it means to flourish or even be truly human in our broader culture. The value of choice has so infiltrated our sense of good news in North American that ministries that serve those without permanent addresses strive to make choice a key facet of programs in order to restore a sense of human-ness or flourishing. For example, at one feeding ministry in the downtown core of Kansas City, Missouri all who come for a meal are given a choice of entree and sides. Those who "shop" for clothes and toiletries in the church pantry can choose what they need and the brands they prefer. Seeking to deepen the humanity of those who are often unseen and devalued is a wonderful practice in Christian service programs but choice is more of a North American cultural value than a specifically Christian value.

When it comes to the religious identities of those in our congregations as well as our Jewish and Muslim neighbors, Berger and Zijderveld

11. Ibid., 13.
12. Ibid., 13–14.

note that chosen religion is much less stable than deeply ingrained or institutionally orchestrated religion.[13] But addressing this reality is part of what it means to be religious in our cultural context. We have increased awareness of different religious options coupled by increased opportunity to make choices about religious affiliation. One who is a multi-generational Catholic may have the same beliefs and practices as a new Catholic convert but they likely carry their religious identities differently.[14] Further, the choice orientation of our culture means that many people engage with their religious tradition in a buffet-style, choosing to take or leave particular doctrines.[15] For example, a young woman is a new attendee in a small town United Methodist congregation seeking to become a member. She informs the pastor that she does not believe that the Bible is sacred or the Jesus is God but that she appreciates the community-feel of the church, the beauty of worship and congregational singing, as well as the social and outreach programs of the church that address real need in their small town. She has approached becoming a member of the church with a list of conditions, like she is ordering from a restaurant. She will have the cheeseburger—hold the burger—with a side of coleslaw and a gluten-free bun please. Certainly most members of our congregations are not so extreme in qualifying their relationship to Christianity, but when every member of our congregations has put his or her own unique spin on our faith traditions, it is challenging to preach in ways that speak to all the listeners and it becomes very difficult to represent Christianity to those who are outside our faith. Because the cross and resurrection have always been scandalous and difficult facets of Christianity, it makes sense that this event that lies at the heart of our faith may be de-emphasized by those who find it distasteful, incomprehensible, or somehow unnecessary. Because choice is also accompanied by homogenization and syncretism, the lines that once separated denominations and even different religions are increasingly blurred. In some ways this has been helpful, opening up new possibilities for mission and cooperation in service, but it has created unique challenges for the witness of the church particularly in interfaith dialogue and relationships.

The result of these movements is that we must find a way to assert and strengthen Christian particularity in the midst of both cultural

13. Ibid., 18.
14. Ibid., 19.
15. Ibid.

choice and religious homogenization. For Berger, the strongest way forward is what he names as an "inductive" approach that acknowledges the power of religious experience and the ways that these experiences lay at the heart of the church's rituals and liturgies.[16] While Berger's Christology tends to focus more on the cosmic love of God that is exemplified in Jesus than on the nitty-gritty details of Jesus' life and work and more on individuals than the church community, we can still find important clues for strengthening the church through his work by naming the importance of experience for Christian identity in a pluralistic context.[17] Indeed, beyond faithfulness to biblical references, an experience of newness in Christ is part of the historical and experiential foundation for the continued practice of baptism and encounter with the crucified and risen Christ rests at the heart of the celebration of Communion. For Berger, churches are necessary for supporting the individual believer, but part of their weakness is that they tend to "domesticate" encounter with the divine and favor patterns that can be replicated rather than the divine "supernatural" breaking into our world.[18] Berger's concerns don't fully acknowledge the formative potential of ritual and learning the language of faith so that when God does invade our lives with profound encounter, we can recognize it, integrate it into our Christian identity, and allow it to bear fruit as part of the witness of our lives.[19] Besides sacraments, for preachers the more recent turns towards narrative and collaborative styles down play an authoritarian tone and "up the experiential ante" so that members of the congregation actually experience something during participatory engagement with the sermon. The challenge is for Christians to engage experience of encounter with God from the very particular position of Christianity itself, to use unabashedly Christian language to describe our encounter with God and to understand our experiences as continuous with historic Christianity. This makes preaching the cross and resurrection a vital way to provide an atmosphere and language so that listeners might experience and name an encounter with Jesus Christ, embracing the impact of the cross and resurrection not only in a historical sense but in their own lives as a move from death, loss, addiction, and brokenness to life and new possibilities in Christ. The cross and resurrec-

---

16. LaFountain, "Theology and Social Psychology," 24–25.

17. Ibid., 26–27.

18. Ibid., 27.

19. See also ibid., 28.

tion are so central to the work of Christ and so crucial for communal and individual Christian identity that preachers should work to connect the cross and resurrection to their preaching regularly—if not every Sunday by placing every biblical text they preach and every story or example they employ into conversation with the cross.

Part of the challenge may be whether or not we accept the idea that the world is becoming homogenized. An alternate view is that we cannot speak in absolutes when it comes to any posture or culture. Rather we speak of cultures, or positions, or churches. Not to minimize the dangers of global franchises, but just because there are McDonald's restaurants in Berlin and Tokyo does not mean that eating there is the same. Indeed one might find beer or seaweed seasoned fries on the menu! If everything is particular, then our context of pluralism means that we have many different particularities coming into conversation with each other.[20] The diversity of perspectives can create an intense need for validation and connection. Given the former Judeo-Christian gloss that coated North American culture, some Christians may feel threatened by "others" who they view as eroding what was once a "Christian" nation. We do not need to compromise our faith in order to live peaceably with those of other religions, but scripture is clear that we do need to live peaceably. In his Sermon on the Mount, Jesus blesses the peacemakers and calls for disciples to turn the other cheek and love their enemies.[21] In his letter to the Romans, Paul describes living peaceably as one of the marks of the transformed Christian life, instructing believers, "if it is possible, so far as it depends on you, live peaceably with all."[22]

THE CROSS AND THE ABRAHAMIC RELIGIONS

To some extent it is easy to see how Rasoul found similarities between a "cross-less" Christianity and Islam as he visited congregations. Congregations where preaching and conversation about the cross are absent bypass the truth; the cross is a stumbling block for those who would try to iron out the differences between Christianity and the other Abrahamic religions. Islamic belief and practice centers around five pillars: confession,

20. Ibid., 30–31.

21. Matt 5:9, 38–39, and 43–48.

22. Rom 12:18. For an interfaith interpretation of this see, Bock and Rosario, "Table Briefing," 99–100.

prayer, almsgiving, fasting, and pilgrimage. The first pillar is confessional, "There is no God but God (Allah) and Mohammed is his apostle." Jews and Christians would also agree with the first half of this sentence although they would disagree with the second clause.[23] The second pillar concerns prayer. While Muslims are to pray five times a day, aside from mentioning Mohammed, Muslim prayers are not so different from what Jews or Christians might pray.[24] Almsgiving and fasting are also practiced within Judaism and Christianity and pilgrimage has been a Jewish and a Christian practice as well. However, when one acknowledges the cross that lies at the heart of Christianity, making tidy comparisons becomes much more difficult. Not only is the cross confounding and challenging for Christians; Jews and Muslims stand as complete "others" to the passion narrative—they cannot find a proper home in it.

Jesus' Death and Return in Islam

Classic creedal interpretations of both the person and work of Jesus Christ are highly problematic for traditional Muslims. While the Qur'an speaks of the prophet, Isa or Jesus, he does not die by crucifixion, as an all-powerful God would never allow this to happen to his prophet. Rather, he is taken up into heaven and someone else assumes his place on the cross. From the standpoint of Islam, Jesus' identity as fully God and fully human is impossible and the Christian understanding of the cross is a sign of "corruption."[25] Jesus' identity as God is not possible because God cannot be subject to the change and vulnerability of incarnation.[26] For God to allow Jesus to suffer and die is an affront to God's sovereign power and will.[27] Further, even if Jesus did die, for Muslims the death would be viewed as pointless since there isn't the same sense of collective sin or that Jesus' sacrifice could somehow mend a rift between people and God caused by sin.[28] Because God is all-powerful, God does not need the death of Jesus, God alone is all-powerful and can grant forgiveness or

---

23. Bock and Rosario, 97.
24. Ibid.
25. Singh, "Rethinking Jesus," 240, 247–48.
26. Ibid., 249.
27. Ibid., 247–48.
28. Ibid., 249.

not.[29] While some branches of Islam share aspects of the resurrection and return of Jesus with Christianity, the details and implications are different. Iranian Shi'ite Islam has within its beliefs the concept of Mahdism—or the belief in a coming savior.[30] There is an interpretation held by some that Mohammed prophesied that only twelve imams would serve before the Mahdi or savior would come. Some Shi'a hold that the twelfth imam who disappeared as a child in the ninth century is the Mahdi and that when the time is right he will return with Jesus as his immediate predecessor who prepares the way and then operates in a deferent and lesser role to prepare the world for final judgment.[31] Some hold that the Mahdi left because of a "rebellious spirit" and that he will return when people demonstrate a proper faithful posture in agreement with his teaching.[32] The Mahdi will be both a supreme religious and political leader.[33] Mission consultant, David W. Shenk explains the means by which the great leader will bring peace and transformation, "Like Mohammed, Iranian Mahdist eschatology envisages the effective use of political and military power to bring about justice and universal peace in the concluding drama of history."[34] Martyrdom as an act of faith can help to convince the Mahdi to return.[35]

Some Islamic engagement with Christians has been troubled. Whenever violence occurs, it makes the news, but Christian encounters with Muslim people have long been troubled and this trouble continues today. The symbol of the cross has long been equated with the "crusading spirit" of medieval Christians who fought Muslims, trying to retake lands that had been in Arab hands for centuries.[36] For many Muslims, the cross continues to be a symbol of colonial power and the political arrogance of the West, despite our scriptural and theological roots that show the cross as an alternative to transformation through violence or political means.

29. Ibid., 249.
30. Shenk, "Muslims and Christians," 120.
31. Ibid., 120–21.
32. Ibid., 120.
33. Ibid.
34. Ibid.
35. Ibid., 121.
36. González, *Story of Christianity*, 345–51.

The Cross and Judaism

In the Jewish tradition, Jesus is historically viewed as a false messiah, yet he was not killed by Jewish leadership. The kind of arguing and disagreements between Jesus and Jewish groups such as the Pharisees and Sadducees portrayed in the gospels would have never led to Jesus' execution.[37] Crucifixion is a Roman means of torture and execution and Roman authorities killed Jesus.[38] Nevertheless, when it comes to Jewish-Christian relationships and engagement around the theology and symbol of the cross, Christians have plenty to be ashamed about. Some of Christianity's most revered theologians and leaders from across history have anti-Semitic passages in their writing, from John Chrysostom to Augustine and Martin Luther. In particular, blaming Jewish people for their role in crucifying Jesus has led to horrible anti-Semitism. Most recent in memory for many is the Holocaust or Shoah during World War II, which took the lives of some six million Jews, but smaller more-insidious instances continue to persist in some Christian materials and among some Christian believers. More than ten years after its extremely popular release, Mel Gibson's *The Passion of the Christ* is still generating news about its anti-Semitic undercurrents. According to an interview with Rabbi Yitzchok Adlerstein, director of interfaith affairs at the Simon Wiesenthal Center in Los Angeles, in an article in the National Catholic Reporter, among the most harmful aspects of Gibson's artistic portrayal of the crucifixion was that he positioned his work as being the most accurate portrayal.[39] Meaning that for many Christians, the film showed what really happened. The article recounts several of Gibson's artistic choices that portray the Jewish tradition inaccurately or with unhelpful stereotyping, including making the Jewish officials into stock "bad-guys" complete with pointy teeth, inaccurately showing an earthquake that destroys the temple at the moment of the crucifixion (implying that the synagogue has been usurped by the church), and not including any Jewish advisors when making his film.[40]

While most Christians and Christian pastors today hate anti-Semitism and look to be responsible in preaching about Israel and the death of Jesus, many well-meaning preachers continue to offer misleading

37. Inbody, *Many Faces*, 168.
38. Ibid., 173.
39. Pacatte, "Decade Later."
40. Ibid.

interpretations of the role of Jewish religious officials in the gospel accounts of Jesus' life, ministry, and death. Preachers tend to downplay Jesus' Jewishness and attribute some sense of strong systemic political power to Jewish religious groups, such as the Pharisees, when the truth is that Israel was a subjugated people, with leaders struggling to maintain an authentic and faithful identity under the rule of Rome. This happens regularly as we move from discussing the text to making connections or applications with our world by equating New Testament Jewish religious systems and leaders with powerful and corrupt systems and leaders today. As Christendom continues to decline, it may get easier for Christian pastors to exercise empathy towards biblical Jewish leaders trying to survive and be faithful in a hostile broader context. It may be that the High Priests, which were well-placed figures with more political than religious connections, did play a passive and derivative role in some of the events that led to Jesus' crucifixion, but Jesus died at the hands of Rome.[41] Even the angry crowd whose shouts of "crucify him," find dramatic resonance on our own contrition on Good Friday, cannot be understood to be representative of the broader Jewish people because 80 percent of Jewish people lived in the Diaspora.[42] The crowd was probably less than one-thousandth of the Jewish population.[43]

New Testament language linking Jesus' death and the Jewish people of the time was written during a period when early Christians may have been seeking to distinguish or separate themselves from Jewish groups who did not follow Jesus.[44] This language may have been meant to encourage repentance rather than exact blame or punishment.[45] Our New Testament shows many points of continuity and resonance with Judaism as well as points of divergence and enmity. While this divergence came after Jesus' death and some is attested to in Paul's letters recounting challenges within congregations containing Jews and Gentiles, perhaps the strongest separation resulted from the Jewish war with Rome in 66–70 CE, which predates the Gospels and may account for some anti-Semitic passages.[46] Post-Holocaust education and awareness around these in-

41. Inbody, *Many Faces*, 169.
42. Ibid.
43. Ibid.
44. Inbody, *Many Faces*, 173–74.
45. Tomson, *Presumed Guilty*, 79.
46. Ibid., 92–133.

terpretive matters means that most pastors are extremely careful not to blame Jewish people for Jesus' death. Nevertheless centuries of blame and abuse cling to the cross, making it a major challenge in Jewish-Christian conversations and relationships. Sadly and incorrectly many people (both inside and outside the church of both Christian and Jewish background) still equate orthodox Christian beliefs and expression about the cross and resurrection with anti-Semitism. As preachers we can help by offering more helpful language to aid our conversations around Jesus' crucifixion. The Jewish people did not kill God. Jesus chose to undergo crucifixion by the Roman authorities in order to unveil sin in all its diverse and insidious forms, and to finally and ultimately destroy its death-dealing power, thereby expressing a powerful divine "No!" to all systems of violence, oppression, and abuse. By taking death into the life of God, it has been completely defeated. The issue of agency around who demanded or caused Jesus' death is not a productive avenue in preaching—the New Testament does not frame the cross in this way. Tyron Inbody aptly summarizes the theological response, "[Jesus] was killed because of and through the power of human violence and sinfulness. That condition, responsibility, and guilt is a reality in which we all participate and share. . . . Best expressed in Robert Petrich's Choral Variations on 'Ah Holy Jesus,': 'Who was the guilty? Who brought this upon thee. . . . Twas I, Lord Jesus, I it was denied thee: I crucified thee.'"[47] Still, given centuries of history, we certainly cannot blame our Jewish brothers and sisters for anxiety surrounding Christian "cross-talk."

It is not only Jewish people who struggle with Christian beliefs and practices. Judaism is challenging for Christians as well. While not wanting to claim that the Church has fully replaced Israel, Christians do believe that Jesus is the long-awaited Messiah and through Jesus' death and resurrection, the church as the body of Christ has become the "new Israel" and is now God's primary agent of ministry and blessing in the world.[48] While we share scripture in common, because of Christianity's understanding of God as being triune, the identity of God for Christians cannot be collapsed into the identity of who YHWH is for Israel.[49] It is confounding for Christians that a majority of Jewish people have not

47. Inbody, *Many Faces*, 175.
48. Davies, "Jews and the Death of Jesus," 209.
49. Lindsay, *Barth, Israel, and Jesus*, xviii.

converted. The "Jewish question" has been a challenge for Christian theologians and leaders as far back as the Apostle Paul.

POSTURES TOWARDS RELIGIOUS "OTHERS"

From the earliest origins of Christian belief, dynamic engagement with "others" has been a part of our tradition and embedded in faithful practice. The theological vision that God's blessings for Israel are meant to spill over and extend from Israel to the broader world undergirds Scripture. Because Israel lived as enslaved "strangers" and as religious "others" in the land of Egypt, God's people are called to behave differently to not harm or oppress the strangers in their midst.[50] Because the Lord, the one true God is with them, Israel does not need to fear the other. Many Old Testament texts speak of offering care and extending welcome to the "aliens" in Israel's midst and the New Testament gospels offer accounts of Jesus relating positively to those who represent other traditions, particularly those who are vulnerable and marginalized and those who follow Jesus are called to extend Jesus' love and welcome to the "others" they encounter.[51] In Matthew's Gospel Jesus instructs us to care for the vulnerable and the strangers as if they are Christ himself, "for I was hungry and you gave me food, I was thirsty and you gave me something to drink, I was a stranger and you welcomed me, I was naked and you gave me clothing, I was sick and you took care of me, I was in prison and you visited me."[52]

Christians today navigate the terrain that exists between God's expansive love for the whole world and the particularity of salvation through Jesus Christ. While a slim minority may view those of other religions as being enemies of Christianity, most Christians and church leaders today assume a variety of friendly postures towards believers from other religions, ranging from seeking to convert the other, to being present with the other without acknowledging religious difference, to active conversation with the other about religious difference, to a kind of pluralistic melding of religious identities with the other. These postures are reflected in the work of sociologists and theologians who explore interreligious dynamics and theologies. Most of these postures were also anecdotally

50. Jensen, *In the Company*, 3.

51. Ibid., 3–4.

52. Matt 25:35–36; Jensen, *In the Company*, 4.

reflected in Rasoul's experiences encountering pastors, church members, and seminary classmates. Theologians have sought to explain how different religions relate to each other. For example, Paul Knitter offers four basic models for understanding how Christianity relates to other religions:

1) "the replacement model," which holds that Christianity is the only true religion,

2) "the fulfillment model," in which Christianity fulfills the other religions,

3) "the mutuality model," which calls the many true religions to dialogue, and

4) "the acceptance model," which simply accepts that there are many true religions who can coexist together.[53]

I will place my own observations and categories in dialogue with Knitter's models.

Enemies with the Other

Many Christians were horrified several years ago when the media picked up stories about a pastor in Florida who was promoting the burning of the Qur'an. We were similarly concerned when some Christians lashed out against Muslims following the September 11 terrorist attacks. While few of us would go to these extremes, with violent actions by religious extremists regularly in the news, we can understand how fear coupled with centuries of enmity between religious groups can create a culture where the religious "other" is viewed as an enemy to Christianity. Fortunately Rasoul was spared this hateful response in the churches he visited. Scholars trace this viewpoint back to the peace of Constantine and the merging of state and church agendas and destinies. With Christianity as the official state-sanctioned religion, religious others are not merely potential converts but also potential enemies of the state.[54] While this view has never been the only or even the dominant view within Christianity, it has emerged again and again in events such as the Crusades; Conquistadors; colonialism; slavery; Christian settlement schools working with Native American groups; and Anti-Semitic housing, hiring practices, and

53. Knitter, *Theologies of Religions.*
54. Jensen, *In the Company*, 8.

the Holocaust.[55] Linking the power of the state with the church has had dire consequences. Vestiges of the view of religious "other" as enemy still exist when Christians view religious others as a threat to the "Christian" values of our nation.

Viewing the religious other as an enemy is an extreme form of Knitter's "replacement model" which holds that Christianity is the only true religion. In Knitter's words, other religions are "so lacking or so aberrant, that in the end Christianity must move in and take their place."[56] Theologically this model is influenced by Karl Barth and stands on Jesus Christ as God's most complete revelation attested to in scripture and sees all religious systems (even Christianity) as potential obstacles that play into humanity's temptation to try to figure out things for ourselves.[57] Christianity is saved in spite of this idolatry only by Jesus Christ, which means that there are no points of contact with other religions.[58] This does not mean that we do not respect those who follow other religions or allow them to freely practice their faith—this much is promised by national governments. More than that, scripture is clear that the Christian mandate towards "others" even towards our enemies is very different from the mandate of a national government. Loving the other does not weaken our witness. Preachers can take a prophetic stand on these matters by highlighting the differences between national citizenship and discipleship in the way of the cross on national holidays or when current events again bring hatred or violence among religious groups to the fore.

Seeking to Convert the Other

If we are passionate in our faith and honest about the orientation and roots of our Christian calling, we will long to share about our faith in authentic ways. We see such deep importance and truth in our relationship with Jesus Christ that caring for the "others" in our lives means that we long for them to also know Jesus.[59] Even if we are not being explicit

55. Ibid.

56. Knitter, *Theologies of Religions*, 23.

57. Ibid., 25–31.

58. Ibid., 26.

59. Jensen roots this posture primarily in the early centuries of the church and describes it as viewing the "other" as being in need or at a deficit and notes that this is a different orientation than described in Scripture. Jensen, *In the Company*, 6.

in our witness, it follows that our beliefs and acts of discipleship will naturally emerge in all our relationships with others. Those who view the other positively may see all practitioners of other religions as potential Christians.[60] Yet there is some difference between an intentional and thoughtful but essentially passive witness and actively sharing the content of Christianity with the intent to convert. Conversations oriented towards conversion work best when we encounter an opening, a receptive posture and a desire to consider learning about Christianity with the possibility of becoming Christian. One seminary student in the class with Rasoul reflected a posture of seeking his conversion. She was open about this posture with classmates before we agreed that Rasoul would join us and she talked to me about it throughout the term. She appreciated Rasoul, enjoyed conversation with him about his beliefs and practices, and deeply desired that he would come to know Jesus and accept him as Lord. Because Rasoul came to our class as a deeply committed Muslim who had served as an imam in his home community, he did not present as open to conversion. The most faithful response for this fellow-classmate was to pray for Rasoul and his conversion before class and regularly throughout the week. She also sought to engage thoughtfully with him, seeking to be a witness to Christ while not explicitly pushing him towards conversion. Her response was natural for her and appropriate.

This response also fits within Knitter's "replacement model." Besides the posture of "total replacement" that finds no point of connection with other religions, some also follow a "partial replacement" understanding where other religions may provide some sense of revelation and set the stage for questions that lead to Jesus Christ, but on their own do not lead to salvation.[61] While dialogue might be helpful to move others towards Christianity, this model does not see grounding for a cohesive theology that can allow for multiple religions.[62] Only Jesus saves. God is active in human history and created all humans to move towards God and experience salvation through Jesus Christ.[63] Those who dialogued with Rasoul, hoping to create an atmosphere where questions might lead towards the truths of Christianity would likely feel comfortable with this model.

60. One expression of this can even see "proto-Christian" behavior in those of other religions. In part, this is what Karl Rahner is describing when he writes about anonymous Christians.

61. Knitter, *Theologies of Religions*, 33–41.

62. Ibid., 43.

63. Ibid., 34–36.

In the arena of preaching, it is helpful to regularly give catechetical sermons that are oriented towards teaching both committed believers and newcomers or visitors in our midst about the core beliefs of Christianity and about Christian sacraments and discipleship practices. This kind of preaching can bring both new commitments as well as renewal for long-time believers. The season of Lent, when the church journeys through Jesus' crucifixion and resurrection is traditionally a time of preparation for baptism in the early church. The texts and theological themes in this season of the church year may help to orient and inspire preachers. Catechetical sermons may provide an opportunity to compare differences between religions, if such discourse is relevant for a particular context. Because we trust the Holy Spirit to be operative in our sermons, we can trust the Spirit to move in ways that may bring about conversion. Preaching is often just one step in a process that can bring new believers into the church and renewed faith to long-time members.

Present without Acknowledging Difference

A common response for Christians who regularly engage with those who practice other religions in a workplace setting is to engage with the other without acknowledging or discussing religious difference. This is the posture that allows for what Berger described as "civic peace" within a context of plurality. In some ways this approach reflects the "good neighbor policy" Knitter describes as one facet of his "Acceptance Model."[64] The Acceptance Model is built in part on the work of George Lindbeck who views our language and experience as being so dependent on our religious worldview that it creates boundaries between the religions and highlights the limitations of true dialogue and exchange.[65] Representatives of different religions can talk to and engage each other as neighbors but must do so firmly from the context of his or her "own backyard."[66] Seeking to find common ground for conversation can lead to the temptation to try to "make someone else's backyard look just like ours."[67]

This posture may be easier for Christians for whom their religious identity is not a central part of who they are, those who reflect the

64. Ibid., 183.

65. Ibid., 180. See also Lindbeck, *Nature of Doctrine,* 33–40.

66. Knitter, *Theologies of Religions,* 183.

67. Ibid.

broader tendencies in our culture to personalize and privatize religion. While there are times such as casual engagement in a non-religious work-setting where this would be an appropriate response, this level of engagement cannot be seen as reflecting a posture that makes sense in the arena of Christian proclamation. If a relationship with someone of another religion moves to any point of depth or sharing, we must share that which is truly central to our identity. If we come to care deeply for someone, we will want to "jump the fence" or invite him or her over for a backyard barbeque. Even though he was a student at a Christian University, this was the response that Rasoul experienced most often from casual acquaintances and Christian staff members on campus. No seminary classmates or church members reflected this detached posture—possibly because Rasoul was vulnerable and bold enough to come into our Christian backyard, seeking encounters in explicitly religious Christian contexts where we could not avoid the risk of engaging with him and our own deeply held beliefs.

Active Conversation about Religious Difference

Most of Rasoul's classmates and professors at the seminary and in his own graduate program engaged in active conversation about religious differences between Christianity and Islam. Rasoul preached sermons from the Qur'an about figures who also appear in the Bible. We would discuss how the figures and narratives were different. Many Christians and Muslims approach scripture differently so we talked about differences in common interpretive practices among leaders. For example, Rasoul was incredulous at the way some Christian seminary students openly voiced disagreement with plain-sense interpretations of some passages of Scripture. He explained to us that in his tradition, if the basic meaning of a Scripture text was understood and not contested, then faithful Muslims must believe it. He also felt that we treated our Scripture too casually at times, noting that conservative Muslims treat scripture with reverence by not eating, drinking, or sleeping in its presence. We also discussed differences in the purposes of preaching. In my preaching classes we talk about many purposes for preaching. While preaching can include teaching about the faith, extolling faithful living or discipleship practices, consoling, challenging, nurturing, or dialoguing among other purposes, I frequently encourage my students to think of preaching as an opportunity for listeners to have an experience of encounter with God through the words of the preacher and the activity of the Holy Spirit so that they experience again the drama of the good news that moves us from death to resurrection. Rasoul's sermons did not reflect this breadth of purpose and generally took the form of wise advice drawn from Scripture that could be applied to daily life, for example, "best practices for parenting." The academic context made discussing differences feel natural and appropriate. This is a dynamic that is also present in other interfaith conversations and encounters, yet the discussions were generally dispassionate and lacked a sense of gravity. The conversations didn't seem to have lasting importance. While Rasoul learned about Christianity and we learned about Islam, the university was not a space of high enough vulnerability or risk and therefore probably not really an opportunity for deep transformation.

Having active conversations within a house of worship carries more risk and vulnerability—particularly for the visitor representing another religion. To facilitate a more even-exchange, vulnerability should be reciprocated. Some Christian congregations have relationships with congregations from other religions where each house of worship plays host to an activity or conversation. A shared practice or service project can provide an environment where conversations can begin that acknowledge differences even in the presence of some shared commitments. In the arena of preaching, preachers should be honest about differences among different religions when it is relevant within sermons. Pastors can affirm shared commitments and collaboration such as jointly hosting a travelling cold-weather shelter or relief in the wake of a natural disaster without suggesting that motivations for service or religious beliefs and practices are the same.

A focus on dialogue and mutual transformation shares some aspects with Knitter's "Fulfillment Model" which holds that religions besides Christianity can also lead to "God's saving love."[68] Theologically this means affirming that God is free to act outside the church and beyond traditional Christian practices such as the sacraments and sermon.[69] Yet, people can only receive God's saving love when God wills it. We can only meet God when the Holy Spirit moves through a channel of embodied communication. This affirms the goodness of creation—diverse aspects

68. Ibid., 100.
69. Ibid., 100–101.

of creation beyond religions such as the arts and popular culture—and allows us to claim these as channels that the Spirit may use to grasp us. While not seeking to sanction "careless teaching and preaching or theological relativism," Emil Brunner reminds us that God can overcome our inadequacies and faltering witness. He writes, "God can, if he so wills, speak his Word to a [person] even through false doctrine and correspondingly find in a false Credo-credo the right echo of his Word."[70] This way of thinking is not new for preachers as we humbly engage our calling to preach the Good News, making connections between Scripture and our world, viewing ordinary life through "God-goggles" that inspire us to see the surprising ways that God is actively engaged in our world, even in unexpected places. This also honors the surprising way that God in Jesus Christ was able to use a Roman cross to open up the possibility of resurrection and salvation—a most unlikely source!

Still, in the mist of dialogue and acknowledging glimpses of God in our world including other religions, we must maintain a clear sense of our own Christian "non-negotiables," those areas that are held close and that we do not offer up to be changed by our encounter with religious others.[71] Knitter names Jesus Christ as representing a non-negotiable for Christians. While uncomfortable and confounding, the cross and resurrection also belong to this territory as they help define who Jesus Christ is. Gerhard Forde reminds us that the cross and resurrection change the way we interpret even the life and teaching of Jesus. He writes, "When he [Jesus] was dead and buried, his followers did not get together in a little liberal clique and comfort themselves with the fact that they still had his teachings."[72] The risen Christ transforms those who follow him. The old self, which is bound to sin, is put to death and buried so that the new self can rise in witness to God. Helpfully, Forde reminds us that Christian faith itself is a Spirit-infused gift that comes from outside us. We cannot control it and even knowledge of the life, death, and resurrection of Jesus Christ cannot guarantee it. Rather it is, "the state of being grasped and captivated in the Spirit by the proclamation of what God has done in Jesus."[73] In this sense, faith is a joyful and hopeful by-product of the new

---

70. Bruner, *Truth as Encounter*, 137.

71. Knitter, *Theologies of Religions*, 102.

72. Forde, *Theology is for Proclamation*, 73.

73. Ibid., 137.

life and freedom experienced by people who have been grasped by God.[74] Faith, like salvation does not come by choice or activation of our wills but as a freely given gift. We can hold our calling as preachers a little more lightly, uplifted by the freedom of the saving Spirit of God.

Pluralistic Synthesis: Blending Religious Difference

In his visits to congregations, Rasoul routinely experienced conversations with church leaders and members that tried to erase the differences between Christianity and Islam. This practice also regularly happens with our Jewish neighbors. Those who suggest that we share a common "God" or who lift up shared practices without naming the differences in theology behind those practices make actual exchange and conversation difficult. In these cases, the conversation lacks an honest base and vulnerability that truthfully acknowledges the "non-negotiables" of faith. In the pulpit, this kind of religious blurring is particularly challenging because it not only sends unclear signals to those of other religions who may be visitors among us, but it also does not contribute to ongoing formation of committed Christians or nurture the particular witness of the church. The motivations behind this stance are similar to those that undergird Knitter's Mutuality Model:

1. A desire for authentic dialogue between Christians and those of other religions.

2. A "level playing field" for conversation.[75]

Where these believers part from Knitter's model in their practice is that they fail to uphold the uniqueness of Jesus.[76] The Mutuality Model seeks to hold Jesus' particularity in dynamic balance with the other two goals so that Christian focus on Jesus doesn't tilt the tables in the quest for balanced and fair interreligious dialogue.[77]

To address the conundrum at the heart of the Mutuality Model, Knitter names three possibilities or "bridges" whose spans are traversed by theologians such as John Hick:

---

74. Ibid., 141.

75. Knitter, *Theologies of Religions*, 109–10.

76. Ibid., 111.

77. Ibid.

1. The "philosophical-historical" route that grows from the " . . . historical limitations of all religions and the philosophical possibility (or probability) that there is one Divine Reality behind and within them all."[78]

2. The "religious-mystical" route that focuses on a commonly held religious belief, "that the Divine is both more than anything experienced by one religion and yet present in the mystical experience of all of them."[79]

3. The "ethical-practical" route that focuses on how religions function in a world of suffering and immense need and that these create " . . . a common concern for those of all traditions."[80]

The context of attending to the needs of the world creates an occasion and space for interreligious engagement and conversation.[81] This was the case for a Mennonite congregation where my husband served as pastor. Due to changes in laws surrounding the temporary housing codes in our town, the Mennonite Church now lacked appropriate facilities to host the temporary emergency homeless shelter that travelled from church to church in the winter months. Because some in the church cared very much about continuing to work with the shelter, a partnership was formed with the local mosque, whose facilities were better suited to hosting. As part of the partnership, the Mennonite church assisted with meals and provided some chaperones to spend the night with the guests at the mosque.

The "religious-mystical" and "ethical-practical" routes may have been the ones chosen perhaps even unconsciously by those who engaged with Rasoul as he visited different congregations. They mainly saw similarities between his beliefs and practices and their own. They may have been informed by friendships with those of other religions. Maybe the congregations he visited had engaged in interreligious service projects like the Mennonite-Muslim winter-shelter partnership.

One of the gifts of the Mutuality Model is that it lifts up the importance of living and acting with deep awareness of the perspective and experience of the other. This is a helpful posture for preaching—if

78. Ibid., 112.

79. Ibid., 112–13.

80. Ibid., 113.

81. Ibid.

not every Sunday, then as a homiletical exercise, to engage with other religious perspectives around potential sermon texts. The practice of scriptural reasoning, discussed later in this chapter, is one possible way to bring awareness of the other into our preaching. After all we worship and serve a God who is other than we are, although God has also chosen to be known in Jesus—one who embraces both similarity and otherness, human like us but also fully God. God continues to bridge the gap between God and humanity in the Spirit of the risen Christ who reveals God's will and presence to us and advocates for us in ways that encompass needs that we name and that which alludes naming. In fact, God's actions in Jesus Christ serve as a model for us in how we can engage and preach in the presence of religious others with theological integrity, honesty, and radical hospitality.

THE CROSS FORMS US TO PREACH IN THE PRESENCE OF THE "OTHER"

Jesus on the cross most starkly shows us the quality of God's self-giving love for others, even enemies.[82] Therefore, preaching the cross forms Christians for encounters with those who are "other" than us. By encountering a God who is "other" than us through the medium of the cross, a way that is confounding to us, we encounter those who are different in a posture of humility or confession rather than arrogance. Using the cross as a lens for all our preaching provides a way of relating to religious others.

The way of the cross is also instructive for showing us how to authentically and humbly preach to the "others" in our midst, both fellow-Christians and believers from other religions. While we carefully prepare our sermons with our congregations in mind, the truth is that our listeners are "other" than us. They have different perspectives on the text and different experiences that resonate with the gospel. The Spirit uses these differences to help preaching serve God's purposes in wonderful ways that extend beyond our control or intentions. In an age when our sermons often have lives that extend to unknown listeners through the internet, even preachers who do not have believers from other religions in their congregations are indeed preaching to those who are unknown and "other." The cross illustrates a key virtue of Christian discipleship, that of

82. Volf, *Exclusion and Embrace*, 24.

relating to others in humility and self-giving love. The act of preaching is one of vulnerability and audacity. We must confess our own deficits before the God we proclaim. In Jesus Christ God has drawn near to us, marking ways in which we are able to follow Jesus and the ways in which we are markedly different from our Savior. As broken and imperfect instruments we must nevertheless allow God to work and speak through our imperfect lives and words. Karl Barth captures the conundrum well, as preachers we are called to risk standing in the pulpit, praying before God, and in Barth's words, "adding something out of our heads and hearts to that which was read out of the Bible."[83] Preachers must attend to the complexities in the Bible and our present world, engaging with challenging ancient Scripture that comes from a culture that feels alien to our local contexts and cultures, while also unpacking equally challenging life events in local and global arenas, claiming that the same God is working through both and that God is still speaking in our lives from Scripture. To this steep charge, Barth incredulously asks, "Who should be a pastor, who should preach!"[84] Translating this into the context of preaching in the presence of other religions, we must remember that no matter how long we have been preaching or studying the Bible, we do not know everything. Our God is unfathomable and we only can know what is revealed to us. The Apostle Paul reminds us that we "see in a mirror dimly."[85] We must speak boldly that which we know to be true, but we must also preach in humility, recognizing our finitude and limitations. Regardless of the presence of religious others, we always preach in the presence of the God who is "other" and among a congregation of many "others" who will perceive and shape the meaning of our sermons in conjunction with the movement of the Spirit. Once our sermons have been spoken—even our own preaching becomes "other" as the Spirit gives our language power.

As we acknowledge the formative power of preaching, our sermons, like prayers, must move from the realm of "explanation" to the realm of "doing."[86] Gerhard Forde writes, "The proclaimer should attempt to do once again in the living present what the text once did and so authorizes doing again."[87] He continues, "The texts do not leave us in the dark. The

83. Barth, *Word of God*, 109.
84. Ibid., 106.
85. 1 Cor 13:12.
86. Forde, *Theology is for Proclamation*, 155.
87. Ibid.

people were shocked, incensed, amazed, offended, they took up stones to kill. Or they comforted, healed, and gave life. The words drive inexorably toward cross and resurrection. Indeed they are the Word of the cross."[88] According to Forde, when the preacher moves to proclaim, he or she has been given authority to announce God's grace and forgiveness not only in the text, but in the present tense.[89] He writes, "The point is that the proclamation itself ought to bear the form of the Word of the cross. . . . The proclamation is to kill and make alive. It purposes to make an ending and a new beginning."[90]

The cross readies us for our task as preachers. It highlights the radical juxtaposition between people who are trapped and limited in their attempts to exercise power and control, and Jesus Christ the Savior who becomes human, and offers himself up to suffer and die for all humans.[91] When preachers proclaim, they witness to the gospel that has also grasped them.[92] The place where the human situation meets God is on the cross. Thus, the shape of proclamation is also cruciform.[93] Human inability and sin and all the broken parts of our lives must come to an end in order to be reborn according to God's intentions. Proclamation is part of that rebirth process, but the way in which proclamation of the gospel grasps people is not through the means that we as preachers would necessarily choose or plan; it feels risky to us.[94] Part of preaching the presence of Jesus Christ is surrendering our own agenda and being caught up in God's broader story.

In this way, Forde claims "Proclamation occurs . . . when the hearer is drawn into the picture, into the story. . . . "[95] Despite its challenges, the cross is a central part of that story. Forde writes, "We forget that [Jesus] was, after all, despised and rejected, and that we crucified him."[96] He further elaborates, " . . . The fact is—and none of his followers could ignore it—that his preaching, teaching, miracles, and whatever claim he made or implied about himself led only to the cross. All of his followers forsook

88. Ibid., 156.
89. Ibid., 156–57.
90. Ibid., 157.
91. Ibid., 56.
92. Ibid., 64.
93. Ibid.
94. Ibid., 56–57.
95. Ibid., 67.
96. Ibid., 72.

him and fled. . . . Yet in the resurrection God had simply cancelled out the rejection, done a new thing, brought life out of death."[97] This means that the cross is an unavoidable part of preaching and teaching. The old self, which is bound to sin, is put to death and buried so that the new self can rise in witness to God. Discontinuity is an essential part of the human encounter with God.[98] Such discontinuity saves us in a way the law never can; it "sets us free so that we will want to believe."[99] While Forde has emphasized the discontinuity we experience in the gospel, there is also continuity in that "God continues the story in spite of the discontinuity. That means that God alone is the carrier of whatever continuity there is, both in the story of Jesus and consequently in our stories as well."[100] When we claim preaching as the "Word of God" we link our preaching with the disorienting and reorienting "otherness" of the crucified God.

By allowing both the otherness of God and the otherness of those who hear our sermons to affect our preaching, we are surrendering control. Preachers cannot ultimately force hearers to receive God's Word.[101] We cannot control revelation, but we can trust it, and this creates the possibility for preaching. A transcendent view of revelation offers us grace because it is only God's active Word that allows us to stand in the pulpit. Just as God's power manifested in the cross puts worldly uses of power to shame, the transcendence of God's Word puts the scope of human words in perspective and frees us from the burden of an often-fruitless

97. Ibid., 72–73.

98. Ibid., 78–82.

99. Ibid., 81.

100. Ibid., 83–84.

101. Nevertheless, preachers can not shirk their responsibility. For example, Fred Craddock writes, "Our task is not just to say the word and to tell the truth but to get the truth heard, to effect a new hearing of the word among those who have been repeatedly exposed to it." Craddock, *Overhearing the Gospel*, 11–12. Along the same lines, Eugene Lowry offers a helpful distinction between preaching and proclamation. He writes, "Preaching I can do. I choose it. I prepare for it. Prayerfully I engage it, and I perform it. I do it. I will do it Sunday next. Proclaiming the Word is what I *hope* will happen next Sunday. I will attempt my preparation strategy in such a way as to maximize the chance for it. But proclaiming the Word? Nobody has the grip of control for it. You cannot capture it; you cannot possess it; you cannot package it; you cannot deliver it; and you cannot control the receipt of it. Sorry." Lowry, *Sermon*, 37. Another perspective is offered by James Henry Harris, who contrasts caucasian preachers' tendency to claim authority with interpretative patterns in African American preaching, which invite the hearer to participate in a dialogue with the preacher so that the meaning is "polyvalent." Harris, *Word Made Plain*, 53.

search for God's revelatory Word based in our own limited experiences and power alone.[102] God's Word revealed in the crucified and resurrected Christ shows us that God is radically for us, dies and is raised for us so that we might never experience separation from God. Through the witness of scripture, we hear that nothing is impossible for God. We hear God speaking through the transformed and redeemed words of diverse people—broken and common. This power of God makes preaching possible for broken and common people today, bringing redemption and hope in the face of death and loss. The ongoing witness of preaching bears this out as Spirit-empowered human words are used to do the impossible. Through God, they can actually become God's own revelatory Word in every language and culture so that God might be glorified.

PRACTICES FOR PREACHERS

As pastors and preachers, we feel called to nurture faith and prepare our congregations for discipleship in a religiously diverse world. Preaching the cross and resurrection with interfaith awareness creates an additional challenge in attending to these events in the life of Jesus Christ which are central to our theology and deepest beliefs. I will discuss three inter-related postures or virtues reflected in the biblical material around Jesus' crucifixion and resurrection that may also be beneficial for preachers seeking to preach with interfaith sensitivity: vulnerability, compassion, and bearing witness.

Vulnerability

Jesus' incarnation and way being in our world was marked by intentional vulnerability, starting with his birth as a helpless newborn in an unortho-dox setting where his mother was likely not attended by her own mother or family members, through his ministry and travels among diverse people, his candid conversations and tussles with religious authorities, right up to his palm-heralded entry into Jerusalem, not on a war horse but on a donkey. In the days leading up to his crucifixion, Jesus demonstrated a sense of openness and receptivity to God's movement and direction in his

102. Nevertheless, while God can work through, and at times shatter, the perspectives of both preacher and listeners, Joseph M. Webb points out that worldview and perspective still certainly shape our understanding and interpretation of the biblical text. Webb, *Old Texts*, 13–28.

life. He gave himself fully into God's care. This vulnerability came with steep costs. Judas betrayed him. As he prayed in the garden, weeping and sweating blood, his disciples were unable to stay awake. After his arrest, he was abandoned and denied by Peter. After an unjust trial, Jesus was tortured, stripped, hung on a cross, and died. Jesus lived an authentic and open life—deeply bound to God—and his death remained true to that way of living. The resurrected Jesus was also vulnerable to his followers, allowing Thomas to touch his still wounded hands and side. In his ascension, Jesus promises to be with his followers until the end of the age.

As Jesus' disciples, we are called to follow him in vulnerability. In our calling as ministers, preaching is a particularly vulnerable act. By the sustaining power of the Spirit, we are called to stand before a congregation and say something true about God using ancient Scripture and present-day experiences as our points of entry. The virtue of vulnerability in preaching invites us to ask different questions of ourselves as preachers. Rather than only asking if the sermon is biblically accurate, timely, memorable, etc., preachers should ask themselves, "Am I engaged completely in the full process of preaching? Am I paying attention?"[103] It is all too easy to "check out" at some point in the process of preaching, whether in the creation process or in the actual preaching moment. When we allow ourselves to check out, we lose the possibility of connection that is fundament to human relationships regardless of religious tradition. Seeking to be more vulnerable in preaching is not a license to make us the center of the sermon, rather it is preaching in a way that engages us fully as the people we are (the ones God called.) Vulnerability in preaching means fully engaging the process of sermon-creation with investment and honesty. In Brene Brown's words, "Its being all in. . . . Our willingness to own and engage with our vulnerability determines the depth of our courage and our clarity of purpose; the level to which we protect ourselves from being vulnerable is a measure of our fear and disconnection."[104] The challenge of vulnerability is that it often makes us feel uncomfortable, yet it crops up in many contexts associated with ministry. Vulnerability is triggered by feeling uncertain of the outcome of a situation, when one may be on the receiving end of judgment or critique, when one is aware of dependence and deep love for others, and

103. Questions adapted from Brene Brown's advice for parents. Brown, *Daring Greatly*, 15.

104. Ibid., 2.

when loved ones are suffering and struggling.[105] Vulnerable preaching starts with vulnerable study and exegesis in which we are aware of our pre-associations or biases around a text or topic and purposely seek out conversation partners, resources, and perspectives that stretch our point of view or challenge our assumptions. After an initial reading of the Scripture, it may be helpful to make a list of our gut- reactions, tendencies, views, and biases around the passage. The sermon-creation process can unfold as a way of openly engaging and challenging these views. For example, is our initial sense of sermon theme born of the Spirit's leading or born from what we experienced somewhere else or preached last time we used this text?

Vulnerability requires strength. It also may uncover past hurts and wounds in our own lives that prevent us from bringing our whole selves to preaching. I've seen student preachers silenced by wounds inflicted years ago. One woman struggled to speak in the pulpit, remembering a careless comment made about the quality of her voice as an adolescent. If the process of sermon creation uncovers an old wound, depending on your context, you may want to name it in some way in your preaching. Jesus promises to bind up and bring healing to our wounds. Bringing our own woundedness tangibly to the sermon, whether it is in the form of a bias towards some aspect of the text or brokenness from damage done to us by another, removes stigma around wounding experiences and invites others to also seek healing. All preaching is self-referential, but styles and cultural mores often determine how open we can be in acknowledging our position and our voice in the sermon. Some preachers and congregations are uncomfortable with stories and points of view explicitly attributed to the preacher, where others are used to preachers openly bringing their own lives into view through story and example. Preaching with awareness of the "other" is preaching that acknowledges the perspective of the preacher. Such vulnerability moves contrary to the ways that authority so often moves in other venues. Rather than issuing timeless truths or propositional edicts from the pulpit, vulnerable preaching invites us to take a confessional stance. We are human and do not have all the answers. Our life experiences color our understanding of the good news. The choices we make about engaging with the world around us inform our experience of the gospel from week to week: what we purchase, social media presence, the websites we frequent, and the

105. Ibid., 6.

newspapers we read (or don't read). When we put on our God-goggles, we see our own lives, families, and neighborhoods. Being upfront about our own experiences and perspectives does not weaken the truth in our claims, rather it gives others permission to view their own particular lives with God-goggles. For those of other religions, it can create an entry point for conversation.

Compassion

Jesus life and ministry were marked by compassion and his compassionate character continued to mark his behavior through his crucifixion and resurrection. In the upper room, Jesus lovingly shared his own body and blood with his disciples and washed their feet as a model for compassionate service. When Jesus is arrested and one of his followers cuts off the ear of the High Priest's servant, he stops and heals the man before allowing himself to be led away. While hanging on the cross, gospel accounts offer examples of his compassion. He makes provision for his mother Mary, commending her into John's care. He also extends grace and mercy towards the thief who hangs near him and asks God to forgive those who have crucified him. His post-resurrection appearances show his sensitivity and compassion for his disciples who struggle to understand what is happening. He offers them peace and an opportunity to restore relationship with him as well as direction for next steps in compassionate ways that acknowledge their humanity and needs.

Compassion is a deeply needed virtue in our world today. In a recent TED talk, pundit Sally Kohn encouraged people to move beyond political correctness, to what she calls "emotional correctness" that empathetically validates another person's experience and perspective even if we do not agree with them.[106] This practice was key for Kohn, a politically-progressive lesbian woman working for Fox News, which is known for its politically and socially-conservative hosts and pundits and allowed for her to connect to members of the audience in ways that allowed for true listening and conversation despite difference.[107] To practice compassion means that we need to be clear about our own identity—who we are and what we believe. In order to set aside our needs to engage another, we need to have clearly marked boundaries. Preaching which aims to form compassion-

106. Kohn, "Is it Enough."
107. Ibid.

ate Christians needs to do the important work of Christian formation. In terms of interfaith awareness and sensitivity, compassion is a virtue that is present among otherwise diverse religious perspectives. Religion scholar and author Karen Armstrong has written about compassion and helped to create a "Charter for Compassion" that uses the Golden Rule as a way to encourage peace among religions.[108] The charter calls all people to treat others as they wish to be treated, to work to end suffering, and to refrain from violence of all kinds. In the arena of religious scriptural interpretation, the charter holds that, "any interpretation of scripture that breeds violence, hatred or disdain is illegitimate."[109]

Pastors are often naturally compassionate people; we honestly care about others and want to relate in ways that concretely show others their value in God's eyes. Compassion can be a virtue that we express not only in informal conversation and pastoral care settings but also in our preaching. Compassion is deeply linked to empathy, or the ability to see something from another person's perspective or point of view. Compassionate sermon-creation begins with reading the biblical text empathetically so that we avoid painting even the most morally questionable biblical figures with absolute brush-strokes.[110] Can we understand what might have motivated someone like Queen Jezebel or Judas Iscariot to behave as they did? Fear can be a powerful motivator and often lies behind reprehensible actions both in the Bible and in our world today. The Charter for Compassion talks hopefully about compassion's potential for "breaking down, political, dogmatic, ideological and religious boundaries."[111] The kind of boundaries that need to be transcended by compassion are not boundaries that define our Christian identity, but the kind of boundaries that prevent us from engaging the humanity of those who are different than we are and the boundaries of our own fear that hold us back from fully living into our Christian calling.

Bearing Witness

Jesus' life was exemplary in bearing witness to his identity as Messiah, God Incarnate. In the gospel accounts, either the Spirit or voice of God

108. Armstrong, *Twelve Steps to a Compassionate Life*.

109. Charter for Compassion, *Charter for Compassion*.

110. Wilson, *Four Pages*, 128.

111. Charter for Compassion, *Charter for Compassion*.

at times announces and reinforces Jesus' divine identity in the events of his baptism and transfiguration. His witness continued in his suffering, death, and resurrection—in fact the integrity of his witness led to his suffering and death. Although they struggled and failed to understand, he was open about his destiny of death and resurrection to his disciples. Throughout his trial Jesus would not step away from his true identity, even when it may have spared his life. He withstood torture and died on a cross under a sign, "King of the Jews." In his resurrection, Jesus maintained continuity with his witness, calling his followers to report what they have seen—that the tomb is empty and he is risen from the dead. Matthew's gospel even reports a false witness among the soldiers who were paid-off to say that Jesus' disciples stole his body.[112] Additional endings may have ben added to Mark's gospel to give a sense of disciples bearing witness to the resurrection as the original closing ends with the women who encounter the risen Christ fleeing in fear and amazement without telling anyone.[113] Luke's gospel includes an account of Jesus appearing to disciples traveling to Emmaus. They are so energized and inspired by the encounter that they return immediately to the road so that they can bear witness to the others in Jerusalem.[114] Luke uses the language of witness, telling the disciples, "You are witnesses of these things. And see, I am sending upon you what my Father has promised . . . ," which links the power to bear witness to the resurrected Christ with the gift of the Holy Spirit.[115] John's gospel, which was written after the others, also lifts up those who are able to bear witness and believe in the resurrection even when they did not see it with their own eyes.[116] This is important for the young church after the first generation of those who walked with the earthly Jesus have died. The witness of believers who are willing to die for their faith was foundational for the early church and continues to be a real part of Christian faith in some parts of our world today. While few in North America will lose their lives for their faith, following Jesus means following him to the cross. Life this side of God's Kingdom is marked both by the suffering of the cross and the glory and

112. Matt 28:11–15.

113. Mark 16:8.

114. Luke 24:31–35.

115. Luke 24:48–49.

116. John 20:29.

joy of resurrection. Ignoring this reality in preaching is not being true to our calling as witnesses.

In his classic textbook for beginning preachers, *The Witness of Preaching*, Tom Long seeks to recast and rehabilitate the image of witness for preachers from negative connotations which link terms such as witness or testimony to particularly "aggressive forms of evangelism" that can manipulate or bully others into believing as we do.[117] Rather, the virtue of bearing witness is crucial for preaching. Long describes the role of a court-room witness,

> The court has access to the truth only through the witness. It seeks the truth but it must look for it in the testimony of the witness. The very life of the witness, then, is bound up in the testimony. The witness cannot claim to be removed, objectively pointing to the evidence. What the witness believes to be true is part of the evidence, and when the truth told by the witness is despised by the people, the witness may suffer, or even be killed, as a result of the testimony. It is no coincidence that the New Testament word for witness is *martyr*.[118]

The image of witness helps the preacher to exercise authority in ways that are helpful for preaching in our broader interfaith context. Our own encounters with the crucified and risen Christ—in a myriad of ways—have changed us; this experience of transformation grounds our authority in a receptive posture that is open to hearing God's voice in new ways, through Scripture and in our world, perhaps in conversation with those who represent another religion.[119]

Vulnerability, Compassion, and Bearing Witness through the Lens of Scriptural Reasoning

The virtues of vulnerability, compassion, and bearing witness are important attributes to cultivate in ministry and preaching. One practice that has affected my own preaching in ways that have strengthened both Christian identity and interfaith awareness is scriptural reasoning (S.R.), an orderly way of reading, interpreting, and discussing Jewish, Muslim, and Christian scripture with Jews, Muslims, and Christians through close

117. Long, *Witness*, 46.

118. Ibid., 47.

119. Ibid.

and careful engagement with pre-selected pericopes. My own interests in
S.R. sprang from working with Rasoul and grading his sermons, which
were anchored in the Qur'an rather than the Bible and a desire to learn
more about interreligious practices around scriptural interpretation. I
embarked on a summer training course in S.R. with Peter Ochs at the
University of Virginia. Learning about and practicing S.R. positively affected not only my awareness and relationship with religious "others" but
also my own use of scripture in preaching.

Scriptural reasoning is a beneficial practice for Christian preachers
seeking to engage with other religious traditions in a way that maintains
authenticity of the Christian witness and offers us new insights into our
own scriptural tradition. In a sense, S.R. offers a means of radical deconstruction, a way of "othering" our own scripture in a form that is offered
as a gift to us from others around the circle.[120] Scriptural reasoning is
an ordered practice of reading, reasoning, and discussing the scriptures
of Judaism, Christianity, and Islam in a group of believers from each of
those faiths. Scriptural reasoning practitioners generally have been both
academics and believers, representing educational institutions and their
particular "house" of worship.[121] Scriptural reasoning groups meet independently from either of those settings in a manner likened to biblical
"tents of meeting." Participants engage with each other and their sacred
scriptures in these "tents of meeting" and then return to their institutions
with "new energy and deeper wisdom."[122] Scriptural reasoning is not
interreligious dialogue although it does foster relationships between believers of different religions and it does desire healing and peace among
those of different religions. Scriptural reasoning resists homogenization
or any attempts to iron out the differences between the different religions.
Believers represent their particular traditions in the tent of meeting. The
goal is not to create a religious mash-up of the Abrahamic faiths. It "is
about serious conversation between three religious traditions that preserves difference as it establishes relationships."[123] Scriptural reasoning
can be understood as an eschatological act in which we sit at God's table
with those who are "other," free from the pressure to convert. Scriptural
reasoning includes times of new insights that are still being formed even

120. For more on deconstruction in preaching see, McClure, *Otherwise Preaching*.
121. Kepnes, "Handbook," 368.
122. Ibid.
123. Ibid.

as they are being voiced by participants as well as reflection when we seek to summarize and organize the new insights that emerged. Scriptural reasoning is still experimental in that the practice is still growing and changing and practitioners are still exploring how it might change the world and help to facilitate peace among religious groups.

As a potential practice for preachers, scriptural reasoning challenges and strengthens vulnerability, compassion and bearing witness. Peter Ochs has described the act of sharing one's sacred scripture with those who are not believers as being similar to a mother lion bringing a beloved and treasured cub into a circle of other mother lions. We feel defensive and protective of our own tradition. Love for God and for Holy Scripture opens us up to being hurt or transformed. We are vulnerable. My most vulnerable experience with S.R. happened during a session where our group explored 1Cor 1:18–31 as the Christian scripture. This text is about the cross and was the foundation of a chapter in my doctoral dissertation. Further, I had preached on it numerous times and listened to student sermons on the text. The practice of scriptural reasoning asks participants to focus only on the text at hand—not on surrounding passages and not on an "internal library" that might move reading and engaging beyond an initial plain-sense of the text. Without the broader context of the rest of the letter, the Corinthian context, and the Apostle Paul, parts of this passage can come across as difficult and hard to understand. It was excruciating to listen to my Muslim and Jewish colleagues ask difficult questions around this passage. Several times the convener had to remind me to refrain from bringing information in from outside of this particular passage. Yet my vulnerability allowed me to have a sense of letting-go and trust. In releasing my hold on my own deeply invested interpretive history with this passage, the text became something new and I was open to a new leading from the Spirit. With vulnerability, I had to allow my "cub" to interact with the other lions.

Scriptural reasoning not only caused me to feel vulnerable in relationship to my own sacred scripture, but also challenged my sense of compassion. Interestingly but not surprisingly, at times I have had the hardest time extending compassion towards other Christians who hold or interpret Scripture differently than I do. In one incident, the group of Christians who were around the table argued so much that one of the Muslim participants intervened and scolded us for not taking our scriptural tradition and relationship with each other more seriously! Sometimes it is not the one who is radically different but the one who is quite similar who is more threatening. On his way to the cross, Jesus experienced betrayal by leaders in his own Jewish tradition and even from his own disciples. Yet knowing all of this did not stop him from extending love, compassion, and ultimately healing forgiveness. Interpretation of scripture is one factor that is dividing us today—not just for Christians but for Muslims and Jews as well. Before attempting traditional S.R. a Christian congregation and Muslim congregation decided to practice S.R. with members of their own congregations. Several times a year the S.R. groups meet together to share what they have learned from working with texts in-house.

Scriptural reasoning also affected my sense of bearing witness. It can feel weighty to represent "the Christian perspective." I am aware of my own particular formation and beliefs as a Mennonite seminary professor who teaches preaching. One of the biggest challenges in practicing S.R. is that we are asked to try to "bracket-off" our witness or testimony for part of the discipline so that the text can speak to others without our interpretation. The act of suppressing or bracketing this off had the effect of making me even more aware of my own confession of faith and narrative journey with Christ as it has played out in the context of engaging with particular passages of Scripture. Because I am a preacher and teacher of preachers, this is a primary way in which I study, pray, and engage with scripture. My sermons reflect my deepest beliefs as they come in contact with scripture and the world around me. Because S.R. is practiced around a table where leadership is shared and each person eventually has a chance to bring insight into Scripture that is unique to his or her religious tradition, the experience of being authoritative, or considered an authority, is rooted in Long's understanding of witness or testimony rather than credentials or educational background. In the settings where I have experienced S.R. the participants have all been academics with similar professional credentials. The authority of bearing witness would be a much more powerful experience in a S.R. group, which included believers that represented not only academics but also clergy and laity.

CONCLUSION

In this chapter, I have argued that while the cross and resurrection can create unique challenges in dialogue and relationships between Christians and our Jewish and Muslim neighbors, the cross and resurrection

STUMBLING OVER THE CROSS

also form and equip Christians theologically and ethically for navigating our world in ways that tell the truth about who we are as Christians while also extending hospitality and love to religious others. Cultivating the virtues of vulnerability, compassion, and bearing witness in preaching can create a sacred holding-space where church members are deeply steeped in Christian identity but religious others are also welcome and where questions do not threaten but rather create an opportunity for nurturing and deepening faith. The practice of S.R. provides a unique opportunity for preachers to study and discuss scripture in an interfaith setting and supports the virtues of vulnerability, compassion, and bearing witness in ways that extend into our broader ministry experiences.

FURTHER RESOURCES FOR SCRIPTURAL REASONING

The internet is a source of many helpful resources for those who would like to experiment with S.R.:

- The website http://www.scripturalreasoning.org/ offers information, definitions, and bundles of pre-selected texts for those who do not feel comfortable choosing scripture from other religious traditions. One can also sign up to be part of a virtual S.R. group, which may be a great option for pastors who need flexibility in schedules and who may live in a rural area or not have relationships with clergy from other religions.

- The University of Virginia publishes an academic journal related to S.R., *The Journal of Scriptural Reasoning.* http://jsr.shanti.virginia.edu/

- Oxford University has been part of the S.R. movement from its inception. The U.K. website is also helpful, particularly their "Scriptural Reasoning Covenant." http://www.scripturalreasoning.org.uk/

- There is also a Facebook page for scriptural reasoning, which provides another geographically-flexible way for pastors to learn about and engage with others who are interested in S.R.

4

Equipping Disciples
for the Global Marketplace

On any given Sunday, faithful Christians worship God in a variety of ways—some of those ways feel very different from what we experience in our ordinary workaday lives. We may wear different clothes, sing songs with ancient texts, or our pastor may wear robes or vestments that set her or him apart from other worshippers. While our preacher may use a tablet instead of a paper manuscript, her sermon is delivered from behind a large and elevated pulpit. On the other hand, some of us may worship in settings that hold continuity with our weekday lives. Our pastor may wear jeans, we may sip coffee during worship, and the music may sound similar to what plays on a top-40 radio station with the exception of explicitly Christian lyrics. The preacher may move around the worship space while preaching or sit on a stool while his notes rest on a music stand. Because the church exists as an embodied group with historical and present-day incarnations, it has always had to navigate its life within human cultures. God engages with humanity in its varied cultures. God means for the good news to exist in human cultures and God's good news both challenges and affirms aspects of every culture. Thinking and writing about culture is challenging because we cannot escape it—even for a moment. To be alive is to be situated in culture or cultures. Culture is the air we breathe—we are so deeply enmeshed that we don't tend to notice unless we encounter a different culture. When it comes to Christianity, David Buttrick aptly notes, that part of how Christians are aware of their faith is "by contrast with the ethos of their culture."[1]

My own Mennonite tradition has a long history of uncomfortable relationships with the cultures in which the church exists, stemming back in part to a parting of ways between Ulrich Zwingli and some of his students in sixteenth-century Zurich. For Zwingli, the State should reflect the Christian witness. For his former students, now Anabaptists, the church was called to a specific ethic that was different from the State. This discomfort persists among some Anabaptist groups today, including the Amish and some Old Order Mennonites who eschew most of the modern conveniences that mark modern life. Even relatively mainstream Mennonites tend to readily question many aspects of North American culture. Part of this contrarian streak is a desire to protect the Christian community and foster allegiance to God above all. Wearing different clothes and having different daily practices serves as a constant reminder that the church is called to a specific witness in the midst of cultures. Sometimes critique is part of that witness.

This chapter explores how proclaiming the reality inaugurated by the cross and resurrection can equip our people for discipleship amidst the competing cultural narratives of weekday life. Some ninety years ago in his essay, "The Need and Promise of Christian Proclamation," Karl Barth wrote about the challenges facing preachers as they seek to integrate their own culturally mediated perspectives with Scripture and speak to the deep-seated question that draws people then and now to churches to listen to a sermon "Is it true?" He writes,

> Is it true, the vision of unity for those who are scattered; the anticipation of a steadfast pole amid the flight of phenomena; a righteousness that does not lie somewhere beyond the stars but within the events that make up our present life; a *heaven* above the earth . . . ? Is it true, the speaking of the love and goodness of God who is more than some friendly deity of transparent origin and short-lived dominion? Is it true? This is what people want to hear, to know, to understand. . . . They do not want to simply receive mere assertions and advice, no matter how heartfelt and sincere they may be. . . . They passionately desire to have the Word spoken to them, the Word, which promises grace in judgment, life in death, the beyond in the here and now. . . . We are

1. Buttrick, *Captive Voice*, 56.

deluded . . . when we think that they will be put off with temporary, easy answers. Oh yes, these methods work for the time being. The people are moved, pleased, satisfied, even if they do not find what they are actually looking for but rather that which they could basically get in a better way elsewhere.[2]

Barth's insights speak with a surprising freshness for preachers today. Our broader North American cultures have shifted so that the church no longer holds a position of privilege or power. Being a "good person" no longer means that that person necessarily regularly attends church. Out of a desire for the church to "step-up its game," many denominations and congregations have followed after cultural trends, from integrating the latest technology to building worship around a "Starbucks" model. The truth is that the church does need to step-up to the challenges of being Christian in twenty-first-century North America, but the best way forward may not be playing up the common links between the culture of the church and the surrounding cultures. Rather, the church needs to tighten its work of distinctive character formation through preaching that speaks to the theological and narrative heart of our faith, the death and resurrection of Jesus Christ.

The cross has never been an "easy sell." We may remember Paul's profession in his letter to Corinth, "We proclaim Christ crucified, a stumbling block to Jews and foolishness to Gentiles."[3] Cultural values of consumerism are seductive and form a deep cultural narrative that is shaping our congregations and us. We are habitual creatures, deeply formed and shaped by the narratives and cultural liturgies in which we are immersed. Within our lives and the varied cultures of our world and congregations, the narrative of the cross and resurrection serves as a powerful counter-narrative, a true and life-giving narrative for our lives, but unless we experience this narrative on a regular basis it is easy to give our lives over to self-centered, consumer-driven narratives that lead to death rather than life. As the quote from Barth implies, when the church short-changes its uniqueness, it cannot compete in a race that it was never meant to run. That is, with what can be done in "a better way elsewhere." If people want a really good concert, they will go to a music venue or arena. If they want really good coffee they will go to a gourmet coffee shop. The church today doesn't need another generation of shallow sermons that reduce

2. Barth, *Word of God*, 110–12.
3. 1 Cor 1:23.

the gospel to feel-good platitudes, self-improvement, and individual achievement. We need a renewed sense of preaching that gathers the community around the cross and reorients us for our participation in God's redemption of the world. Set within the context of worship, the sermon has a unique opportunity to offer a transformative tuning note that can help interpret and reorient the congregation's corporate actions and witness as well as guide individual members in personal discipleship. To this end, we will explore some working definitions of culture and name some aspects of North American consumer-driven culture that are especially seductive for the church, noting how these tendencies sound hollow or dissonant when placed alongside the eschatological crisis of the cross and resurrection. Then I will discuss how the cross speaks to our culture before naming ways in which preaching can contribute to counter-cultural Christian formation and renewal that forms preachers and the Christian community according to the cross, equipping members for discipleship amidst the many competing cultural pressures we balance today.

WHAT IS CULTURE?

Christians all over the world are seeking to faithfully embody worship in ways that reflect the gospel of Jesus Christ while engaging their local setting and connecting to their culture.[4] Because we are embodied within particular cultures, it is notoriously challenging to define culture or even describe it with clarity. Usually our perceptions about culture are most heightened when we are visitors or guests in another culture. Nevertheless, it will help our discussion to have in mind a couple working definitions for "culture" in hand. Anthropologist and ethnographer Clifford Geertz defines culture as "a multiplicity of complex interweaving structures with people suspended in webs of significance that we ourselves have created."[5] Analysis of these webs is a quest for meaning and understanding.[6] Culture is like a text and exploring it is like doing literary analysis.[7] Humans can't exist without a culture—without culture

4. Plantinga and Rozeboom, *Discerning the Spirits*, 47.

5. Ibid., 53; Geertz, *Interpretation of Cultures*, 5.

6. Ibid.

7. Plantinga and Rozeboom, *Discerning the Spirits*, 54; Geertz, *Interpretation of Cultures*, 9.

life would be meaningless. Geertz particularly emphasizes the public and social aspects of culture.[8] Along similar lines, theologian H. Richard Niebuhr in his influential lectures, *Christ and Culture* defined culture as, "The total process of human activity and the total result of such activity."[9] He saw culture as something manufactured and "secondary" that we as people inevitably "superimpose" or lay over a natural environment, such that culture includes all aspects of life in our world.[10] Picking up on similar themes, Clifford Orwin, political theorist says that culture is "the totality of [any people group's] social practices."[11] Orwin is using "social practices" as shorthand to mean everything we do from our thoughts and motives to our choices and outward behavior.[12] A final definition may be helpful as we seek to explore the church's relationship to and in culture. Communication theorists Larry Samovar and Richard Porter discuss the phenomenon of what they call "co-cultures," that is "groups of people that exist within a society but outside the dominant culture."[13] My own Mennonite tradition would represent one of these co-cultures, but Samovar and Porter would also include groups that move past traditional racial or ethnic categories such as those with disabilities, generational groups like baby-boomers, and those who live in a particular town, neighborhood, or other niche.[14] Samovar and Porter hold that these smaller groups use language in particular ways, which in turn helps to form and reinforce their own particular culture.[15] From these definitions, we can note some generalities about culture. Culture is inevitable. It is of our own making but we can't exist apart from it. Culture has to do with our regular habits and behaviors—both intentional and subconscious.[16] It is also dynamic, relational, multifaceted, and polyvalent as our lives include multiple cultures and co-cultures.

8. Plantinga and Rozeboom, *Discerning the Spirits*, 54; Geertz, *Interpretation of Cultures*, 17.

9. Plantinga and Rozeboom, *Discerning the Spirits*, 54–55; Niebuhr, *Christ and Culture*, 32.

10. Plantinga and Rozeboom, *Discerning the Spirits*, 55.

11. Ibid., 55; Clifford Orwin, "All Quiet," 3–21.

12. Plantinga and Rozeboom, *Discerning the Spirits*, 55.

13. Ibid. Samovar and Porter, *Communication between Cultures*, 158.

14. Plantinga and Rozeboom, *Discerning the Spirits*, 55. Samovar and Porter, *Communication between Cultures*, 159.

15. Plantinga and Rozeboom, *Discerning the Spirits*, 56.

16. Ibid.

As preachers we are always engaged with cultures, always making choices about cultures. Adaptation and engagement with cultures is inevitable and desirable, but risky! Part of pastoral and Christian formation is growing as discerning practitioners who can navigate our native cultures, drawing from scripture, communal discernment, tradition, experience, and prayer, among other tools, to make choices about how we interact with our world. Congregations routinely make culturally based choices that play out in many ways, from what people wear to church, to how we celebrate communion, the leadership style in the congregation, what the worship space looks like, and so on.

What makes the relationship between cultures—particularly popular culture—and worship especially challenging in some of our contexts is that in our attempt to be relevant we have to do a careful dance so that popular culture doesn't violate core aspects of the gospel or our theology that are not supported by the broader cultures in which our churches exist.[17] But the other side of the scale is equally vital. Worship dare not cast itself as irrelevant or miss a chance to connect the gospel to people's real lives.[18] What we're talking about here is the situation that mission-workers or Bible-translators regularly face. Obviously none of us represent the original culture of Israel, Jesus, or the Bible—so even our inherited "traditional" practices are the end result of translation and cultural choices. Ultimately, no culture has the corner on God. The gospel affirms and challenges or critiques aspects of every culture or context. How do we inculturate the Gospel? The gospel cannot exist apart from being in some form—but any translation involves making choices. The message is also affected by its medium. Consider whether you hear a preacher in person or watch the preacher on T.V. Even if the sermon is the same, the power and content of the message is received differently. Pastors who preach the same sermon in different congregations or in worship services with a different style can testify to a similar reality. The context is not simply a set of eye-glass frames in which preachers can pop their sermon lenses. The relationship between all aspects of worship and the context is dynamic, complex, and deeply relational. While preachers today are still guided by Barth's infamous axiom that we must preach with the Bible in one hand and the newspaper in the other, this quote really doesn't tell the whole story. We cannot merely attend to both realities in our preaching but

17. Ibid., 48.
18. Ibid.

need to recognize that our situation in the world has completely affected the way that we read and interpret scripture. In the midst of this dynamic, the cross and resurrection function theologically to remind us that Jesus does not follow our rules and morays and that God is not bound by the realm of what we might consider possible. Our commitment to God will always complicate the church's relationship with the cultures in which it exists. Naming the crucified and risen Jesus as Lord destabilizes the marketplace commercial tendencies that run our workaday lives.

THE "CAPTIVITY" OF THE CHURCH AND THE NARRATIVE OF CONSUMERISM

In 1520, a young Martin Luther harkened back to themes of captivity and exile from the Hebrew Scriptures and published a treatise detailing the ways that the Roman Catholic Church had gone astray, naming the use and abuse of the sacramental system as a new "Babylonian Captivity" for the church. Borrowing Luther's language we might note that throughout history, the church is prone to captivity in different ways. Ultimately freed by Christ, we are called to serve as witnesses and our lives are meant to reflect, at least in a mirror dimly, the Realm of God. The cultures in which our congregations exist are rightly enmeshed with our Christian identities as we seek to serve God in neighborhoods and communities where we worship, live, love, work, and play. When and how does embedded ministry become ministry held captive? Where are the powers and principalities harmfully encroaching in territory that is rightly God's?[19] In the following paragraphs, I will make a case that the North American church experiences captivity in two arenas that have deeply affected our ability to live into our unique calling in relationship to cultures. One arena concerns our understanding of time, the other is our understanding of "the good life." The economic powers and principalities play a significant role in both of these arenas, steering us towards consumerism in subtle and often subconscious ways. Dynamics within these broad arenas generate powerful narratives that steer our lives both communally and personally.

19. Walter Wink's work on the powers and principalities undergirds some of my thinking on the captivity of the church. According to Wink, the powers and principalities are the large and often invisible spiritual forces and systems that run much of our lives. While not always harmful, these spiritual systems can become depersonalized pathways for sin and brokenness. People experience being powerless, caught in a system they cannot change. Wink, *Powers that Be*, 2–5.

In the Synoptic Gospels, one of the events leading Jesus to the cross is the cleansing of the temple. With only slight variations, Matthew, Mark, and Luke describe a narrative unfolding something like this: Jesus enters the temple with his followers. He sees vendors selling animals for sacrifice and money-changers who will exchange currency to facilitate purchase.[20] In addition to blurring ritual purity boundaries, the officials involved are likely not playing fair and are offering dishonest exchange rates and skimming some off the top for themselves. Jesus becomes incensed by exploitative practices that detract from worshipping God and drives them out. The Gospel of John, with characteristic dramatic flair, puts this event towards the beginning of Jesus' earthly ministry rather than towards the end and has him brandishing a whip made of cords.[21] The situation that Jesus encountered in the temple has persisted in one form or another. Recent reports from the Pew Forum on Religion & Public Life / U.S. Religious Landscape Survey describe the American religious landscape as a "market-place."[22] As congregations compete for members in a marketplace where the fastest growing group are those who have no religious affiliation, one wonders if Jesus would turn over tables and clear house as he did in the Temple.

In many respects, churches or preachers borrowing tools, techniques, and rhetoric from the realm of effective advertising is nothing new. However, the embedded and simultaneously elevated nature of advertising in our culture means that we are less and less aware of its presence in our lives and how consumerism is shaping and forming us according to a particular narrative. The narrative of consumerism goes something like this, "identify and reinforce a sense of need, then introduce a product to meet that need." For example, some of us may be familiar with the recent series of popular commercials for Snickers candy bars that show a person acting unlike him or herself—so much so that they have actually physically become another person; for example, in one ad, ravenously hungry 1970s goody-two-shoes icon Marsha Brady physically becomes hyper-masculine tough-guy Danny Trejo of "Machete" fame. With just a few bites of the candy bar, Marsha's wild hunger is satisfied and she returns to her smiley feminine self. It is a narrative we see again and again; the need is established whether it is for a car,

20. Matt 21:12–17; Mark 11:15–19, Luke 19:45–48.
21. John 2:13–16.
22. "U.S. Religious Landscape Survey," 6–7.

shoes, a phone, or detergent. The advertiser then introduces us to the Lexus, Nikes, iPhone, or Tide to satisfy the need. The narrative is not always explicit when products are inserted into films or when products show up in our facebook news feed. In these cases, the products become inserted into the narratives of our own day, so that when we experience a need—real or reinforced by advertising—we are drawn to purchase the products and brands that have been showing up in our lives. The drive of the consumerist narrative forms us, in the words of Debra Dean Murphy, "to expect the immediate satisfaction of all desire—physical and emotional, material and psychological."[23] Consumerism creates, shapes, and sustains our desire "to acquire and accumulate temporal goods in ever-increasing amounts (and the experiences of pleasure associated with this acquisition and accumulation)."[24] Moreover, Dean Murphy also notes that most Western cultures encourage and defend consumerism as crucial for a healthy broader economy while downplaying its serious effects.[25] Bluntly, Dean Murphy notes that in its "manipulation of desire," consumerism, "thwarts imagination and creativity, and destroys genuine community."[26] And so storage units sprout like mushrooms at the edges of our communities and in re-developed urban cores as we set aside older stuff in pursuit of new stuff. The truth, at least in part, is often that it's not so much the stuff itself that we desire as the opportunity to communicate an identity that others will recognize as worthy of love or to embark on a quest that will provide meaning and allow us to divert our eyes from challenges in our lives and our world. Consumerism exploits our weaknesses for gain.[27]

Consumerism is a cultural threat that has crept into the sermons of unsuspecting and well-meaning preachers. The language that we use betrays this dangerous undercurrent. We may not all talk about our sermons as "packaging" for the gospel. But many of us speak of a desire for people to "get something out of our sermons that they can take home with them." In part this issue is challenging for preachers because on the surface, the narrative of consumerism, that is, "establish need and provide a solution (product)" sounds similar to a formula long employed

23. Murphy, *Teaching that Transforms*, 119–20.

24. Ibid.

25. Ibid.

26. Ibid., 120.

27. Ibid., 122.

by some effective preachers—particularly in contexts oriented around inviting newcomers or seekers to get to know Jesus. The need may vary— loneliness, addiction, financial or relational struggles, lack of meaning or purpose, etc—but the solution or product we promote in this instance is "Jesus." Our consumerist culture has trained us to be hyper aware of ourselves and our own needs so it is often relatively easy for preachers to tap into these desires with just a few well-placed images or a story. The theological challenge of employing this narrative for preaching is that it lacks a sense of cost, engagement, or demand; it brings together our own therapeutic longing to help people feel better with deep-seated human tendencies to serve our own self-interests, ultimately trumping the hard- er edge of the gospel. Much like a purchase or economic transaction may offer a temporary balm to distract us, a purely therapeutic approach from the pulpit does not offer deep-seated or lasting hope or real transforma- tion. In our desire to evoke warm feelings and invite participants into a worship experience, we forget that "authentic worship" is not achieved by the feelings of participants, but by the presence of God; and God is not reliant on our feelings.[28] God using the cross evades our understanding. The cross refuses to lull us into an easy, warm experience that only af- firms us and nurtures our self-reflective needs.

When preaching borrows too much from our therapeutic market- driven media culture, we not only risk offering a temporary fix, but we may also inadvertently deepen isolation and divisions. The marketplace divides people into target demographic groups based on gender, age, race, education, marital status, postal code, and habits. It is tempting for churches to employ this model as they target programs or sermon series towards particular groups, such as single parents or recent retirees. Fo- cusing on subgroups isolates us from people who are different from us and weakens the church's ability to work as a whole body. It also heightens a consumerist approach for those who are seeking a worshipping com- munity. Rather than committing to a church that is serving their com- munity in its diversity, we understandably seek out a church that relates to us or has programming designed to target us and meet our perceived physical, social, or spiritual needs. This targeted approach to ministry, coupled with the increasing use of media that allows us to "participate" without extending ourselves, risks making church too much like the mar- ketplace, where a common consumerist approach is a significant part of

28. Ibid., 128.

what binds us to each other.[29] As Debra Dean Murphy puts it, "How do we reckon with the truth . . . That when we enter into worship we bring a numbing passivity born of media bombardment and image overkill, a self-preoccupation created and nurtured by an increasingly therapeutic, individualistic, and narcissistic culture, and the not so tacit assumption that worship is but another attractively packaged commodity to be consumed by a savvy, discriminating, church-shopping public?"[30]

Consumerism is a cultural threat, but for the church the cross provides a catalyst for resistance. The stark reality of the cross cuts through our delusions and unveils the truth. So many of our consumer practices lead to death and suffering—of underpaid workers, our planet, our own future plans when we rack up more debt than we can repay. On the cross, Jesus takes on the real issues in our lives, the shame, brokenness, biases, and mistakes—the pain we have caused to others and the pain that has been inflicted upon us. All of this dies with Jesus. The cross and resurrection reorient us towards God who alone can bring life from death. All our efforts reach an end at the cross; the cross represents our unredeemed destiny, the way of death, the way of seeking self at the expense of others, and the way of fear. The cross highlights our captivity, which is the way our insatiable quest for stuff binds us in an unending cycle that is fed by pervasive advertising.[31] Where the marketplace divides, Jesus' death and resurrection reunites. Jesus' death and resurrection heal real rifts in relationship between God and people and between people. But consumerism is not a fatal condition. On the cross, Jesus has exposed the hollow drive of the marketplace and offers us life with real value. The physicality of Jesus' death on the cross re-connects us with our human-ness and mortality. The cross highlights our own weakness and fallenness, while the resurrection comes as a gift that highlights our dependence on God for life.[32] Furthermore, we cannot purchase the gift of life that God offers to us. God has purchased it with God's own blood. God's perfect love splayed out on the cross casts out our fear. We are set free.

29. Ibid., 126.
30. Ibid., 126–27.
31. Ibid., 129–30.
32. Ibid., 129.

Captivity: Time

Lawrence Hull Stookey describes Christians as always needing to live at "the intersection of time and eternity."[33] We live as sinners justified by God's grace in a world that simultaneously bears witness to God's ultimate transformation of creation, which is evidenced in the resurrection of Jesus Christ and the human fallenness that costs Jesus his life on the cross. Nevertheless, it is very easy for us to get caught up in the immediate needs and pressures of our day-to-day lives. Even the seminary where I teach has recently struggled to reserve time for chapel worship that is free from other scheduled meetings. Time is an increasingly valuable commodity as technology has enabled us to work from everywhere and to be constantly available. Furthermore, there are many different cultural calendars that exercise control over our lives that have also become important markers for our congregations. Observance of the Christian year has been passed over or integrated with school calendars, Hallmark holiday calendars, sports calendars, and increasingly the political calendar as election cycles garner greater media attention than in the past. Observing the Christian year reminds us that there is a God who is at work within, but also above and beyond, our own calendars.[34] The Christian year is an alternative calendar that has the potential to order our lives and spirituality as we navigate living between time and eternity. The Christian calendar reminds us that God is the Lord of time as creator of time, redeemer of our lives and time, and sustainer of our lives. God created time and continues to break into our calendars and lives. The Christian year specifically organizes our worship and congregational life together around the life, death, and resurrection of Jesus Christ. These matters are key to the work of preachers as we are called to lead our congregations between the realities of our lives and the ultimate in-breaking reality of the Kingdom of God.

While the Christian year has its roots in the ancient practice of keeping Sabbath, setting aside a day of rest to specifically honor and worship God as a tithe of our time that acknowledges God as the Lord and giver of all time. The Christ event forms the core of the Christian year by acknowledging Christ as the center of time. Our origin and our ultimate destiny lie in Christ. When we keep Sabbath, we recognize our finitude and dependence—attributes that are also undercurrents in a

33. Stookey, *Calendar*, 17.
34. Ibid., 18.

well-rounded understanding of the cross. To preach the cross is to profess that the church values people regardless of their productivity by remembering those who suffer, the poor, the vulnerable, the oppressed—those who experience limitations in productivity and who carry little power in broader culture.

The celebrations of the Christian year are ancient and grow from Jewish festival practices where an event like Passover was not simply remembered but experienced afresh. Practically speaking, the Christian year, also called church year or liturgical year, is a cycle of theologically rooted seasons that move us biblically and doctrinally through the events unfolding the life of Christ, his death and resurrection, and his promised return.[35] The arrangement of these events into larger and smaller festival seasons, bracketed by Ordinary Time, purposely blurs the lines between events that unfolded chronologically in the life of Christ and prophesy and the promises of God—those already fulfilled in Christ and those waiting to be fulfilled. The past, present, and future overlap each other as we move from season to season. Between some of the church seasons we have special Sundays that help to bridge the seasons or provide a window into a particular church teaching. For example, the last Sunday in the church year before Advent, which starts the cycle over again, is Reign of Christ or Christ the King Sunday—this day proclaims the Lordship of Christ on the heels of end-times texts that come at the end of Ordinary Time and foreshadow the future-sense and eschatological hope of Advent, which simultaneously celebrates Christ's coming to a stable in Bethlehem, Christ's continual coming into our hearts and lives, and his promised return to finally restore all of creation. Thus all that happens before Christ finds its fulfillment in Christ and all that comes after only finds meaning in referring back to Christ.[36]

Celebrations of the Christian year fell away in most protestant traditions during the Reformation in an attempt to simplify worship and allow for deeper engagement with the biblical text in preaching. However, the second half of the twentieth century and early twenty-first century have seen a reclaiming of the church year by protestants in a way that mirrors the Christocentric focus of the early church. Observing the Christian year does not in any way lessen the potential to deeply engage scripture or preach in a timely manner. On the contrary, it heightens the view that

35. Webber, *Ancient Future Time*, 31.
36. Webber, *Services*, 79.

the church is an alternative community centered in Christ. As we move through the seasons year after year, our spirituality deepens and calls us to bring our present lives and questions into the crisis of the cross and resurrection that lie at the heart of our faith.

Advent: *What aspects of our lives and world are marked by longing for Christ?*

Christmas: *How is Christ made incarnate among us today?*

Epiphany and Season after Epiphany: *How is God revealing God's-self to us in new ways—deepening our knowledge of who Christ is?*

Lent: *Reflecting on the challenge of discipleship, traveling the way with Christ towards the cross. What do we learn from Jesus?*

Easter Triduum: *How do Jesus' death and resurrection affect our lives and our world? How do we experience anew the death of sin and our old selves as we experience liberation, forgiveness, and new life in Christ?*

Easter: *Where do we see and experience New Creation, the Risen Lord among us?*

Pentecost: *How is the Holy Spirit active in our lives? What new things is the Spirit of the Risen Christ doing in our world?*

The cross and resurrection are key aspects of Christ's identity and thus are present throughout the church year. While Lent, Good Friday, and Easter lend themselves to explicit preaching about the cross, the cross can help us refocus time itself so that we can understand the eschatological upheaval present in the death and resurrection of Jesus. In this vein, the sermon becomes a vehicle for Christ's promise of life to us. The cross stands both inside and outside of human cultures, in the borderland between this age and the next, offering a distinctive difference from traditional understandings of linear time and history. Christ's death and resurrection save this world while it is yet imperfect, breaking into the present age with a promise from the age to come. The new reality exposed by the cross and resurrection "confronts" us in the vulnerability of our present lives, making "a claim" on us that calls for an answer.[37] Thus, while the church exists between the giving and fulfilling of God's eschatological promise, experiencing both the agony of a broken world and "the 'guarantee' of God's final victory" through the presence of the Holy Spirit, the sermon tears through time and human history to expose reality as rendered by Christ—a reality promised in him and through his

37. Lose, *Confessing Jesus Christ*, 205–6, 215, and 221.

atoning work.[38] Moltmann's depiction of promise as "a declaration which announces the coming of a reality that does not yet exist . . . ," which "'initiates' and 'determines' history," "binding" hearers to a certain impending reality, is a kind of "speech act" guaranteed by God and when proclaimed through the sermon, creates reality in the present moment—making something happen here and now.[39] James Kay explains, "In saying 'I love you,' the speaker does not discourse about love but enacts love concretely. This word of love is the love of which it speaks."[40] When the sermon functions as a promissory Word of God, despite the delivery of the Word by a human preacher, God is the guarantor of the promise—the one who offers is "actively committed to others in the present for the future."[41] Preaching as promise involves the "real presence" of the one who promises, so that "when the kerygma is heard as a promise of Christ's death and resurrection on behalf of our salvation then it is heard as a promise from Christ himself."[42]

The cross and resurrection as an eschatological promise means that preaching that is deeply attuned or formed by the cross and resurrection will have a "both-and" quality in relationship to our eschatological placement in time and our relationship with culture. All cultures are a mix of already redeemed aspects that the gospel affirms and broken areas that are still waiting for complete transformation, which means that what one congregation may embrace another may reject.[43] This does not mean that either church is being unfaithful. We exist in time as embodied congregations attuned to the narrative of Christ and must discern how to best enact our calling as stewards of time and culture.

Captivity: The Good Life

So many advertisers use comfort in their commercials, from shoes to mattresses and medications, we are reminded that feeling good and

---

38. Kay, *Preaching and Theology*, 121–22

39. Moltmann, *Theology of Hope*, 103. See also Kay, *Preaching and Theology*, 121–122. That God uses broken and vulnerable human words to express this reality corresponds to God's use of power in the cross. Lose, *Confessing Jesus Christ*, 228–29.

40. Kay, *Preaching and Theology*, 123.

41. Ibid., 123–24.

42. Ibid., 124.

43. Plantinga and Rozeboom, *Discerning the Spirits*, 90.

comfortable is not a luxury or a temporary condition, but that it is our
"right." The desire to feel good in all areas, from physical and emotional
to spiritual and relational, is deeply human. This is precisely why Satan
chose this angle with Jesus shortly after his baptism as he prepared to
begin his ministry, "He ate nothing at all during those days, and when
they were over, he was famished. The devil said to him, 'If you are the Son
of God, command this stone to become a loaf of bread.' Jesus answered
him, 'It is written, "One does not live by bread alone."'"[44] At the end of
his earthly ministry, shortly before his arrest and crucifixion, Jesus again
struggled with the human drive to avoid pain praying, "Father, if you are
willing, remove this cup from me; yet, not my will but yours be done."[45] I
want to be clear that having needs and experiencing a drive to meet those
needs is not a sign of our sinfulness but a sign of our humanity, and when
rightly oriented, marks our dependence on God and others. To be part of
creation is to be defined by finitude (a concept that is key to transforming our approach to energy resources.) In the midst of finitude, a drive
towards "the good life" can also be a rightly oriented impulse if "the good
life" that we desire is a life marked by the Reign of God, which is recognized by God's abundant generosity rather than a mad dash to gobble
everything up before it's gone or a desire to hoard good gifts until our
lives are held captive to managing the good things we own. When a few
of us hoard God's good gifts and withhold these from others, what was
intended as a means to life abundant becomes marked by suffering. We
need the cross, God's radical and complete self-giving, to set the world
right.

"The good life" is a long-standing philosophical ideal and our descriptions of "the good life" are likely as diverse as the cultures, traditions, communities, and families we represent. However, regardless of the
specific details, such as whether we would rather spend a free afternoon
at the beach, in a museum, with friends, or alone, a recent article in Psychology Today lifted out four factors by which a surveyed group evalu-
ated their lives according to an idealized "good life." According to this
group, "the good life" is characterized by "experiences of pleasure, lack of
negative and unpleasant experiences, developing personal strengths, and
contribution to others."[46] Many people linked the good life with develop-

44. Luke 4:2–4.

45. Luke 22:42.

46. Howell, "How Do People." The survey focused on users of the website Beyon-
dThePurchase.org so there may have been a bias against material aspects of "the good

ing personal strengths. A focus on self-development corresponds to other trends and resonates with what some scholars have called the "Oprahfication" of American culture, a focus on nurturing the self that encompasses an almost spiritualized approach to self-help alongside professional support.[47] Self-development is not new, but some have credited Oprah with making it popular and an attainable goal for the masses. Beyond its broad popularity, self-development as key to "the good life" also resonates with recent trends in church programming and preaching.

In reflecting on some common cultural understandings of what "the good life" looks like, it is not surprising that the church has often fallen into patterns that are steered by the marketplace. After all, the most celebrated "religious events" in our culture are increasingly commercial and economic enterprises. For example, recreational gatherings for Super Bowl Sunday have a "quasi-religious" quality. Advertising spots during last year's big game cost $4.5 million for a thirty second slot, a mind-blowing $150,000 per second.[48] In his research, around what he calls "cultural liturgies," James K. A. Smith refers to shopping malls as being the "cathedrals" of our culture today, embodying "the good life," employing effective iconography, and serving as a kind of "worship."[49] He writes,

> . . . We are invited to enter. . . . Sometimes we will enter cautiously, curiously, tentatively making our way through this labyrinth within the labyrinth, having a vague sense of need but unsure how it will be fulfilled, and so are open to surprise—to that moment when the spirit leads us to an experience that we could not have anticipated.[50]

Smith addresses both those who show up as "seekers" and those who shop with purpose; naming our found objects as "holy" and the checkout counter as the "altar" where we participate in a culturally pervasive "religion of transaction, of exchange and communion."[51]

Smith's use of religious language to describe a shopping excursion highlights his concerns about formative Christian practices and our understanding of "the good life." He explores practices using the language

---

life."

47. See Cotton and Springer, *Stories of Oprah*.

48. Kramer, "Super Bowl 2015."

49. Smith, *Desiring the Kingdom*, 20–23.

50. Ibid., 22.

51. Ibid.

of liturgy—or quasi-liturgy whether the practice is "secular" or "sacred."[52] By using the term *liturgy*, Smith is making a claim that human beings are religious beings and that all people are believers in some way, although not all human beings desire the Kingdom of God and not all people are believers in Christ.[53]

The core premise of Smith's book, *Desiring the Kingdom,* is that these collections of practices or liturgies "make us a certain kind of people, and what defines us is what we *love*. . . . Liturgies aim our love to different ends precisely by training our bodies. They prime us to approach the world in a certain way, to value certain things, to aim for certain goals, to pursue certain dreams, to work together on certain projects."[54] This means that not only do our most core values dictate our behaviors but that our habitual behaviors also inform our values. Where we spend most of our energies reveals that which we value above all; we are willing to undergo hardship and sacrifice for what we value most. According to Smith, the church has too often focused only on right thinking without engaging us as whole people and has missed an opportunity to shape our deepest desires so that they are oriented towards the Realm of God. We are living beings with bodies, minds, hearts, and souls. Have you ever gone to the grocery story hungry? If you're like me, then you find yourself making decisions with your stomach rather than your head. This is part of what it means to be human. We are people with all kinds of drives, impulses, and views that affect how we live day to day and determine our goals—the end towards which we are striving. The things that we love and desire drive our lives and we are willing to make sacrifices and choices to pursue these loves and desires.

Preaching about the cross provides an opportunity for pastors to focus on communal formation that is particularly Christian and operates according the Christ's call and the upside-down Realm of God rather than allowing a marketplace mindset to dictate the habits of the church.

PREACHING CROSS AND CULTURE

The relationship between cross and culture is challenging. In some ways it mirrors the complex dynamics that exist within the call and practice of

52. Ibid., 24–25.

53. Ibid., 23.

54. Ibid., 25.

preaching. In order to successfully communicate the gospel, we seek to harness all the tools available to us—these are the gifts of God's creation, our embodied nature as people within the cultures of the world. We engage with the full spectrum of biblical scholarship. We employ the most winsome stories and rhetoric. Yet we also hold tight to the "edges" of the gospel that critique the places where we fall short of God's intentions for us. We cast every part of our sermon into the crisis of the cross and resurrection, allowing the Spirit to hone our craft, allowing God's self-giving on the cross to counter the many conflicting impulses that so often guide us.[55]

The Cross Against Culture

As a theological symbol, the cross displays resistance rather than accommodation to society. Drawing from Rene Girard's work on sacred violence, Walter Wink holds that the powers and principalities often move through cultural institutions and trends, exacting a small amount of violence upon the most powerless who are often silenced in order to keep the system going.[56] It was in this spirit that civil and religious authorities sought to silence Jesus on the cross. But rather than allowing the powers to continue, Jesus' death broke the cycle of violence and shook the powers to their core, allowing us to experience the reverberations today through moments of clarity, seeing our world afresh through the lens of cross and resurrection. God has freed us from the powers of domination that so often hold us captive. In Wink's words,

> The Powers scourged him with whips, but each stroke of the lash unveiled their own illegitimacy. . . . They stripped him naked and crucified him in humiliation, all unaware that this very act had stripped the Powers of their last covering that disguised the towering wrongness of the whole way of life that their violence defended. They nailed him to a cross, not realizing that with each hammer's blow they were nailing up, for the whole world to see, the affidavit by which the Domination System would be condemned (Col 2:13–15).[57]

55. See also ibid., 129.
56. Wink, *Powers that Be*, 83–84.
57. Ibid., 83.

With the powers revealed, they lose their insidious strength and we can begin our witness, joining God's work of eradicating the powers and principalities from every corner of our world. While they are ultimately dethroned, resistance carries with it a cost. In my own tradition, Mennonites who resisted going to fight in World War I suffered social ostracizing and physical abuse. This was viewed as part of the cost of cultural resistance. Invoking the cross is synonymous with a vision of discipleship as a journey of sacrifice accessed through a narrow gate. It follows that language or preaching about the cross will also display areas of resistance to human culture rather than wholesale accommodation.[58] Honest and attentive preaching about the cross will not downplay these difficult and painful aspects of our faith. Some prominent and popular preachers want to preach a ruthlessly positive word. They want to preach "yes" in the face of all the "no's" that hurting people encounter in their lives. But these promises can ring hollow when they don't ring true to the life of Jesus or the power of God to bring life and good news from death and despair. In an increasingly competitive religious marketplace, it is so tempting for us to domesticate the terrible horror of the cross, but in order to be Savior of the whole world God must be wholly free to engage the powers and principalities that hold humanity captive, not on the world's terms but on God's own terms.[59] As David Buttrick notes, "If we are justified by the free grace of God, we must be willing to say no to all forms of social self-justification."[60] It follows that the resistance of the cross informs the nature of the gospel, our redeemed selves in Christ, and our preaching.

Part of the counter-cultural aspect of preaching the cross is that the preacher in a sense must desire to "get out of the way." It's impossible for preachers not to have their egos invested in their congregations and their sermons but preaching according to the cross serves as a stark reminder of the limitations of human wisdom and power. Andre Resner's work, *Preacher and Cross: Person and Message in Theology and Rhetoric*,

---

58. Buttrick, *Preaching Jesus*, 31–32. The idea that following Christ can set the church apart from the world is voiced by Niebuhr, *Christ and Culture*, and this discussion is in part shaped by his work.

59. Robert Farrar Capon notes with irony that preachers "can't bring themselves to come within a country mile of the horrendous truth that we are saved in our *deaths*, not by our efforts to lead a good life. . . . Nothing counts but the *cross*." Capon, *The Foolishness of Preaching*, 8. McClure's use of Levinas upholds an understanding of preaching which acknowledges the God who is other as "interrupting" our sense of the familiar. McClure, *Otherwise Preaching*, 8–9.

60. Buttrick, *Preaching Jesus Christ*, 32.

acknowledges the reality of the preacher's ethos, or gifts and character, but stresses that it is "God's trustworthiness" rather than "the human preacher's *ethos* which makes efficacious the gospel."[61] Resner sees a kind of counter-intuitive "cruciform" power in acknowledging human brokenness before almighty God, transforming the weakness of the human condition into a rhetorical strength in communicating the gospel. Following the example of Paul, the preacher must "acknowledge his or her own complicity in sin—sin for which Christ's sacrifice was alone efficacious."[62] Because the cross so starkly displays the devastating effects of human sin, laying bare our weakness and inability to save ourselves despite our occasional "delusions of self-righteousness," Christian preachers are called to embody a pattern that contrasts with traditional rhetorical patterns that emphasize the power and credibility of the speaker.[63] Thus, the weakness of people is met by the strength of God (powerfully displayed in ironic weakness). The crucified Christ is made Lord of a new creation where the world's understanding of power holds no sway.[64] Such a reversal is completely counter to the way humans naturally operate, which means that the preacher must constantly test his or her words by laying them alongside and beneath the cross where human expectations die and are raised with the crucified Christ. When the cross is proclaimed, the radical counter-cultural and world-transforming event of the cross happens anew.[65] Yet the power still lies with God rather than human preachers

61. Resner, *Preacher and Cross,* 107. David Lose draws heavily on Resner's work to suggest that preaching as confession is a way to remain faithful to the reverse rhetoric of Christ's cross and resurrection within a postmodern context. Lose, *Confessing Jesus Christ,* 205.

62. Resner, *Preacher and Cross,* 107.

63. Ibid., 107. Resner quotes from McGrath's article "Cross, Theology." An alternative point of view is offered by David M. Greenhaw, who writes, "The gospel cannot be proclaimed without authority." Greenhaw asserts that the preacher must transmit interpretive authority to the congregation so that "they can speak the gospel in their own lives." Greenhaw, "As One *with* Authority," 105–22; Finally, Mark Galli and Craig Brian Larson note that it is precisely because people are imperfect that preachers will need to employ rhetoric in service to God. They write, "Rhetoric is like fire: it can burn and destroy; but when used in love, it can bring warmth and light." Galli and Larson, *Preaching that Connects,* 20–22.

64. Resner, *Preacher and Cross,* 110–11. Buttrick names this "scandalous" aspect of the cross as a major hurdle for cultural "assimilation" of the message of the cross. Buttrick, *Captive Voice,* 59–60.

65. Resner, *Preacher and Cross,* 112. While not focused on the cross specifically, Walter Brueggemann uses the metaphor of prophetic or poetic preaching to address

who are understood best as Paul understood himself, "servants fulfilling tasks assigned to them by the Lord."[66] Because the world is still hostile to the power reversal of the cross, it follows that those who live in the light of the crucified and resurrected Lord will experience some of the same trials and suffering which he also experienced.[67] Resner writes,

> When one stands in the cross's shadow, the same stigmata attend to the follower as they did to the master. In fact the attending stigmata are the disciple's marks of genuineness or credibility. . . . To preach the cross of Christ and not to live out the cross for others effects a separation of witness: one's lived witness is separated from one's verbal witness.[68]

The Cross for Culture

As much as the cross and the gospel itself run counter to culture, they are also radically for the world and in the world.[69] From the very moment of creation, God has entered into relationship with the world and its varying and diverse human cultures. Ebeling addresses the profound connection as mediated through words, " . . . God cannot be spoken of in theology without the world thereby coming into expression as event, and the world cannot be spoken of in theology without God thereby likewise coming to expression as event."[70] Christ died for the world—affirming its preciousness to God and God's intentions to save, restore, and

---

similar themes. Brueggemann, *Finally Comes the Poet*.

66. Resner, *Preacher and Cross*, 121–23.

67. John Killinger cautions Christians against approaching changing cultural trends with a fearful sense of self-righteousness, viewing themselves "as guardians of truth and correctness in a world gone awry." Killinger, *Preaching to a Church*, 75. His quote from W. H. Auden's "Age of Anxiety" poetically compounds his point through the metaphor of the cross, "We would rather be ruined than changed, / We would rather die in our dread / Than climb the cross of the moment / And let our illusions die." Auden, *Collected Poems*, 533.

68. Resner, *Preacher and Cross*, 149.

69. This section is influenced by Niebuhr's view that followers of Christ can also affirm culture. Niebuhr, *Christ and Culture*. Marjorie Hewitt Suchocki notes that God meets us so intimately that God knows us better than we know ourselves. She writes, "God's creative word meets our condition, emerging quietly and most unnoticeably in the midst of who and where we are. . . . God's word is hidden incarnationally in the world. It is a whisper." Suchocki, *Whispered Word*, 4–6.

70. Ebeling, *Word and Faith*, 324–25.

transform the world, not abolish it.[71] Just as the cross does not exist as judgment alone but also mercy, the gospel does not only criticize culture but also affirms it.[72] Further, judgment is a necessary step along the path to experiencing salvation or redemption. Because the church is called to participate in God's redemption of the world and its cultures, cultural critique in our sermons can be seen as part of this process.[73] Miroslav Volf emphasizes that the reconciliation and unity among people brought about through Christ's death on the cross does not erase the particular cultural differences that mark human life. He writes,

> . . . the unity of all humanity is *not disincarnate transcendence, but the crucified and resurrected Jesus Christ.* . . . the cross is the *self-giving of the one for many.* Unity here is not the result of "sacred violence" which obliterates the particularity of "bodies," but a fruit of Christ's self-sacrifice, which breaks down the enmity between them.[74]

God's love for the world and affirmation of culture matter for preaching because preaching is not mainly "an alien word," that stands outside of our cultural realities, but the "mother tongue"[75]—the language of God's redemptive activity that is very much rooted in this world as it imagines and heralds the Kingdom of God, which is transforming this world.[76] God has been an active part of human history and human culture most fully in the person of Jesus Christ, who lived in the world as a human

---

71. Because God saves the whole person, Henry Mitchell's focus on "holistic" preaching is significant. Mitchell wants preaching to reach people at multiple levels including intellect, intuition, and emotion. Mithell, *Celebration and Experience*, 18–35.

72. Charles L. Rice supports a positive relationship between culture and preaching. Rise, *Interpretation and Imagination.* Similarly, Alyce McKenzie encourages preachers to put "cultural wisdom" and "Christian wisdom" in conversation with each other. McKenzie, *Preaching Biblical Wisdom*, 44–45; Henry H. Mitchell connects different styles of preaching to different cultures and asserts that one specific culture should not be "promoted" by the preacher, rather the preacher is called to "work within the culture of the congregation." Mitchell, *Black Preaching*, 11–14; On the other hand, Paul Wilson highlights North American preachers' narrow habit of singularly focusing on their own culture, noting how this is counter to the gospel, which encompasses every culture. Wilson, "Beyond Narrative," 145–46.

73. Plantinga and Rozeboom, *Discerning the Spirits*, 84, 88.

74. Miroslav Volf, *Exclusion and Embrace*, 47.

75. See also Mitchell, *Black Preaching*, 76.

76. Lischer, *Theology of Preaching*, 47.

representative of a particular human culture.[77] Because they are fully enmeshed in the world through their own struggles and the struggles of the
congregation, preachers can only preach from an "embedded position."[78]
Despite the struggles associated with being in the world, because God
in Christ has shown that God is for the world, the church as the body
of Christ and preaching as the Word of God, are also empowered by the
gracious gift of the Holy Spirit to exist in and for the world.[79]

It follows that the church's whole being is committed to the role of
witness to God's love and activity in the world. Preaching should also
echo this purpose as the world must understand the gospel that the
church proclaims.[80] The language and concerns of the sermon should be
culturally relatable because the gospel is infinitely translatable into every
culture and can address every human concern. In addition to announc-
ing God's good news of healing and hope, the sermon also guides and encourages believers as they engage the world as Christ's hands and feet, as
the necessary ingredients of salt and light. The cross illustrates how Christ
chose to relate to the world and thus, it is a model for the church today.
It is a temptation for preaching to tend toward the theologically abstract
but hearers live out the gospel in very particular situations. Therefore,
locating the sermon in a particular local context of the gospel, such as
families, neighborhoods, and towns, anchors the event of preaching as
being for a particular people in a particular moment.[81] Preaching that

77. Craig A. Loscalzo uses the Incarnation of God in Christ as a model for the
particular incarnation of preaching. Loscalzo, *Evangelistic Preaching*, 15–17.

78. Lischer, *End of Words*, 42.

79. Suchocki describes God's word as directing us "forward toward the world"
rather than "back to God" so that we can be drawn "into God's own creative work."
Suchocki, *Whispered Word*, 10.

80. David Buttrick asserts that preaching which "names God in connection with
a wide range of human experience" shapes the ways in which hearers understand
scripture and participates in the transformation of "human consciousness" over time.
Buttrick, *Homiletic*, 19–20.

81. To help people better understand the sermon, Mark Galli and Craig Brian
Larson suggest turning to communication methods used in the "worldly" realm of
journalism. Galli and Larson, *Preaching that Connects*, 11; Loscalzo calls for preachers
to take care to include everyone in their preaching to make sure that people know that
the gospel is for everyone, which means that sermons will need to bridge generations,
racial and ethnic groups, and people representing a variety of life situations. Loscalzo,
Evangelistic Preaching, 25. Concern for preaching to diverse congregations led Joseph
R. Jeter Jr. and Ronald J. Allen to look at ways to address different types of listeners with "the one Gospel" through different methods. Jeter and Allen, *One Gospel*,
9–13; A similar concern lies behind James R. Nieman's and Thomas R. Rodgers's use

attends to the immediate context also communicates that God's Kingdom is coming here and now—not in some abstract unworldly future.[82]

RE-FORMATION ACCORDING TO THE CROSS: PRACTICES FOR WORSHIP AND PREACHING

Preachers are under tremendous pressure to please their congregation, to please broader denominational structures, and to satisfy their own sense of call in relationship to preaching that communicates the good news in all its complexity amidst the many challenging contextual situations that we and our congregations face. The alluring pull of the consumerism narrative in our broader North American culture communicates fear and mistrust as it drives us to keep our eyes focused on ourselves. We are drawn to avoid the themes of sacrifice and challenge that are part of the Christian narrative of the cross and resurrection. It is tempting to use our sermons as opportunities to promote self-improvement for individuals and families within our congregations rather than to engage broader social realities and brokenness that seem overwhelming and impenetrable. In the midst of these pressures, refocusing our preaching through the cross and resurrection allow us to re-center and re-orient our congregations in ways that strengthen their witness as they also grapple with what it means to be a Christian in twenty-first-century North America. The following techniques or approaches offer a range of ways in which the cross empowers preachers and congregations to bear witness to the Christian narrative amidst competing cultural pressures.

Go Social

One critique often voiced by those who are uncomfortable mentioning the cross in their sermons is that much preaching about the cross tends

of "frames" of reference to explore different cultural perspectives and offer relevant options for preaching. Nieman, and Rodgers, *Preaching to Every Pew*, vii–viii.

82. Wayne V. McDill understands the sermon as only coming into existence in the "moment" of preaching. McDill, *Moment of Truth*, 1–4; Paul Scott Wilson highlights the importance of using "ordinary life" in the sermon as preaching recasts everyday events into "sacred stories," and "the congregation experiences a transformation of life before the gospel." Wilson, *Broken Words*, 99–101. Similarly, Richard Lischer emphasizes the often unmet need that ordinary people feel to hear about God's presence in " . . . their lives of faith—not Mother Theresa's, Gandhi's or Gandolf's, but theirs." Lischer, *End of Words*, 39.

to focus on individual rather than community or social benefits of the gospel. On the other hand, when sermons do express the social aspects of the gospel, the cross tends to be absent or not fully integrated into the sermon. Unfortunately, these weaknesses often fall along divisions already present in the church between non-denominational or evangelical and mainline or more socially liberal denominations and congregations. One way in which the cross can be instructive for us counter-culturally is to allow the cross to function more holistically in order to address both individuals, what some call "vertically" oriented reconciliation that is between "God and me," and "horizontally" oriented reconciliation that is between "neighbors." The truth of the gospel is that we don't need to choose between individual and social approaches. God's new covenant, established through Christ for me, must affect my relationships with others.

While concerns for time-limitations and sermon-unity might mean that not every sermon can address both individual and social implications of the gospel, congregations should have balanced enough preaching that members see the connection between their own faith, bound to and originating in Christ, and the way they live and relate to others. This means if you tend to focus on the individual, you may want to try a social approach. If you tend to preach socially, engage the cross as a catalyst for radical social change. While some of us have always engaged the social realm, preaching social aspects of the good news warrants retrieval and sustained focus in some of our traditions.

One entry point is to employ Walter Wink's language about the "Powers" or "Domination system" surrounding Jesus' death on the cross. Over the course of the church's history, preaching gradually grew quiet about the powers and became less comfortable challenging the powerful systems of our world, whether economic or political. This had an unfortunate side effect, where the good news became that which preserved present social power structures rather than necessarily and primarily bearing witness to the Realm of God—even where it might challenge the social order.[83] This also contributed to an imbalance in many of our traditions concerning the breadth of the gospel, deepening the private and personal side to the exclusion of naming social aspects of the good news that challenge the powers.[84] Sermonic language linking the "powers" to

83. Wink, *Powers that Be*, 90.
84. Ibid.

Jesus suffering and death on the cross moves us away from problematic transactional metaphors that cast God as the one demanding Jesus death. It also invites us to participate in the continued liberation of the church from its union with political "empires" that have appropriated some cultures into the church without nuance while suppressing or destroying others under the sway of western Christendom.[85]

Don't Just "Sell" the Gospel—Engage the Imagination

Our consumer culture has inspired a mindset that people need to be "sold" on something in order to "buy into" it. When it comes to the church and the work of preaching, this is a rather pessimistic view of the body of Christ. The cross invites us to follow Jesus in letting go of those cultural expectations. Rather than getting people to buy into something, preachers might try portraying a vision of the Realm of God, using description so that people can begin to imagine or envision themselves as a part of this in-breaking kingdom. Using well-placed details and focused narrative can invite listeners into the Kingdom-vision. Empathy is also an important tool as we decide where and how to offer examples and glimpses of resurrection life. Portraying biblical and real-world "villains" with understanding creates an opening for listeners to also surrender the parts of their lives where they may experience shame and fear judgment.[86]

Preaching the Call of the Cross

Quite rightly many of us find comfort and hope in preaching about God's love for us that overcomes and surpasses our sin and brokenness. Yet as Walter Brueggemann notes in his classic article, "Duty as Delight and Desire," preaching that focuses only on God's gift without any sense of reciprocal relationship or demand distorts the gospel. According to Brueggemann, a shift away from preaching obedience has its roots in at least two phenomena, the first being some readings of the apostle Paul that have been routed through Luther's theological slant during the sixteenth century and adopted wholesale in our preaching vocabularies.[87] Maxims such as "we are saved by grace alone" or "God loves us uncon-

85. Ibid., 87.
86. Wilson, *Four Pages*, 128.
87. Brueggemann, "Duty as Delight," 2.

ditionally" are not wrong but they lack theological and biblical nuance, and often function as comfortable "churchy" shorthand for preachers. While we may understand the nuances, many in our congregations do not; having been conditioned by therapeutic self-oriented cultural contexts, many misconstrue what it means to experience salvation or live as a disciple of Jesus.[88] Brueggemann also notes a second cause surrounding the decline in preaching about obedience also rooted in broader cultural narratives, a strong emphasis on individual freedom, particularly common in Western political and social rhetoric.[89] In fact, a very common narrative for coming of age in Western society involves rejecting the authoritative claims of parents or elders and claiming an unfettered freedom as one's own.[90] It is safe to say that both of these narratives have crept into Christian preaching in ways that counter theological claims made by scripture. As Brueggemann notes, "Only the exposure of these false articulations can permit the community of the gospel to discern and accept its true position before God, who loves, delivers, summons, and commands."[91] Brueggemann invites us to employ a "both-and" approach that complicates and deepens our relationship with our God who loves us to the point of dying for us, meaning that " . . . our most serious relationships, including our relationship to the God of the gospel, are, at the same time, profoundly unconditional and massively conditional."[92] Our Old Testament is comprised of both unconditional (Abraham and David) and conditional (Moses) relationships with God.[93] God's commitment to Israel continues even when Israel is unfaithful, although in these cases the relationship is marked by consequences including pain, brokenness, rejection, and loss.[94] Scripture draws upon the metaphor of the relationship between a parent and child or between marriage partners.[95] Such an image may also be helpful for us to borrow when appropriately qualified to acknowledge situations of abuse where disobedience may be essential to saving one's life and the special qualities present in our relationship to a

88. See also ibid.
89. Ibid., 2–3.
90. Ibid., 3.
91. Ibid.
92. Ibid.
93. Ibid.
94. Ibid., 3–4.
95. Ibid., 4.

God who is inscrutably beyond us but who has chosen to call us "friends." For example, we may choose to check our own freedom or desires out of love to another. The sacrifices we make for a loved one may be relatively large, such as quitting one's job to care for a young child or sick parent, or allowing a spouse to accept a job in another state. They may also be small sacrifices, such as prolonging an evening commute to pick up something from a store, changing a baby's diaper, taking out the trash, or cleaning up after the dog. Being in relationship with those we love means that not only are we willing to do these things but often we desire to do them as an act of devotion, love, and service.

The supreme love of Christ, poured out for us on the cross, is a tremendous sacrifice taken on by God; and our relationship to God calls us to response. Brueggemann suggests that preachers might frame response in part as, "disciplines essential to the revolution."[96] Jesus Christ has turned the world upside-down; such an act calls us to the waters of baptism to give up the present in order to inherit the Kingdom of God.[97] This allows us to invite our congregations to set aside culturally mediated, often self-seeking, practices for a set of alternative ways of life that have been inspired by the powerful love of Christ. We will want to take care to situate our obedience within the broader actions of God, in scripture, and in our world so that God is still doing the "heavy lifting" in our relationship. Starting with God's action in Jesus Christ allows our response to be the joyful overflowing excess of God's love. Our obedience becomes that which we want to do, which means that we can be invitational in tone and do not need to employ "must," "should," or "ought" language in our sermons. In a recent blog post, pastor Joanna Harader reminds us that sacrifices made in service to following Christ set us free and are a means to abundant life.[98] Our preaching can work with this nuance. While Jesus does call us to "take up your cross and follow me," he also says, "my yoke is easy and my burden is light."[99] Sacrifice is something that is redeemed in Christ's own sacrifice. Sacrifice and suffering

96. Ibid., 5.

97. In the early church adult baptismal candidates undertook years of preparation, many had to give up habits, employment, and relationships that ran counter to their budding commitment to Christ. To symbolize this sense of death and new life, the candidate would enter the baptismal pool naked and receive new garments upon emerging from the waters.

98. Harader, "On Sacrifice."

99. Matt 16:24; 11:30. See also Harader, "On Sacrifice."

are not synonymous, rather suffering often accompanies sacrifices made for the sake of discipleship, in part because brokenness still persists in our world and God's Realm has not fully taken hold.[100] In this way, our own sacrifices mirror Christ's sacrifice as they become generative, a positive means to resurrection life. Indeed, sacrifice can be positive; to follow Jesus is to sacrifice our unquestioned link to cultural powers that have formed us—whether familial or broader social forces. We must sacrifice racial biases, patriarchal patterns, low self-esteem, and fear to our own "exceptionalism."[101] Coming face to face with the cross reveals our own brokenness; God asks us to give up the socialization that has formed us up to this point and begin anew.[102]

Attend to the Christian Narrative

In the midst of competing cultural narratives, the Christian narrative is marked by the move from cross to resurrection. There are several ways in which preachers can deepen congregational formation according to the Christian narrative in ways that equip members for faithful witness. One way to deepen congregational formation according to the Christian narrative is to design worship according to the Christian year. The Christian year is guided by the narrative of Jesus. The theological heart of the Christian year is the Easter Triduum or Vigil and the fifty days of Easter, but the Christian year moves through the entire Christ event and its related doctrines. Because the cross and resurrection are so central to Jesus' work and identity, these events also undergird the entire Christian year. Many congregations may move in and out of the Christian year, but preaching through the entire cycle can be helpful for the formation of church members over time, according to the life, death, and resurrection of Jesus Christ.

The form or structure that you choose for your sermon can also implicitly reinforce the narrative of the cross. The approach offered in Paul Wilson's *Four Pages of the Sermon* helps the preacher attend both to the biblical text and to the world through the theological "grammar" of trouble and grace.[103] Because a four-page sermon necessarily follows the

100. Harader, "On Sacrifice."
101. Wink, *Powers that Be,* 94–95.
102. Ibid., 96.
103. Wilson, *Four Pages.*

movement from death to life that is also present in the cross, employ-ing this structure for our sermons imparts meaning to the events and language in our sermons.[104] In the sermon we experience how the move-ment of the gospel is different from the way events often unfold in the 24-hour news cycle that moves from crisis to crisis. Over time we are formed as people who are on the lookout for God's in-breaking action in our lives and world.

Broader worship elements and explicit reinforcement of commu-nity values can also help to form believers into disciples of our crucified and risen Lord. In her book, *Almost Christian*, Kenda Creasy Dean ex-plores four cultural characteristics or "tools" that lead to the formation of "devoted young people."[105] These practices are linked to specific and local congregational cultures but hold potential to be formatively powerful for Christians of all ages and can be implemented in worship and preaching in a way that attends to the particularities of a range of traditions. The tools are 1) confessing "their tradition's creed or God-story"; 2) belong-ing to "a community that enacts the God-story"; 3) feeling "called by this story to contribute to a larger purpose"; and 4) having "hope for the fu-ture promised by this story."[106]

Confessing one's creed or God-story can involve reciting it as part of worship or attending to it through preaching or other teaching op-portunities. A "creed" can be formal, such as reciting the Apostle's Creed, or it can be local, constructed for a particular community. For example, Grand Ave. Temple in Kansas City, Missouri is a downtown church that serves a transient community of people without fixed addresses. Because this community often experienced discrimination, humiliation, and pain, the "creed" recited in that congregation on Sundays was "every-body is somebody special reaching out to unite all in God's love."[107] For other congregations, the "creed" may be a hymn such as "Lift Every Voice and Sing" that is sung every Sunday as a way of reinforcing that which a congregation holds close and believes to be true. The classic Christian creeds give a prominent place to Jesus' death and resurrection—reciting these creeds helps Christians to understand the centrality of these events for the life of the church today. The sermon can be a wonderful place to

104. Wilson, *Practice of Preaching*, 162.
105. Dean, *Almost Christian*, 49.
106. Ibid.
107. Grand Avenue Temple, "Making a Difference."

unpack a congregation's official or unofficial creed. This can be done in a single sermon or in a sermon series and may be especially appropriate as members approach decisions and commitments around confirmation or believer's baptism. Enacting the God-story can take place in worship and preaching as well. The sermon can be an opportunity to bear witness to the ways God acts in our world—reinforcing our beliefs and empowering our practices. Testimony in the broader worship service, or as part of the sermon, can allow for multiple voices to lend credibility to the community's God-story.

The other "tools" cited by Dean, "feeling called by this story to participate in a larger purpose" and "having hope for the future," can also be influenced by worship and preaching. Music, prayers, and the use of drama or art shape our experience and give us a range of entry points for participating in the God-story enacted through public worship. Participation and formation in worship lead to a rich devotional life and commitment to service—this is part of our joyful response to the gospel. While the gospel may sometimes challenge us or "trouble the waters" of our souls, it never fails to instill hope. Preachers seeking feedback may want to include the question, "Did the sermon instill hope?" Christ's resurrection means that death is not the last word. Because we have been given the possibility of new life in Christ, we have hope that death is not the last word for us either.[108] The empty cross, a symbol present in some way in many of our congregations, testifies to this hope realized in Christ. Hope never grows old or tiresome. People come to church longing to hear it week after week—this is, in part, the root of Barth's question, "Is it true?" Whatever else we do or say in our sermons week after week, instilling deep hope that is not afraid to face real pain, trouble, and brokenness head-on, is crucial to our calling as preachers. Hope is born on Easter Sunday and is unafraid of the worst that life can throw at us because ultimately Jesus has faced and defeated pain, brokenness, and death on the cross.

Quit Playing the Church-Growth Game

One of the most pressing factors facing many pastors is pressure to grow churches, to increase membership and worship attendance, and,

108. "He who rescued us from so deadly a peril will continue to rescue us; on him we have set our hope that he will rescue us again. . . . (2 Cor 1:10)."

for some, to add additional worship services and even off-site campuses. This pressure certainly impacts preaching; we feel the need to appeal to people and to be invitational and interesting. These attributes are important but they are not the most important part of preaching. Douglas John Hall reminds us, "The picture of the Christian community that we derive from the scriptural testimony is that of a prophetic minority, an *ecclesia crucis* that must share in the suffering and rejection of its 'head' if it is to participate in the only 'glory' authentic to its vocation."[109] While concerns about church growth can cause us to down-play some aspects of our theology, preaching the cross causes pastors to think about depth and authenticity of witness rather than only a broader witness. While the end of Matthew's gospel does extend a sweeping commission that calls us to preach, teach, and baptize to the very reaches of the earth, metaphors for faithfulness in the gospels tend to be small, like salt, yeast, a mustard seed, and a pearl.[110] By their humble and minor-status these images point to the glory and power of God. Hall shoots a pointed theological and biblical barb towards those of us who fret over declining numbers and uncritically laud the leaders of mega-churches. He emphasizes the critique in the New Testament of a church who would try to draw power to itself, noting, " . . . there is nothing at all supportive of 'church growth' as a legitimate apostolic aim—unless it is the parable about the 'fool' who determined that he would build 'greater barns'!"[111]

Bringing our sermons to the cross means surrendering what we hope will come from our sermons; it means dropping out of the numbers game. While broader culture measures worth by how large, powerful, popular, or wealthy an organization is, the cross offers something different. On the cross, Jesus' own self-giving subverts the rule of the powerful and offers hope that worthiness is no longer anchored to productivity or strength. Rather than concerning ourselves with attracting new members, perhaps we can channel our preaching energies towards encouraging on-going renewal, inviting our listeners again and again to experience the renewing power of the cross and resurrection.

109. Hall, "Confessing Christ," 68.
110. Ibid.
111. Ibid.

Cut-out the Good Parts

When I was a student, my professor Art Van Seters used to suggest adding one final step at the very end of the sermon-creation process. His advice was to "Cut out the good parts." What Art meant by "good parts" were the parts of the sermon where the preacher is trying to be clever or particularly theologically astute, funny, or erudite. Basically those times when the preacher's self-awareness in engaging the craft of preaching swells and we may be inadvertently or even purposely drawing attention to ourselves rather than the gospel. These "good parts" of the sermon can sometimes hog energy that might be better used elsewhere to communicate to others in a way that gets us and our insecurities out of the way. When we bring our sermons to the cross we may be asked to surrender what we consider the "best parts" so that the Spirit can transform and renew our work in ways that allow the Word to live beyond our imaginations or expectations. I am reminded of the Isenheim altarpiece painted by Mattias Grünewald around 1515. The painting portrays Jesus dying on a cross. On the left, John, the beloved disciple, consoles Mary as she appears to almost faint at the sight of her son's stretched-out body. On the other side, John the Baptist stands, bearded and barefoot, straight from the desert and draped in rough camel hair. He holds a book in one hand and the other hand is extended towards Jesus pointing to the cross. The great theologian Karl Barth is said to have kept a copy of this altarpiece over his desk; this image may also be helpful for us. Our work as preachers is to point beyond ourselves to the work of Jesus Christ. The painting's image of John is also helpful in reminding us of the cost of faithfully bearing witness to the in-breaking Kingdom of God. John the Baptist's preaching career was not marked by popularity among the elites of his day. In fact, his preaching may have cost him his life. While preachers today may not lose their lives for bearing witness to the gospel, the cost may still be high. When professional ministry is the way that we support our families, it is challenging to risk security by preaching an unpopular but true word.

CONCLUSION

We are embodied and habitual creatures, deeply formed and shaped by the narratives and cultural liturgies in which we are immersed. The narrative of the cross and resurrection serves as a powerful counter-narrative, a true and life-giving narrative for our lives, but unless we experience this narrative on a regular basis it is easy to give our lives over to self-centered, consumer-driven narratives that lead to death rather than life. Set within the context of worship, the sermon has the potential to offer a transformative tuning note for all of congregational life. Preaching through the lens of the cross and resurrection invites preachers to expand the social vision of the gospel, move beyond commercial techniques to engage the congregational imagination, name the demanding call the cross makes on all disciples, re-orient worship and preaching around the narrative of Christ, set aside church growth as a primary goal, and point beyond ourselves to the power of God.

5

The Cornerstone of the Pulpit

Creating Sermons on the Cross and Resurrection

Good preaching requires more than head-knowledge of exegetical methods and the newest communication techniques; it requires a deep theological steeping that shapes preachers to live out their vocation of thoughtful witness to the gospel through biblical and contextual engagement. This kind of theologically informed preaching can set the tone for congregational life as it provides a point of sustained conversation with the Bible and the realities of our world that take seriously the complexities of what it means to be human. The cross and resurrection are meaning-laden historical and theological events that lie at the heart of Christianity. Intentionally designing sermons with the cross and resurrection in mind encourages preachers and listeners to wade into deep waters both in theology and the expressed mission of our churches as well as inspire discipleship that impacts lives. Many of the challenges of preaching the cross and resurrection that cause preachers to stumble and listeners to balk can be engaged in ways that bring vitality and energy to preaching, allowing the cross and resurrection to serve as a cornerstone for powerful and transformative preaching.

This chapter will serve as a hands-on guide for preachers. I will explore concrete occasions and methods for preaching the cross and resurrection using sermons from a variety of traditions to illustrate. Using these specific methods and occasions to guide our discussion, I will name ways in which we might seek to intentionally engage the cross and resurrection not only during the seasons of Lent and Easter, but throughout the year. Along the way I will note challenges and concerns that may arise, such as designing the sermon to be relevant for listeners across the theological spectrum; balancing the dynamic between teaching and proclamation; and choosing illustrations and examples in light of the concerns raised in previous chapters around awareness of suffering, interfaith concerns, and competing cultural impulses that can foster a consumer-mindset among listeners. I will discuss techniques and circumstances that may allow preachers to choose between starting with a biblical text or from the perspective of a topical sermon.

METHODS AND OCCASIONS FOR PREACHING THE CROSS AND RESURRECTION

Preachers can employ the cross and resurrection in a variety of ways: in the theologically-oriented rhetorical release of celebration, as a means of validating experiences of suffering, as a specific hermeneutical lens for exploring scripture for preaching, as a means for teaching about church doctrine, as a means of preparation for discipleship, as a means of engaging the liturgical events of Good Friday and Easter, or through the use of narrative sermon forms.

Celebrating God's Acts

The piano music swells as the preacher wipes her brow and shifts toward the final push of her sermon, which is on navigating crossroads in our lives using Jesus' parable of the prodigal son from Luke 15. The congregation is standing as some worshippers clap while others offer excited and encouraging words: "Preach!" "My Lord!" "Say it . . . Say it! Rev. Irwin continues with rhythmic pauses, her voice in a deep growl, and words punctuated by excited responses:

> Oh yeah, I'm reminded of how the world was at a "Cross-roads" of sin and how God sent his Son Jesus, who was full of love and Compassion! . . . And although, Jesus was fully divine, Jesus was also fully human and I just believe that even Jesus himself came to some "cross-roads" in his life! Oh yeah, Jesus

even found himself one day in the garden of Gethsemane, at a "Cross-roads," saying "Father, if it is thy will let this cup pass from me!" And when Jesus realized that the cup would not be removed, Jesus was committed to go to Calvary! Oh yeah, they beat my Jesus! They put a crown of thorns on His Head, they nailed Him to old rugged cross, and they even pierced Him in the side, where blood and water came streaming out! Oh yeah, there was even a "Cross-roads" at the Cross! Oh yeah, a Cross-roads with a thief on the right and a cross-roads with a thief on the left! A Cross-roads! A cross-road with the centurion soldier, who said, "Truly this is the Son of God!" A Cross-roads for Mary his mother, a cross-roads for His very Disciples, and yes, even a Cross-roads at the Cross for you and me! . . . Oh yeah, my Jesus, . . . he hung his head . . . and He died! But that wasn't the end of the story! They took my Jesus and they buried him in a borrowed tomb where he stayed, all night Friday night, he stayed all day Saturday and He stay all night, Saturday night, but early Sunday Morning . . . He got up with all power! He got up with healing power! He got up with Saving Power and He got up with Delivering power! And Because Jesus got up, you and I don't have to stay at our "Cross-roads" any longer! Because of the "Cross-roads" at the Cross and because we serve a Christ that is able to take our confused state of life and connect all the pieces, you and I can finally come to a "Conclusion" at our "Cross-roads" and come to Christ! I thank you Jesus for "The Cross-roads at the Cross!"[1]

The music rises to a crescendo and the congregation claps and exclaims "Thank you Jesus!" The cross is used in many African American worship contexts as a rhetorical and theological means of celebrating God's acts as well as a signal for listeners that the preacher is closing the sermon.

Frank Thomas defines "celebration" in preaching as "the culmination of the sermonic design, where a moment is created in which the remembrance of a redemptive past and/or the conviction of a liberated future transforms the events immediately experienced."[2] Thus, it makes sense that celebration in African American preaching often incorporates the cross on more than one level. Rhetorically and homiletically, much traditional African American preaching has a narrative shape and has been described as having a form that follows a "start low, go slow, strike

1. Irwin, "Crossroads."
2. Thomas, *Like to Never*, 31.

THE CORNERSTONE OF THE PULPIT

fire, sit down"[3] or "situation, complication, resolution, celebration" pattern.[4] As I will also discuss later in this chapter, the narrative form itself invokes the movement of the gospel from cross to resurrection. Because brokenness and systemic sin are concrete experiences, it makes sense that grace and good news are also deeply experiential so that in much African American preaching the climax and celebration are pronounced. Depending on context, the preacher's preference, and the text or theme of the sermon, the celebration at the end of the sermon often incorporates a recounting of God's mighty acts, moving through the life of Jesus through the cross and to the resurrection. The cross and resurrection are present both in the words and tone of the celebration while the remembering of the celebrative recounting also becomes almost a sacramental opportunity to experience again the liberating power of the resurrection.

The cross functions theologically through the presence of celebration in the preaching of a people who have been, and continue to be, subjected to intense suffering, racism, and abuse. The way that the cross functions in celebration keeps the use of the cross from being formulaic even when a preacher follows the same celebratory trajectory in nearly every sermon. Rather, the presence of the cross in celebration speaks to the subversive power of the cross, to a rejection of the unjust ways that power often moves in our world, and to an ultimate trust in the inbreaking liberating power of the resurrection—even when it appears that death has won.[5] Richard Eslinger adds that this "bittersweet" engagement with irony may happen at points throughout the sermon rather than only in the celebration at the end.[6] As Frank Thomas notes, the church is a celebratory community defined by the cross and resurrection in which the experience of the good news moves from internal appropriation to external joy, thanksgiving, and celebration.[7] The experience of celebration in worship has been, and continues to be, empowering for the African American community to face and actively engage the challenges of racism both interpersonally and systemically in the broader culture. Indeed, Martin Luther King Jr.'s preaching in the midst of the Civil Rights

---

3. McClain, *Come Sunday*, 68.
4. Thomas, *Like to Never*, 53–55. See also Eslinger, *Web*, 143.
5. Eslinger, *Web*, 115, citing Crawford, *Hum*, 68.
6. Eslinger, *Web*, 115.
7. Thomas, *Like to Never*, 24.

Movement employed celebration to powerful effect.[8] In celebration, Christ's victory becomes the victory of the gathered community.[9] Thomas writes, "Having experienced transformation through celebration, they marched, and their feet changed the face of the evil system of segregation and influenced change throughout the world for years to come."[10]

While celebration can have a sacramental quality, celebrations in sermons are not necessarily one-size-fits-all. Frank Thomas describes the function of celebration as "reinforcing" the gospel theme of the overall sermon.[11] Sermons need to operate on both an emotional and cognitive level so that the use of the cross in the celebration feels organically connected to the rest of the sermon in terms of logical connections and emotional freight.[12] Frank Thomas' guidelines for celebration support using the cross and resurrection carefully and thoughtfully rather than falling into the same pattern for every sermon. He encourages preachers to "avoid new concepts," to keep the themes affirmative, and to stay connected to the overall theme of the sermon.[13] Preachers need to be aware of the lure of "celebrative standbys," and for many preachers going to the cross may fall in this category.[14] Not every celebration needs to go to the cross, but if going to the cross is important for your theology and context, celebrations that invoke the cross are most effective when coupled with one of the other methods or occasions also listed in this chapter. That is, celebration invoking the cross will be much stronger and more powerful when the cross also informs the content of the sermon as a whole. Integration of celebration that goes to the cross with broader sermon content serves to teach the congregation about the cross beyond emotional release and recovers something of the scandal of the cross that resists routine or formulary proclamation.

While I excerpted Rev. Irwin's celebration at the end of her sermon, "Crossroads at the Cross," the entire sermon was designed with an awareness of where this sermon was heading. Her use of the cross in the celebration was intimately connected with her overall theme, which

8. Ibid., 32.
9. Ibid., 33.
10. Ibid.
11. Ibid., 85.
12. Ibid., 89.
13. Ibid., 90–96.
14. Ibid., 96.

centered on Jesus' presence in the midst of messy crossroads moments both in the text and in human lives. The term *"Cross-roads"* functioned as a repeated image that provided unity and helped listeners make connections throughout the sermon. As she introduced the characters from the parable and described the crossroads that each figure faced, from the difficult decision of the younger son to head home, to his father, and to the older son's decision to remain outside the party, she made connections both with the present experience of listeners who may be facing crossroads in their lives, such as marital or financial challenges, and with the life of Jesus.[15] This allowed the celebration to flow naturally from the content of the whole sermon. Her explicit move to the cross in her celebration signaled to the listeners that she was wrapping up the sermon. However, because the sermon had naturally moved to this moment and her use of the cross and resurrection were a natural extension of her theme and central image, listeners were able to engage with her throughout the sermon and move along with her to the climax and celebration.

Validating Experiences of Brokenness in our World

At times the only response preachers can muster when faced with the experience of human suffering and trouble in our world may be to offer up a lament to God. Preaching about the cross and resurrection is a means of dealing with the trouble that we experience in a theologically sound and pastorally sensitive way. By linking trouble to the cross we also find hope for the trouble we experience in the resurrection. A focus on what many in the midst of suffering might describe as "distance from God" is one way to use the work of Christ on the cross to attend to hearers; another is to stress the connection between Christ and humanity shared in the incarnation and in the suffering that comes with being human in a fallen world.[16] God created humanity as good; through the cross, Christ restores and affirms God's good intentions. This connection in suffering leads to a connection in redemption, stressing salvation, that grounds human existence in the experience of Christ.[17] Mary Catherine Hilkert

15. Irwin, "Crossroads."

16. Jung Young Kim points out that because of historical experience, an ethos of suffering permeates Korean identity. The suffering of Christ connects with Korean Christians who believe that "Christ's suffering heals our wound" more than other "religions of our heritage." Kim, *Korean Preaching*, 77.

17. James H. Harris connects human theologies of liberation to "Jesus' power to

explicitly connects "preaching the cross" to expressions of grief and fury in the face of human suffering, encouraging preachers to draw on the psalm tradition of lament to offer "'complaints' against God."[18] Honest expressions of grief and anger towards God on behalf of the congregation maintain open communication and express "a form of hope in the possibility of a renewed relationship."[19] Hilkert asserts that these expressions of distress are a "form of good news" and that "naming pain and claiming forgotten memories are parts of a larger journey towards healing, wholeness, and joy, although that future hope cannot be seen at every step on the journey."[20] In *Lament: Reclaiming Practices in Pulpit, Pew, and Public Square*, Sally Brown and Patrick Miller draw on the biblical tradition of laments as "prayers of trust that God is ever attentive to the cry of the sufferer."[21] Preaching lament in the face of suffering also gives voice to God's own "divine rage and grief over the violation of God's beloved children and creation."[22] In this light, preachers should also name the ways in which the church has fallen short of its calling and exerted unfair domination or abuse of some members.[23] Preaching in a lament style encourages the preacher and the hearer to connect the suffering in the world today with the suffering of Christ on the cross. Savior and saved are linked as both bear the signs of life in a broken world. However, the sermon should not end with lament just as God's actions in Christ do not end on the cross.[24]

The experience of loss or tragedy need not be grand for preachers to attend to human experiences of brokenness and loss in sermons. Luke

---

overcome the suffering of the cross via the resurrection." Harris, *Preaching Liberation*, 31–32.

18. Hilkert, "Folly of the Cross," 43–44.

19. Ibid., 44.

20. Ibid.

21. Brown, "When Lament," 31.

22. Hilkert, "Folly of the Cross," 44. On the other hand, In "Beyond Narrative: Imagination in the Sermon," Paul Wilson is careful to distinguish between a "passive" understanding of God as empathetic to human suffering but not actively engaged and the "God who acts." It is the God of action who acts decisively on the cross through Christ and whose action in the past, present, and future is crucial to the gospel. Wilson, *Listening to the Word*, 141–42.

23. Hilkert, "Folly of the Cross," 45.

24. Hilkert emphasizes that the preacher is called to "name grace" but can only do so when he or she also names "situations of impasse or 'dis-grace. . . .'" Grace-filled preaching must take sin and the reality of pain and suffering seriously. Hilkert, *Naming Grace*, 111.

Powery encourages preaching that names real trouble as an antidote to what he calls "candy theology" in some popular preaching today.[25] Powery advocates for preaching that has a strong awareness of the context of death—not only our final physical deaths that end our lives on this earth but the many small deaths and losses that we experience regularly such as retirement, graduations, or the loss of relationships that may come from a breach in trust or geographic transition.[26] In fact, many celebrations that the church acknowledges also have often unacknowledged shadow-sides of loss. The birth of a wanted baby brings joy but also an end to that couple's life without children. Graduation from a school program offers a sense of accomplishment and a new start but also the loss of routine and a change in relationships connected to being a student. Retirement may bring more free time and new possibilities for meaningful engagement with family, friends, and commitments but also brings the loss of meaning and identity connected to one's work.

Powery particularly critiques prosperity preaching, although he also acknowledges the complexities of preaching to people, namely African Americans and others who have been systematically excluded from economic and social opportunities for generations. Positively, prosperity preaching appears to offer "a message of personal and individual empowerment for those who desire upward mobility in society."[27] For those who have been denied material wealth through the sin of racism, the possibility of monetary and material blessings may be seen as divine provision.[28] Yet, prosperity preaching is insidious because it reduces the benefits of the gospel to only material and monetary benefits—and rather than offering something truly satisfying such benefits often seem to lead to an insatiable hunger for more.[29] The hope of the gospel comes down to how Jesus defines discipleship—a way that Scripture tells us is narrow and not easily traversed by those with material wealth. Scripture and Christian history show us that the way of following Jesus most often does not lead to Bentleys and mansions but to the cross where all must be offered up to God in order for us to experience new life in Christ. Powery accurately names a "hole" in prosperity preaching when it comes to attending to

25. Powery, *Dem Dry Bones*, 2–3.

26. Ibid., 3. See also Lathrop, *Pastor*, 125.

27. Powery, *Dem Dry Bones*, 4.

28. Ibid.

29. Ibid.

trouble, pain, and loss.[30] Without acknowledging these real aspects of human life, preachers cannot fully offer hope that speaks to us in the midst of death and suffering.

To address the "hole" in much of popular preaching, Powery turns to African American Spirituals—these songs offer words of hope, strength, and gospel forged in the midst of death and suffering and offer substance to fill the holes in our preaching today.[31] Powery says that Spirituals speak to the soul of African American people in the depths of enslavement even today, and as such, to sing was to live and assert life in the midst of death.[32] The Spirituals also offer a communal hermeneutic and proclamation which is counter to the individual approach of prosperity preaching that tends to fall into step with our broader consumer and competitive culture.[33] For enslaved African Americans this created an alternative institution of resistance to the demonic institution of racism; the Spirituals offered powerful counter-testimony in the face of the lies of slavery.[34] Finally, preaching that is informed by the Spirituals maintains a sense of cultural memory that remembers the power of God, who delivers us from enslavement, hallows the sacrifices of people of faith who have died following Jesus, and proclaims the truth in the face of the powers of sin, slavery, and death.[35] Recollection of God's deliverance also reminds us of the costs undertaken by God for humanity—the suffering and death of Jesus on the cross. In Jesus we have a Savior who has experienced the worst the world can offer so that through Christ all who suffer are gathered up into God's powerful and redemptive embrace.[36]

In his sermon, "The Death of Hope," Frederick G. Sampson II preaches from Luke 24:17–21, focusing on the despondent posture of the disciples who were walking to Emmaus following Jesus' death and resurrection.[37] Sampson starts the sermon by creating a sense of connection between the listeners and those disciples on the road, calling their experiences "Egypt" experiences, which makes a typological link to Israel's

30. Ibid., 6.

31. Ibid., 13–14.

32. Ibid., 31–33.

33. Ibid., 33–34.

34. Ibid., 34–35.

35. Ibid., 39–42.

36. See also ibid., 42–44.

37. Sampson, "Death of Hope," 818–22.

slavery as well as historic and present-day experiences of enslavement in, but not limited to, the African American experience.[38] "Egypt is that point in life when we experience the death of hope. . . . he loses the map to take him into tomorrow, and all of his days become nothing but yesterdays. . . . When hope dies you need something else." Sampson begins the sermon by describing experiences of trouble and loss in our world, telling several vignettes of those who have lost hope—the characters are broad enough to be archetypal and allow multiple listeners to make connections, however, all have in common a sense of culpability in their own misery. Their own decisions contributed to the death of hope in their lives. Next, Sampson moves to discuss how three different groups who were with Jesus experienced a death of hope in the events surrounding his crucifixion and death: the women who came to care for Jesus' body in the tomb, the two disciples on the road to Emmaus, and Jesus' disciples. Concerning the women, Sampson notes, "They didn't come to get their dreams fulfilled. . . . They came to embalm a dead hero, not to welcome a resurrected savior. And even when he showed up they didn't recognize him."[39] He describes the two disciples heading to Emmaus as walking away from where the action is—he equates this with those who leave the church, they are "going to the west," the way towards "sundown" rather than "sunrise."[40] Meanwhile Jesus' disciples were "trying to recapture yesterday" they had returned to fishing.[41] "They had seen the resurrection and still they did not believe."[42]

At this point Sampson shifts his focus to Jesus—Jesus is free to act as he chooses and neither the biblical figures nor people today can make Jesus do what they want him to do or in a time or manner that can be controlled. Yet, herein lies the hope:

> His delays are not his denial. Come on now. I asked him for water, he gave me a shovel and told me to dig. I asked him for shelter, he gave me a forest and told me to build. I asked him for food. He gave me some seeds and told me to plant. I asked him for courage and hope, he gave me some enemies and put me in the darkness and told me to struggle. But my word tonight is that Canaan is always available. If your find yourself in Egypt,

38. Ibid., 818–19.
39. Ibid., 819.
40. Ibid., 819–20.
41. Ibid., 820.
42. Ibid.

Canaan is always available. If your hope dies, all you've got to do is let Jesus relocate in your heart. Oh, my God. And whenever Jesus shows up, that is the resurrection of hope. And the good thing is that if you've got Jesus as your Savior and your hopes die, you don't have to send for him. For the Bible said, as they were walking and discussing the things that killed their hope, Jesus himself walked in. What I like about Jesus is that he walks into the scene of your misery. He catches up with you.[43]

Sampson describes how Jesus "enlightens" and empowers the men on the road, women at the tomb, and Jesus' disciples, moving directly to Jesus' gift of resilience and empowerment to those facing trouble and the death of hope today.[44] One of the aspects of this sermon that makes it particularly effective in relating to human experiences of suffering is that he doesn't try to solve or resolve the suffering in the sermon—he doesn't return to his earlier vignettes and create unbelievable happy endings. He validates the experience of the cross and acknowledges that the resurrection doesn't mean that the cross didn't happen. Yet the presence of the risen Christ makes perseverance and joy possible even in the midst of trouble. Eschatologically both realities persist for us today. Nevertheless, the sermon ends on a strongly hopeful note and the celebration rings true because the sermon has also addressed trouble, pain, and challenges.

I am on my way somewhere. I don't know about you, but I'm on my way somewhere. Jesus is all the world to me, my light, my joy, and my all. He gives me strength from day to day and without him I would fall. Somebody said, "You're getting old and yet you just keep on plowing. What keeps you going?" Leaning on the everlasting arms. Oh how bright the path grows from day to day leaning. I said, "Leaning on the everlasting arms."[45] I heard, I said I heard somebody say, that when troubles rise I'll hasten to his throne. Jesus, I said Jesus is all you'll need. Jesus will walk by your side. Jesus will come when you need him. Jesus will be there every time. When you've wiped your pillow with your midnight tears, Jesus will walk with you. Your enemies might be all around you. But don't worry. Don't worry. Don't worry. Jesus will prepare a table before you in the presence of your enemy.[46] He's alright. I said he's alright. Is he alright? Is he

43. Ibid., 820–21.
44. Ibid., 821.
45. "Leaning," No. 596.
46. See Ps 23:5.

alright? Jesus. I said Jesus. When Hope dies, Jesus can resurrect it. Is he alright?[47]

Hermeneutical Lens for Scripture

Beyond occasional preaching, the cross and resurrection can become a central hermeneutical lens for reading Scripture and can become part of regular exegetical habits in sermon preparation. This approach may be particularly helpful for preachers who are unsure of how to integrate the cross and resurrection in ways that honor Scripture passages where these events are not referenced. Engaging with the cross and resurrection as an explicitly theological part of scripture study helps to provide unity across scripture, that is, the same God who acted in the Old Testament also died on the cross; it also guarantees that these central events in the Christian faith are also exercising a sense of gravitational force on preaching from week to week. By making the cross and resurrection part of the sermon-creation process from the very beginning, the sermon will have organic unity and theological richness that would be lacking if the preacher instead chooses to create a sermon and tack-on something relating to the cross and resurrection at the end. Engaging the cross and resurrection as a hermeneutical lens need not be complex—but it may entail a wider vision that often extends beyond the particular biblical pericope selected for the sermon.

In addition to their regular exegetical practice or process that explores the historical context, the literary aspects of the text, and the plot of the text itself, among other elements, preachers who desire to integrate their sermons with the cross and resurrection at a deep level should add another step to their study and ask, "How does the cross and resurrection affect this text?" Another option is for preachers to look for resonance between the text and Jesus, because Jesus' death and resurrection is so central to his divine identity. Paul Wilson names the act of "bringing the text to the cross and resurrection" as one of the steps towards preaching the gospel and invites preachers to engage their preaching text as a "look-out place from which to view the cross on the far horizon."[48] Each text will provide a distinct vantage point and allow for infinite nuance.[49]

47. Sampson, "Death of Hope," 821–22.
48. Wilson, *Practice of Preaching*, 250–51.
49. Ibid., 251.

Wilson asserts, "Bringing the text to the Easter event is a process of allowing the significance of what God has accomplished in Jesus Christ to modify, fulfill, or otherwise affect the final meaning of the text at hand."[50] Bringing each preaching text to the cross and resurrection may also magnify good news standing behind some tough texts that seem to be mostly judgment and connect deeply to the challenges of listeners lives.[51]

To be clear, the cross and resurrection should not be used as a quick escape or parachute to allow us to have some sense of hope in an otherwise bleak sermon.[52] Allowing the cross and resurrection to inform the whole sermon helps us to gradually build the bridge needed to help us get to the good news. For example, a sermon focusing on Amos 7:7–17 may feel quite heavy with Israel's failures to live faithfully and to care for the poor in their midst. In 7:7–9, God gives Amos a vision of a plumb line by which God will measure Israel. Israel will surely be found lacking, the king will be overturned, and Israel will be exiled from the land. The good news in this text is that God's righteousness sets a standard for Israel that overturns the harmful behavior that is eating away at the fabric of God's people. Standing in this text and looking towards the cross and resurrection allows us to see that ultimately Jesus Christ will be the plumb line by which humanity is measured. In Jesus' death and resurrection corruption and death are made clear to us and destroyed by God's self-giving love.

To look for deeper resonance with their preaching texts, preachers may wish to return to the characteristics of sermons that are deeply informed by the cross, which we explored in chapter 1, and use them as areas of study in exegesis. Sermons that are deeply informed by the dynamics of the cross and resurrection:

- Acknowledge evil
- Name hope
- Maintain a sense of tension or contradiction
- Are grounded in Scripture
- Address personal and social implications of the cross
- Address the fullness of the Christ event

50. Ibid.
51. Ibid.
52. Ibid., 252.

Preachers can use each of these characteristics as headings in sermon preparation by which to explore both the text and the realities of our world. Returning to our text from Amos, to employ these categories:

Acknowledge evil

Israel's actions and unjust behavior towards the poor have corrupted the people. Leading up to chapter 7 God has threatened great calamity and relented. Now God will set up a plumb line that will show how corrupt Israel has become. God will give them over to their inclinations and their behavior will lead to the overturning of the king and the exile of Israel.

Name hope

God loves Israel and has raised up a prophet to help show them where they have gone wrong. The plumb line shows God's integrity and gives them a clear standard by which to live. In time, Israel will be restored. Ultimately God in Jesus Christ becomes the plumb line or standard by which humanity is measured.

Maintain a sense of tension or contradiction

God's love expresses itself through a fierce sense of righteousness that will not allow Israel to continue to destroy itself. This fierce love will also lead Jesus to the cross. Though we still fail to reach the standards of God's righteousness, God's self-giving love destroys injustice and allows us to continue in full relationship with God.

Grounded in Scripture

As with all biblically grounded preaching, it is important to attend to the details of this specific passage looking for how God's actions can communicate good news. In this case, God's righteous love resonates with the cross and resurrection.

Address personal and social implications of the cross

Personally, preachers might address shortcomings and sin in the lives of individuals, such as dishonesty or adultery. Socially, preachers might address sweeping injustice in our nation. For example, some communities struggle with "food deserts" that keep groceries and fresh foods from poor areas even while grocery chains compete to build new stores in the wealthier suburbs. Other topics might include pointing out the lack of equal access to quality health care, education, and legal support in many towns and neighborhoods.

Through the cross Jesus engaged unjust systems and absorbed their violence into himself. On the cross Jesus offered forgiveness to both individuals and larger groups who harmed him.

Address the fullness of the Christ event.

Preachers might not only explore the cross and resurrection but also Jesus' life and teaching that cared for poor and outcast people.

In addition to attending to these areas, preachers may also wish to employ a set of questions in their exegetical process. Paul Scott Wilson offers a set of questions in *Practice of Preaching* that are comprehensive in their exploration of the text as well as asking broader gospel-oriented questions, including specific questions about the cross and resurrection.[53] Luke Powery also suggests some exegetical questions for preachers to explore as part of their study and preparation process. Powery's questions encourage preachers to look specifically for aspects of death and hope— themes which are deeply anchored in the work of Christ through the cross and resurrection and represented in the African American spiritual tradition.[54] Powery's questions are not presented as a "complete method" but as a means of deepening preachers' awareness of some dynamics in the text; they range from asking about human need and the presence of "little deaths" as well as explicitly seeking "Who needs resurrection?" both in the text and in the pastoral context.[55]

---

53. Wilson, *Practice of Preaching*, 19–25, see especially questions 34 and 35.

54. Powery, *Dem Dry Bones*, 127–28.

55. Ibid., 128.

Tom Long's sermon, "Troubled?" on John 14 spins around the theological axis of Jesus' consolation to his disciples that their hearts not be troubled.[56] For Long, Jesus' comments must be understood through the hermeneutical lens of Jesus' character made manifest through his death and resurrection. Much of Long's sermon explores the drive in much of our culture—including church culture—to not engage with the most troubling aspects of human existence. Playing on the use of the word "troubled" throughout the sermon he says, "It seems to me that one of the problems with Christians in North America today is that we are insufficiently troubled. A kind of easy, 'power of positive thinking,' success-oriented, gospel has seeped down into the pores of the church, disengaging us from the suffering and pain of the world and we are insufficiently troubled."[57] Long juxtaposes stories detailing a range of heartbreaking human troubles from the agony of families with children suffering from debilitating disabilities to the death of a mother and un-born baby amidst the conflict between Israel and Palestine with aspects of the "insufficiently troubled" witness of the church.[58] He names pros-perity gospel promoted by some popular church leaders as well as pithy and trite statements made by unthinking pastors and church members such as the sign on one church lawn that reads, "The birds are back, the grass is green, Happy Easter!"[59]

Long critiques any reading to not be troubled in John 14 that sepa-rates Jesus' words of comfort from the context of the gospel and the com-plete person and work of Jesus Christ by saying, "We lift this [verse] up and let it float as some antiseptic cheerful saying of Jesus disconnected from the suffering of the world. But if you put it back into the gospel of John, back into the ministry of Jesus, it becomes much more complex and much more powerful."[60] The word "troubled" elsewhere in John refers to situations in which Jesus himself is deeply troubled—including when he is facing the cross.[61] Reading through this lens, Long shows how all of the world's deepest and most painful troubles are gathered up by Jesus Christ, who deeply understands trouble and takes the world's pain and

56. Long, "Troubled?"
57. Ibid.
58. Ibid.
59. Ibid.
60. Ibid.
61. Ibid.

brokenness to the cross. Long preaches, "Only the Jesus who had been troubled by suffering and death, and betrayal and evil, had the right to say, 'Do not let your hearts be troubled.' And only disciples who have faced the pain and evil and suffering in life can know the power of a Lord who at the last said, 'Do not let your hearts be troubled.'"[62] At this point, having showed us a glimpse of where this sermon is going, Long offers compelling stories and examples of deep troubles in our world, allowing Jesus to speak directly, " . . . I who have been troubled by suffering and evil and death take this into myself and I take it to the cross and I will be lifted up and this [trouble] will not be the last word. The last word will be the glory of God. Let not your hearts be troubled."[63] Long then moves to offer instances where the church's ministry has depth and where it too has become deeply troubled and is able to engage in meaningful work and service in a hurting world.[64] Through the lens of Jesus' cross and resurrection, the church can rightly claim Jesus' promise, "Do not let your hearts be troubled."

Teaching on Church Doctrine

Our methods and occasions for preaching the cross and resurrection also include catechetical preaching that teaches believers about church doctrines, such as salvation, sin, or even atonement theology. While a pastor may certainly choose to create a topical sermon or even a series on a doctrine or church teaching, sermons on doctrine might most easily begin with using a particular text for a window into the teaching. This keeps the sermon particular and provides helpful limits and focus while also providing a context so that the doctrine or teaching "matters" and feels embodied. For example, options might include a passion account from the gospels or passage from Paul's letters, the near sacrifice of Isaac in Gen 22, or Isaiah's texts about the suffering servant. When the sermon functions not only as the Word of God that comes from outside the community but also as voice for the congregation—showing the Spirit's presence in their midst, the metaphors chosen to disclose the mystery of the cross and resurrection will need to change along with the congregational culture. While the good news may be timeless, language metaphors are

62. Ibid.
63. Ibid.
64. Ibid.

not. Preachers may want to reflect on how they might talk about the cross and resurrection to a junior high Sunday school class or in a catechism context. The Bible, as well as the broader Christian tradition, offers us a wide range of images and metaphors.[65] Preachers today draw on atonement theologies that encompass language of sacrifice, victory, moral influence, and forgiveness or reconciliation among others. David Buttrick writes, "We . . . speak Christ in a social language shaped by social styles and values. . . . By God's grace the gospel does seem to get through to us, although never as a pure gospel undiluted by cultural ideals."[66]

Much of our language about the cross is connected to how the cross functions theologically in forgiveness of sin. Many atonement theologies, disembodied from scripture or a human context can feel transactional and disconnected from our experience. In the words of Pastor Robert Howard in his Passion Sunday sermon, "[We] need interpretation: not just, 'here's what happened,' but 'this is what it means for you and me.'"[67] "Sin" is an abstract concept for many in our congregations and even the word "sin" is rarely used outside of church walls. Further, many pastors don't want church members to feel bad so when we do preach about sin, we only linger there briefly—quickly moving on to the grace. Unfortunately, our experience and understanding of the cross and resurrection are dampened without a deep acknowledgement of sin. Douglas Hall writes,

> The truth that the cross of Christ embodies about us is certainly that we are loved by God, but that we are loved as prodigals, as problematic creatures, as beings whose alienation from God, from one another, from ourselves, and from the inarticulate creation is so great that we will accept love only on our terms. . . . [68]

Some preachers may decide to build their homiletic on the inevitability of human brokenness—both in the biblical text and in our time. Our dependence upon the gospel comes from our inability to escape human brokenness or re-orient our lives on our own. Noting the tendency

65. Buttrick, *Preaching Jesus Christ,* 14–17, 27. David Bartlett notes that "God may be the same yesterday, today, and tomorrow, but words about God shift, even in the Bible." Bartlett further notes that scripture "argues" with itself, giving the preacher permission to actively engage the text in a "lover's quarrel" during the sermon writing process. Bartlett, *Between the Bible,* 16, 35.

66. Buttrick, *Preaching Jesus Christ,* 27.

67. Howard, "Gone Baby Gone!"

68. Hall, *Cross in Our Context,* 102.

preachers have to make "moral instruction or societal reform the *primary* focus of their messages," professor of preaching Brian Chapell writes, "Fundamentally and pervasively the Scriptures teach the inadequacy of any purely human effort to secure divine approval. We are entirely dependent upon the mercy of God to be what he desires, to do what he requires." [69] From this vantage, it follows that humanity's role in serving God's will cannot be situated in a sense of innate human ability, but only in God's provision through Jesus Christ. Therefore, sermons are rooted in the work of Christ in order for the gospel to be present and for hearers to have a basis for leading holy lives.[70] Building sermons that delve deeply into sin and brokenness begin with exegesis and biblical study. To incorporate the whole Bible, including those texts that do not explicitly focus on Christ, Chapell encourages preachers to explore the text "as a unified message of human need and divine provision."[71] Chapell's take on preaching is "Christ-centered" because he understands Scripture as redemptive in that God ultimately answers all human need through Christ. Weekly preaching then repeats the reality of the atonement and rehearses the coming promises of God's Kingdom in his pattern of seeing every scriptural passage as "revealing, preparing for, or reacting to the work of Christ."[72] Thus Chapell's route to Christ-centered preaching begins with acknowledging human need and travels towards God's ultimate answer to human need—the person and work of Jesus Christ.

While God's work through Christ is the center of his homiletic, Chapell displays a decisive concern for hearers and fallen humanity in general as his method provides a narrative undercurrent of law and gospel by following human trouble to resolution in Christ.[73] Thus, the focus of the sermon is determined by how the Scripture passage illuminates some aspect of the "fallen" human "condition," to which God is attending.[74] Further, while Chapell's approach rightly ascribes saving power to God alone, preachers will also want avoid applying "Christ" as a quickly soothing balm. Charles Campbell's critique of sermons, which apply Jesus

---

69. Chapell, *Christ-centered*, 12.

70. Ibid.

71. Ibid.

72. Ibid., 73

73. Chapell's method is expository preaching but the narrative undercurrent is present.

74. Ibid., 40–42.

as a general answer to human dictated problems, is well founded.[75] The specific uniqueness of Jesus needs to be the starting point of the gospel; we as humans can only respond from there, our salvation follows from Jesus Christ. Nevertheless, moving from broken lives to healing through Christ adequately communicates the gospel to those who desperately need it today. Chapell writes, "No text was written merely for those long ago; God intends for each scripture to give us the 'endurance and the encouragement' that we need today." [76] A homiletic that views human nature as broken encourages preachers to focus on real concerns and problems that emerge from life.

Whether one starts with a Scripture text as an entry point or takes a more doctrinal and topical approach, preaching about sin is most effective when preachers are able to describe what sin looks or feels like. For example, in his Passion Sunday sermon "Gone Baby Gone!," Robert Howard takes on our preconceptions of who "sinners" are and how sin functions in our lives, debunking any easy notions that may cause us to glide past the crucifixion narrative without taking a deeper look at our own actions and behaviors. Howard's skill at imaging sin in a variety of ways, both individual and social, broadens the scope and makes it harder and harder for listeners to exclude themselves from the indictment of sin while also deepening the weight of sin so that listeners experience the power of Christ's actions for us. Howard addresses sins of rebellion and rejection of any restraint, sins of "missing the mark" where we may cause harm to others without meaning to, sins of not living up to our potential, and the broad network of social sins. Howard's language is conversational and uses "we" rather "you" to create a sense of common culpability.

> Died for our sins. Hallelujah. Case closed.
> Oh, no. We don't get off that easy. Paul was on the right track—we just turned it into an economic transaction. *He* paid *our* cost, so "now I am happy all the day," right?[77] Oh, friends, that is way too easy. Let's talk about sin for a minute. . . . Look, there are varieties of sin. I'm not talking about better ones and then the nasty ones that those other folks do. I'm talking about different sorts, a Heinz-57-varieties spread of alienating behaviors, and the attitudes from which they spring. For example,

75. Campbell, *Preaching Jesus*, 38–44.

76. Ibid., 42.

77. Isaac Watts, "Alas and Did My Savior Bleed," Chalice Hymnal #204 (St. Louis: Chalice Press, 1995.)

take the sin of *rebellion*. The two-year-old's "no, I *won't!*" Or the Prodigal Son's harsh rejection of dad's authority: "Gimme my share, see you later." Rebellion. Now *that's* sin! Oh, but that's just the easy kind. And all too often colored with dark masculine colors—we are independent, free, self-autonomous, put no re-straints on us! Too easy. For there are so many more varieties. Uglier. Sneakier. What about, say, that nice little biblical word, *hamartia?* "Missing the mark," so say the Bible dictionaries. . . . A fairly good action goes astray, and somebody is hurt. Didn't mean to do it. But the damage is still done. Hydraulic fracturing enables companies to get oil out of the ground that was inacces-sible before the technology was developed. But it damages the environment—polluted underground water, earthquakes where the land was quiet before, as the liquid lubricates the faults un-derground, easing the friction that kept them in place. Missing the mark. Nobody meant for the damage to happen. The chicken we eat at home or Chik-Fil-A, stacks of caged birds overfed to plump them up, horrendously cruel to those creatures, so that we can have our easy meals. Missing the mark. Nobody meant for the damage to happen. Nuclear power creates waste that is dangerous for thousands of years. Where are you going to store it? Not in *my* back yard. Missing the mark.

And it gets worse. Oh, yes. There is a more modern notion of sin as failing to live up to your potential. Or, really, an ancient sin, if you think about it. Weren't we made in the image of God? To show the world the face of God, the fidelity of God's love? How are we doing at it? Oh, dear. Failing to live up to our poten-tial. Every time we tell somebody they are no good. Every time we *think* it. And then *believing* that lie. Trying to mask it, cover it up, by diving into a bottle, injecting substances. Muffling the pain of not being . . . enough. Or lording it over somebody else— I'm better than you, because I take a shower every day, because I dress better than you, because I have more stuff, a newer car, a bigger house, because I'm a citizen of *this* country, not *that* country . . . I'm better than you. . . . Or worse: we are *trapped* in a sticky web of *social* sins that we can't even see, they've got such a headlock on us. Something beyond us, bigger than any individual, in which we *willingly participate*. . . . Trapped in a web that we didn't create. Paul talks about being "enslaved to sin." (Rom 6:6) Sometimes we know it. Often we have no clue. But that web of sin forces us to do some wicked things to our fellow human beings made in the image of God. We participate in wickedness. We didn't know. We didn't mean it. Sin trapped us in its web. And we *cannot* get ourselves out. It just gets worse and worse.[78]

Howard's deep and vivid portrayal of sin opens the way for listeners to experience the power of Jesus' crucifixion. His careful approach to atonement theology keeps a relational focus rather than falling into familiar transactional language that can lighten the agony of crucifixion and the passion in God's love for us. Using repetition adds both emphasis and energy to the sermon and he offers real good news at the end while also staying true to the liturgical season.

> Now hear the miracle, the astounding, incredible, outlandish wonder of it all. "It was God's will," says Isaiah. And Paul. John adds: "and not for *ours only* but also for the sins of the whole world." (1 John 2:2) In Jesus Christ on the Cross, God gathered it *all* in one mighty embrace, in solidarity with every last human being who has ever suffered wrongly, suffered rightly, *caused* another to suffer, sinned by rebelling, sinned by secret cowardice, sinned by missing the mark and damaging others, failed in ten thousand ways to live up to the image of God we were meant to be, sinned by being swept up in prejudice against blacks, Indians, Muslims, women, children, elderly, or *any* other people made in the image of God, sinned by using things made with human blood and tears—sinned against *God Almighty* . . . Gathered it up, all of it, all our sins, all our misdeeds, all our omissions, all our pride, all our waywardness . . . Gathered them all up, every last bruise, every insult, every withered leaf, every dead fish floating in scummy sewage, every wounded heart, every trembling soul, all the damage from every last sin ever done, left undone, imagined, sins there are not even names for yet . . . gathered it *all* up, every last scrap. . . .
>
> And nailed it all to the Cross. Burned every last scrap in the white-hot blast-furnace of God's invincible love. Turned it all inside-out: you thought you were crucifying Me? I turned your crucifixion inside out, and *crucified your sins—all* of 'em! Every last scrap. For, says God, you did sin, you do sin, you *will continue* to sin. But . . . your sins *do not define you!* You are salvageable. You are salvag-*ed*—it is a done deed. The whole world has been *made new*. By his bruises we *are healed*. We just shake our heads in disbelieving wonder. It is just too much to take in. Who has believed what we have heard? *All* of Creation *is redeemed*. Every lapse, every snarl, every stab at the heart, vanished. Canceled.

78. Howard, "Gone Baby Gone!"

Shiny-new. Crucified, dead, buried. Out of sight . . . out of God's mind. Signed in blood. Sealed by the Spirit. *Given* for us.[79]

Indeed, while humans long for an all-powerful God who can make up for all our brokenness and vulnerability with supreme strength, what we get is Jesus Christ beaten, betrayed, and hung on a cross. In the person of Jesus Christ, God lived among us in a manner we could not have imagined.[80] In Christ, humility and vulnerability are transformed into strength that overwhelms power with love and ultimately preserves human freedom to be truly human in Christ.[81] With Jesus Christ as the leader and "perfector," the important role to which God has called the church as Christ's body is revealed through the Holy Spirit in the proclaimed word. Scriptural interpretation and preaching usher Christ's presence into the midst of the people, bringing salvation, hope, and the gift of discipleship through the power of the Holy Spirit.[82] This encounter between Christ and people happens at both an individual and a corporate level when sermons are careful to employ a range of vivid descriptions and examples.

In addition to teaching positively about doctrine, preachers may also engage the cross and resurrection so that they are preaching against some traditions and theologies in the church that have done harm. Sally Brown writes about the importance of "challenging cross talk gone wrong" by offering critiques of some theologies in order to offer up space for new voices to speak of God's redemption in new ways.[83] For example, in her sermon, "The Will of God," Barbara Brown Taylor engages with the belief that God "willed" the death of Jesus.[84] This assertion is linked to critiques made by feminist and womanist theologians who accuse God of "divine child abuse," and has caused many to shy away from preaching about the cross.[85] Taylor names the concerning doctrine and our struggles with it right at the outset of her sermon.

79. Ibid.

80. Hall, *Cross in Our Context,* 77–86.

81. Ibid., 86.

82. While preaching is used by God through the Holy Spirit, Lucy Rose cautions that language is also fallen and "participates in the sins and distortions of the generations and cultures that use and shape it." Rose, *Sharing the Word,* 83.

83. Brown, *Cross Talk,* 49.

84. Taylor, "Will of God," 115–19.

85. See Brock, "Little Child, 42–61. Also Brown, *Cross Talk,* 17–18.

> That God should will the death of Jesus may be the single hardest thing that we Christians are asked to believe. . . . The crucifixion is not negotiable. It happened. And according to the historical faith of the church, it happened because God wanted it to. . . . We call it the atonement—the satisfaction—the idea being that Christ paid for our sins. We were so bad, it seems and our crimes against God were so great, that justice demanded the sacrifice of life. The only way God could honor that demand and still preserve our lives was to find someone else to be sacrificed in our place. Jesus is who God sent—the divine self made flesh—the crucified one who set us free by taking our death sentence upon himself. This last part is the part we hear the most about, thanking God for our pardon, but there is no getting around the detail that God killed Jesus.[86]

Having named our resistance and trouble with a common view of atonement, Taylor moves on to compare Jesus' sacrifice with the near sacrifice of Isaac by Abraham in Genesis 22. She expresses our anger that Jesus was not similarly released. "Where was Jesus' angel? That's is what I want to know. Where was the angel with the flaming sword, to pry him loose and spirit him away? Even a voice would have done. 'Stop this right now. You are about to make a terrible mistake.'"[87] Taylor then shifts the ground of the sermon by naming some other possibilities. Because the crucifixion happened and God did not stop it we presume that God willed it.[88] She points out that this presumes "a universe in which there are no other powers operating besides the power of God."[89] Taylor points out that God's practice from the creation of humanity has been to share power with us, but we have abused it.[90]

> The dark side of our power is our power to resist God—to say no to God's yes and to thwart the divine will. We tend to dilute that fact by believing our rebellions are more or less benign, like two-year-olds pounding their parents' knees. God allows us the temporary illusion of power, we tell ourselves, but God is really in charge, and when things get bad enough God will come back into the room and set everything right. Only what if that is not how things work? What if God has settled for limited power in

86. Taylor, "Will of God," 115.
87. Ibid., 116.
88. Ibid.
89. Ibid.
90. Ibid.

order to be in partnership with us and we really can mess things up?[91]

Brown has offered an alternative view—perhaps it was not God's will that is at issue here, but our own will that is captive to sin and resistant to God and God's intentions for our world. Jesus died because who he was clashed with the way the world works.[92] Even though Jesus could have stopped, he kept being who he was, ". . . I am who I am. I will be who I will be. . . ."[93] Brown has turned our theological assumptions so that we can see them in new light.

> If the cross was in any sense the defeat of God's will, then it was also the perfection of it, as one beloved human being chose to bear the consequences of being who he was and died with the same integrity he had lived. Insofar as it was the will of God that he live like that, then God's will included the possibility of his death—not as something God desired but as something that God suffered. . . . By entering into the experience of the cross, God took the manmade wreckage of the world inside himself and labored with it—a long labor—almost three days—and he did not let go of it until he could transform it and return it to us as life. That is the power of a suffering God, not to prevent pain but to redeem it, by going through it with us.[94]

A final note for preachers who seek to preach the cross and resurrection as a means of teaching on Christian doctrine is to acknowledge the unfinished nature of our work. As Tom Long puts it, "Preachers do not preach because the sermon is finished; they preach because it is Sunday. The time has come."[95] It may be tempting to try to tie up loose ends that exist within our theology and even in scripture itself. Long names "untidiness" as a virtue when it comes to preaching about the most complex aspects of our faith.[96] Preachers need to recognize the incomplete nature of our work—this is the blessing of an unfolding preaching relationship with a congregation over time that allows for multiple opportunities to engage the complex realities of Christ's saving work for us.

91. Ibid.
92. Ibid., 117.
93. Ibid.
94. Ibid., 118.
95. Long, *What Shall We Say*, 114.
96. Ibid., 114–15.

Preparation for Discipleship and Formation
for the Kingdom of God

The cross and resurrection show us that God does not work the way the world works. Some scholars have described God's kingdom as being "upside-down" because Jesus does not respond violently to the power structures that kill him, rather he absorbs the violence and stops its power. Formation for discipleship can feel counterintuitive. Anchoring our preaching to the cross shows us the way that God uses power in the world. It critiques our attempts at empire-building and shows us the limitations of our human efforts. Therefore our discipleship and sense of mission must grow from the power of God who has defeated the forces of violence and death and may work particularly well in concert with concerns around the infiltration of consumer-driven mindsets in the church. Context will be a strong indicator of the best approach to preaching the cross and resurrection within this approach since formation and missional calling are so specific to the people and setting for ministry.

Pastor Robert "Ty" Bradley preaches about Jesus' healing of the man born blind in John 9. He set up the context of this passage as taking place during the Jewish Feast of Tabernacles, which follows Yom Kippur, the Day of Atonement, so that celebrations of the bountiful end-of-summer harvest coincide with a sense of restored relationship with God. Bradley then turns his focus specifically on the officials' question about whose sin had caused the man's blindness. Throughout the sermon, he engages in counter-cultural formation, seeking to make his congregation aware of how the media likes to lift out "enemies" of the United States in ways that dehumanize.[97] While much of the sermon is troubling because it highlights xenophobia and intolerance, Bradley brings in the cross at the end of the sermon—offering a link to the Jewish festival contexts in order to offer hope and grace and to highlight Jesus' means of relating and using power. Bradley encourages his listeners to not "ask the wrong question," and focus on what is wrong with a person who they may encounter but instead to ask "How can God be glorified?" Bradley engages with atonement in a fresh way by using the text's link with the Jewish festival to be a gateway to understanding Christian atonement. By emphasizing the "already completed" nature of Christ's work, Bradley seeks to free his congregation to joyfully participate in the resurrection harvest of the Realm of God. This linking is particularly important for empowering a sense of

97. Bradley "Prophetic Sermon."

mission or justice in congregations and worked well in Bradley's context. In his Metropolitan Community Church many members may have been discounted as "broken" by family and friends and may need encouragement to actively engage in reaching out as part of God's mission.

> Our question, church, is not where is the sin, but where is the glory! You see Jesus is reminding us today that we are living in the age of the Feast of Tabernacles. The Day of Atonement has already come! It came when the Word made Flesh, the Light of the World stretched out his hands and took our sin upon himself by giving himself for the world he loved. That he still loves. He took our sins to the grave with him, and when the stone was rolled away on the third and glorious day, the empty tomb proclaimed throughout the world that the atonement offering was accepted!
>
> The Day of Atonement has come and it is a season now for rejoicing in the restoration of relationship with God. It is a season of harvest, as we continue to find those left by the side of the road and gather them in to great house of God. The great light of God's glorious presence, the Spirit of the resurrected Christ, shines brightly into the dark places of the world, calling out the violated and the violent from all nations that they might come together and rejoice in the light of God's reconciling love.[98]

While Bradley's sermon was prepared for an ordinary worship service, our most significant church celebrations can offer unique opportunities to continue the work of formation of disciples—often with awareness that more listeners may be present for these services. Robert Howard preaches from Mark's resurrection account in an Easter Sermon that is both appropriately celebrative and also engages in serious counter-cultural formation. Drawing from the comment by the young man in Jesus' empty tomb in Mark 16:6, " . . . he is not here," Howard uses this phrase to engage with our tendencies to try to contain Jesus—to say where he is and where he isn't. The good news is that the resurrected Christ is free to engage the world where needed—not always where we would choose. To find the risen Christ, listeners are called to follow Jesus—to do what Jesus does.

> What Mark is saying is this: the risen Lord has been sprung loose to roam this world. Jesus could be *anywhere*. You follow him, circling right back to Galilee, whatever *your own* version

98. Ibid.

might be. And there is where you *will find him.* How? By following him. By doing what he did. Teaching. Healing. Mixing it
up with folks at all levels of society. Getting your hands messy
up to the elbows, tying to bring the presence of God to them.
Look, if we are baptized, we are baptized into his *continuing
life.* "Body of Christ," remember? We can *learn about* Jesus
from the scriptures—and please *do* read them! But you want to
find him? Really find him? Go do *what* he did—*where* he did it.
Tell folks about Jesus, certainly—but with lips *and lives.* Spread
the alarm—he has been raised! All powers hostile to God's love
for *every* last person take warning! Tell the good news of God's
love for every last creature. And . . . *show* God's love. With your
body.[99]

The final section of the sermon has an appropriately celebrative Easter tone as Howard reminds the congregation of experiences of resurrection and encounters with the living Christ in their own experience and
congregational ministry. The inclusion of small details, such as the exact
wording from a child's note of thanks, helps make this section relatable
for the listeners.

. . . Remember, *nobody* expected the resurrection. And nobody
really expects it today, either. Resurrection still comes out of
death. Inability. "I don't know how I made it through those dark
days." You met Jesus, in Galilee, and saw a little Easter. A note
scrawled in the notebook found in a hospital chapel: "thank you
Jesus for healing my brother. I can rest easier, knowing he is finally with you." A little Easter, in Galilee. A note from one of the
kids who ate the food *we* gave for the backpack program: "Thank
you people for doing this for me because you didn't have to do
this for me. You could have gave it to another kid—some who
needed it more then me. But still, why? Why me? And thank you
for everything your doing for me—I'm not good with words at
all."[100] Another little Easter, for a kid living in Galilee, right here
in Globe [AZ.] Mark is right. Jesus could be anywhere. Even
here.[101]

99. Howard, "Risen Lord!"
100. Punctuation added, grammar and spelling uncorrected.
101. Ibid.

Liturgical Events of Good Friday and Easter

The cross and resurrection can be a significant part of preaching because the text or liturgical season lead us there directly. These are occasions for staring fully at the cross and resurrection; an opportunity to probe again into the rhythms that give the essential shape to our Christian identities. Preaching in this mode includes sermons that may be given during Holy Week, particularly Palm/Passion Sunday, Good Friday, and Easter. Liturgically the dynamic of the move from cross to resurrection is marked most fully through the Easter or Paschal Triduum, which begins with the evening service on Maundy Thursday, extends through Easter Vigil or Easter Sunday services, and is echoed through the whole fifty days of Easter. While we move into the agony of Christ's death, we always do so with an awareness of where this journey is going. As we join the crowds on Palm Sunday, waving branches to welcome Jesus into Jerusalem, we do so with awareness that we too are "fickle" when Jesus doesn't conform to our hopes and plans.[102] We also stand with the crowd whose cries of "hosanna" turn to cries to "crucify him!" Thus, our wilted and burned palm branches will become the ashes that are applied to our foreheads in contrition next ash Wednesday. But even in the midst of this march to the cross, the resurrection is also exercising its gravitational pull; we re-enact the story, but we know where this is going, through death into life.

Both crucifixion and resurrection are inseparable parts of the unique person and life of Jesus Christ, yet people struggle with one or both of these definitive gospel notes and preachers must strive to sound them together. Some view the resurrection as a scientifically impossible myth because it falls outside the realm of everyday human experience. It is easier to lift up Jesus' teaching and political character. These people have no problem ending the story on the cross where Jesus willingly dies for others. For others, the agony of the cross is more challenging to claim than the triumph of the resurrection.[103] The cross separated Christ from his disciples and followers, and the cross separates Christians from the world today. The difficulty of the cross further confounds our un-

102. Stookey, *Calendar*, 88–89.

103. Sally Brown notes that some preachers are aware of theological debates surrounding atonement theology and have a pastorally rooted concern with unintentionally lifting up suffering in a way that perpetuates abuse and the victimization of some. Later she notes " . . . many North Americans prefer either the life of Jesus as ethical example or the resurrection of Christ as triumphal denial of death rather than the cross." Brown, *Cross Talk*, 11–13, 23–24.

THE CORNERSTONE OF THE PULPIT 177

derstanding of Christ's freedom in choosing it; as divinely powerful, he could have chosen otherwise. Yet it is this free act that makes us free to be the preachers we really are—the preachers God intends us to be—as we witness to the inbreaking and God-driven eschatological reality of the world. Ultimately, both crucifixion and resurrection are necessary for human salvation to be complete and for humanity to be changed—made new in the image of Christ. Jesus' death and resurrection changed him. He was no longer immediately recognizable to his disciples and he did not stay with them in the same way in which he had before—this is the dynamic tension that we preach through the season of Easter. Following his resurrection and a few opportunities for teaching and preparing his followers, Jesus ascends into heaven to be with God but promises to be near to people through the Holy Spirit. It is this same Spirit who inspires preaching and forms the church into Christ's body here on earth.

For Palm/Passion preachers, the lectionary gives us two gospel readings and two psalms for the day. I would encourage limiting the preaching text to just one of these, discerning from engagement with context which text to focus on. However, in the sermon preachers can fill in the rest of the story. If the Good Friday service is well attended, preachers may choose to place an accent on the triumphal entry, however, stay true to where this story is going. Preachers will want to avoid a sense of moving from the triumphal entry to the triumph of Easter and bypassing the way of the cross. Most preachers choose to accent the passion. This is a harder road to travel because, in a sense, the whole of the week's drama needs to unfold in this sermon. For Holy Week preaching in general, the sections of sermons dealing with the biblical text may be a little larger than contextual sections—this is especially true for Palm/Passion Sunday. This is a week for remembering and reliving the old, old story. Nevertheless, preachers will still want to deal with the realities of our world to make this old, old story as relevant as possible to the realities that listeners are facing. During the services prior to Easter, preachers may find that the grace in the sermon feels somewhat muted—this is okay and embodies the liturgical and theological realities of Holy Week. However, preachers will still want grace to be present even in the midst of trouble that may remain somewhat unresolved. Grace can even be envisioned as something that exists on the horizon—much like the sunrise where we can begin to feel the warm rays even before it is fully risen. By Easter, the experiences of trouble and grace will be reversed so that we spend much less time exploring trouble. In his classes, Paul Wilson often advised his preaching students to write their Easter sermons before Lent begins in order to capture a deeply joyful tone—recognizing that after weeks leading up to the cross, it can be hard to lift our language and presence to the heights of Easter. In situations like this, our own preaching can serve as a means up lifting us up and fostering joy not only in our listeners but in ourselves as well.

The Triduum begins in the evening on Maundy Thursday and carries through three days, ending with the announcement of resurrection in the wee hours of Sunday morning. The events of the Three Great Days are constitutive of Christians; these days are the source of our core identity, our baptismal identity. It is important that worshippers have a sense of unity in moving through these three days, so it may be helpful to view them as one worship service or event broken into three parts. Lawrence Stookey suggests having no benediction until the end of the Easter Vigil service (or Easter Sunrise/Sunday service), and instead listing in the bulletin or order "our service continues," noting the time of the next service.[104] Similarly, refrain from repeating an opening or call to worship for Good Friday or Vigil/Sunrise services.[105] Thus you have one opening and one closing for a single service of worship spanning three days.[106] Linking these services makes an important theological statement, reinforcing the unity of the cross and resurrection. Jesus' suffering, death, and resurrection are part of one single divine act.[107] We spread this act out over several days and times of worship to allow time for it to sink in, to form and re-form us.

Tips for Maundy Thursday

The season of Lent officially ends the evening of Maundy Thursday. The word "Maundy" means "new." While preaching could certainly have a place in Maundy Thursday worship, the three most significant acts in this service are footwashing, Eucharist, and stripping the altar.[108] Footwashing may be done in a way that encourages the most participation given the culture of the congregation or ministry setting. In my Men-

104. Stookey, *Calendar*, 91.
105. Ibid.
106. Ibid., 92.
107. Ibid.
108. Ibid.

nonite tradition, some congregations separate men and women. Some congregations encourage participants to pair-up and wash each other's feet while others create circles where each person washes the feet of the person next to him or her until all have washed and been washed. Foot-washing can also be an opportunity to share prayer concerns and may end with a hug. Some congregations offer hand-washing or massaging lotion onto hands as an alternative to footwashing. The important thing is the physicality and the focus on care and service to one another. Maundy Thursday Eucharist should have a joyful tone.[109] The somber part of worship is the stripping of the altar, which ends the service. This celebration of Eucharist sustains us for the journey ahead it's a way of "shaking our fists" at evil and of celebrating the presence of the risen Christ even as we move into commemoration of his suffering and death.[110] It allows us to experience a foretaste of the heavenly banquet. The "Last Supper" is not Jesus' last supper as Jesus stands at the head of a feasting table in the Kingdom of God.[111]

Because this service is rich liturgically, instead of a full sermon, pastors may want to offer a briefer meditation oriented toward inviting participants into the acts. Clear written and spoken instructions will help newcomers feel more comfortable participating.

Tips for Good Friday

The designation of the day of Jesus' death as "Good Friday" may come from the phrase "God's Friday," which reminds us that God is in charge of these events, Jesus' suffering and death are willingly undertaken by Christ.[112] As Robert Webber points out, we can indeed claim this day as "good Friday" because that is the day in which Jesus faces the powers of evil and death and they crumble away.[113] Congregations do different things in terms of liturgical practice and scripture choices for Good Friday. Some traditions have a word-centered service focusing on the last seven words of Christ as drawn from all the gospels, with different preachers offering a sermon on each word. Other congregations

109. Ibid., 95.

110. Ibid.

111. Ibid.

112. Ibid., 96.

113. Webber, *Ancient-Future Time*, 130.

observe a service of the Stations of the Cross. For protestants, this often takes place ecumenically. In several different settings, I've participated in ecumenical Stations of the Cross services that take place in the urban core of the cities where we have lived—pointing out instances of suffering today and places where God might be calling churches to act in the name of God's justice.

For Lectionary preachers our Good Friday texts always come from the Gospel of John. John is the latest of the gospels and offers the most theological reflection. The sense that God is in control of these events comes through even in the small asides that characterize the gospel of John. Laurence Stookey highlights four key ways in which God' sense of presence and being in control of this event are brought to the fore by John's gospel:

1. In Gethsemane, Jesus does not run away when the guards fall to the ground. Instead he asserts impatiently that he is the one they are looking for; Jesus is more authoritative than the soldiers.[114]

2. When he is brought to Pilate, Jesus says, "You would have no power over me unless it had been given from above." Pilate assents to divine control by not changing the sign and leaving the words, "Jesus of Nazareth, The King of the Jews."[115]

3. In John, Jesus says three things from the cross, all of them are actions of authority:

   a. "Woman here is your son . . . here is your mother." Jesus takes charge of Mary's destiny.[116]

   b. "I am thirsty" is not so much about literal thirst but a statement made specifically to fulfill Scripture.[117]

   c. "It is finished" means that the goal is accomplished, a far off reality has been brought near and to completion. The Greek verb *tetelestai* is connected to words like television and telephone—meaning that something is being transmitted to bring something from far away near.[118]

114. Stookey, *Calendar*, 98.
115. Ibid.
116. Ibid.
117. Ibid.
118. Ibid., 98–99.

4. Death by crucifixion is essentially asphyxiation that happens when the legs of the crucified are too weak to hold the body upright. This can take days. In the case of Jesus, the soldiers were planning to break the legs of those on the crosses so that they wouldn't be hanging there over the Passover, but they discover that Jesus is already dead. How can this be? He was presumably healthy and fairly young. When I was a child I remember asking this question. While my mother said that Jesus died so quickly because he was carrying the weight of all human sin, Stookey positively asserts that in the Gospel of John, Jesus has foreshadowed that this would happen, "I lay down my life in order to take it up again. No one takes it from me, but I lay it down of my own accord. I have power to lay it down and I have power to take it up. I have received this command from my Father."[119] Jesus has laid down his life with his own power. God is in charge here.

This is the good news of Good Friday. There is a time for Jesus' quiet suffering in solidarity but this is not John's message on Good Friday. God is not weak, not even for a moment! God is in charge, even in the terrible events of Good Friday. While Jesus is not yet risen at the end of this service, God is already exercising power over the forces of darkness and death, facing them on God's terms, something that brings great hope when we experience terror, chaos, loss, and death in our own lives. But this is still hard theology and there is mystery here; this is not how we would expect a powerful God to behave. We struggle to understand how submission to the powers, suffering, and death illustrate being in charge. Indeed, this is part of experiencing the "stumbling block" of the cross.

Good Friday is a day for proclamation and for intercessory prayer, traditionally there are no Eucharistic prayers or consecration of elements at this service, if you want to celebrate communion, it is done with "leftovers" from Maundy Thursday, but perhaps this service is better observed without the Lord's Supper.[120] This is a time to pray for the whole of creation for which Jesus suffered and died. The Scripture for this service is compelling and long enough that the sermon should focus in on one theme to carry the sermon; there will be other years to address other themes. The text moves all the way from the arrest in the garden to the high priests, to Pilot, to the crucifixion, and then to Jesus' death. One

119. John 10:17–18. Stookey, *Calendar*, 99.
120. Ibid., 100.

way to limit the text is to look at one figure or scene in detail or to move thematically, allowing your theme to highlight certain aspects of the text. Any other tools the preachers may use for sermon unity are useful for this sermon, too. To keep a unified sermon, Paul Wilson suggests using the mnemonic device, "The Tiny Dog Now Is Mine" with each letter of a word standing for an element of which a sermon should have just one.[121] A sermon should focus on one text, have one theme, one key doctrine or church teaching, address one area of need, have one central image, and move towards one mission, which may also be a deepening of something that is already present.[122] In parts of the sermon that focus on application or engage with our world we may turn to the places where Jesus still suffers and aspects of our eschatological situation that are "not yet" according to God's ultimate vision. It may be helpful to look at our own role as those in power who felt threatened and participated in Jesus crucifixion. We could also look at ourselves as Jesus disciples who fled and denied him. Or we may look at ourselves as present-day followers who may undergo suffering in Christ's name, praying that the Spirit of God infuse us with the strength to endure this suffering as Jesus endured it for the glory of God. While a Good Friday sermon will have a heavier tone, it can certainly still lean towards hope—listeners should never be left without hope or without knowledge of the resurrection. For preachers who are used to a more equal balancing of trouble and grace in sermons, it may be helpful to envision the sermons on Good Friday and Easter as one act of proclamation that has most of the trouble falling on Good Friday and the grace coming on Easter Sunday. Preachers may not be able to literally count it as one sermon since not everyone will be at the Friday service but it may be helpful to view it this way theologically and structurally.

Barbara Brown Taylor's book *God in Pain* offers many examples of Good Friday preaching that demonstrate strong proclamation while also leaving space open for theological questions as we grapple with the mystery of the cross. In "The Silence of God," Taylor paints a vivid picture of "the wreckage," as we grapple with the death of Christ. "This is our own flesh and blood—God's own flesh and blood—the one we pray to, the one with power to heal, to case out demons, to raise people from the dead— dying himself now, as helpless as a kitten. It is all he can do to hold up his head. Everything else is tacked down now, nailed firmly in place. He

---

121. Wilson, *Four Pages*, 33–57.
122. Ibid.

cannot wipe the blood from his temples. He cannot cover his nakedness. The rescuer, unrescued. The savior, unsaved."[123]

Taylor moves to name the truth hanging in the air. The truth is that in many ways we are not shocked about what happens to Jesus on Good Friday. We see suffering all around us. Many of us are experiencing our own personal "Good Fridays." Resurrection is much harder to believe.[124] "We live in the land at the foot of the cross."[125] It can be hard for those who are in the midst of suffering to relate to John's portrayal of Jesus. In Taylor's words, "It is so cleaned up and brave."[126] Jesus in John is "in charge," and exercises active agency. Taylor muses,

> Maybe that is the gospel we are given today because someone thought it might help us a little, to have such a strong and fearless savior. He is nobody's victim. He is God's own martyr, who goes to his death with all the eagerness of a bride. I have read about it in other times and places: civil rights workers going down under the fire hoses, Archbishop Romero gunned down at the altar, the Yugoslavian cellist who placed his folding chair in the street in Sarajevo—right in the path of sniper fire—and played Albinoni's adagio in memory of the dead.[127]

Taylor's use of small details in her examples allows each one to be a vivid vignette and to take a hold of our minds and imaginations. Taylor turns from these instances of bravery in the face of death in more recent history to Jesus on the cross, reminding listeners of not only the physical pain but also the betrayal by Jesus' friends and the "silence of God"—we have no confirmation here as we do in Jesus' baptism and the Transfiguration.[128] Those who suffer today also grapple with the silence of God. "Good Friday is the day we receive no answer and must suffer that silence with the crucified one—wondering what it says about us, wondering what it says about God."[129] Taylor picks up on the repetition and freight of the word silence by using an extended story taken from the book *Silence* by Japanese writer Shusaku Endo that tells of a seventeenth century Por-

---

123. Taylor, "Silence of God," 110.

124. Ibid., 111.

125. Ibid.

126. Ibid.

127. Ibid., 111–12.

128. Ibid., 112.

129. Ibid., 113.

tuguese missionary named Rodrigues who meditates on the strong face
of Christ in his devotional practices. Taken captive in a national uprising
of Christians, his captors seek to make him renounce his faith by offering
a terrible conundrum.[130] Either he "trample" the image of Christ that he
has so revered or fellow Christian prisoners will continue to endure horrific torture. From the image, he hears the clear call of Christ, "Trample,
Trample."[131] Taylor continues,

> The silence of God is broken. Christ speaks, not from some safe
> place outside human suffering but from the very heart of it. He
> is the trampled one, the crushed and soiled one whose loyalty
> to humankind leads him to endure all that we endure—right
> up to and including the silence of God. When Jesus howls his
> last question from the cross, it is God who howls—protesting
> the pain, opposing it with his last breath. Only this is no defeat.
> This is, contrary to all appearances, a triumph over suffering. By
> refusing to avoid it or to lie about it in any way, the crucified one
> opens a way through it. He hallows it by engaging it. He shows
> us how. We are not supposed to love suffering. We are allowed to
> hate it and to do everything in our power to bring it to an end,
> only we may not avoid it. That is not one of our choices. Today
> we look on the one who we have pierced. More important we lis-
> ten. To the silence. To the howl. What is the gospel in the land at
> the foot of the cross? When God is silent, people of faith cry out.
> When people of faith cry out, it is God who speaks. Amen.[132]

Taylor amplifies Christ's suffering by dirtying-up John's version of
the crucifixion event but remains true to Christ's active agency in his suffering and death. She also continues to speak a word of hope to those
who are in the midst of suffering—who live in "the land at the foot of the
cross" without moving to the resurrection. She names death's defeat while
staying liturgically appropriate to Good Friday.

Tips for Easter Vigil/Sunrise Service

In an Easter Vigil, the extensive liturgy does the heavy lifting, with each of
the four main parts of the service contributing to the proclamation of resurrection: Service of Light; Service of the Word, which involves Scripture

130. Ibid.
131. Ibid., 113–14.
132. Ibid., 114.

readings recounting God's mighty acts from Hebrew Scriptures through Romans, Psalm 114, and the Gospel lesson for that year; The Service of Baptism and Reaffirmation; and Service of the Eucharist all contribute to an extended experience of joyful Easter celebration. Because the service is so rich and freighted sacramentally, the sermon becomes more of a homily on one of the scripture texts (usually the gospel reading) that echoes the themes brought to the fore by the whole worship event. A full array of Scripture texts guides worshippers through the experience of the vigil; preaching can be an important part of extending the proclamation of good news. In his Easter Vigil homily on Year C's gospel reading from Luke, Hank Langknecht briefly recounts the journey of the Vigil, turning from the creative power of God as witnessed in Hebrew Scriptures to the question hanging in the air this night in the wake of crucifixion and death. "Is the creative power of God's love sufficient to overcome evil? Sin? Death? Is the creative power of God's love sufficient to overcome how much we make of ourselves . . . Or how *little* we make of ourselves?"[133] By the end of the homily, Langknecht has brought the worshippers into the experience of the first witnesses of Jesus' resurrection so that they too might experience the presence of the resurrected Christ.

> My dear brothers and sisters in Christ, our vigil nears its end.
>
> And soon we shall have our answer . . . again.
>
> Is the creative power of God's love sufficient to overcome evil? Sin? Death?
>
> Is the creative power of God's love sufficient to overcome how much . . . and how little we make of ourselves?
>
> Listen.
>
> Maybe in the next little bit you'll hear the words, "Peace be with *you*."
>
> Maybe in the next little bit you'll hear the faint whisper that bread makes when it is torn open *for you*.
>
> Oh, didn't Jesus tell you . . . he is risen!
>
> Our vigil is nearly over.
>
> Is the creative power of God's love sufficient to overcome evil? Sin? Death?
>
> Is the creative power of God's love sufficient to overcome how much . . . and how little we make of ourselves?
>
> Of course.[134]

133. Langknecht, "Easter Vigil Homily."
134. Ibid.

Langknecht's homily amplifies the overall proclamatory thrust of the liturgy and maintains a sense of continuity with the drama of the whole Paschal Triduum.

If your congregation celebrates with a Sunrise Service, Eucharist, and singing, accompanying these with a brief meditation or a homily is completely appropriate. This approach should be similar to the Vigil, allowing the story of resurrection to be upfront and to guide the message.

Tips for Easter Day/Easter Season

Stookey reminds us that we really shouldn't call "Easter Day," "Easter" because that ignores the fact that Easter is a whole season, the longest of the church year at fifty days. Each of the Sundays of Easter has a particular focus in the texts, but the doctrine of resurrection ties this whole season together. Worship should be permeated with a sense of joy. These sermons can return to a balance of trouble and grace but the good news needs to be very strong. Easter Day is the inaugural event of the season of Easter; it needs to be grand in its scope to open the way for the coming seven weeks. Here are some possibilities for specific sermon themes for Easter Day:

1. The story of Easter as situated in God's broader salvation story. This is where all of our theology is headed; every doctrine echoes from this doctrine and this is the culmination of the arch of Scripture.[135]

2. Personal sense of our own rising with Christ. This also could connect to a social and eschatological vision of Jesus' resurrection as having broader dimensions in which everything is made new.[136] Preachers will want to guard against making the resurrection only a personal event. Preachers might seek images of the healing of creation as diverse as a putting in a ramp to make a space accessible for wheelchairs, or an instance of racial reconciliation between a police department and an African American neighborhood.

3. Preachers have a choice on Easter of staying with John's gospel or going back to the gospel of the particular year and can choose to focus their resurrection preaching on the particulars of the specific text at hand, following general rules for good preaching. Expository

135. See also Webber, *Ancient-Future Time*, 144–45.
136. Ibid., 143–44.

or narrative sermon forms are deeply text-centered; they follow closely through the text, allowing the text to shape the flow of the sermon, making application to our world throughout the sermon or often towards the end. It can be particularly effective to highlight for listeners what makes each gospel account unique.

4. Regardless of the particular path chosen, Easter sermons should focus on the magnificent and amazing power of God that enters our lives as pure gift. While our actions so often lead to the cross, to suffering and death, only the power of God in Jesus Christ can bring completely new life from death. Resurrection never gets old and there are no direct natural metaphorical comparisons in our world. Sections of our Easter sermons that focus on our world offer us small glimpses of resurrection reality, a small foretaste of ultimate glory and life everlasting.

In an Easter sermon that accompanies Matthew's gospel in Year A, Hank Langknecht revisits an earlier sermon on Ezekiel's dry bones, making a contrast that focuses on the radical newness of resurrection. Resurrection is not merely a restoration or a reconstituting but something entirely different—a break with the past. He preaches, "Where we are going next . . . nothing is going to be put together like it was before. . . . There are no blueprints . . . Our memories could be our downfall . . . And our bones will be no help."[137] Langknecht turns to the women who visit Jesus' empty tomb and encounter an angel with a message,

> "He has been raised from the dead, and indeed he is going ahead of you to Galilee; there you will see him." This is my message for you.
> This angel matter-of-factly accepts their terms,
> Shows them what they need to see,
> Gives them a message and sends them on their way
> And then they go. They go with "fear and joy" . . .
> that amazing combination of emotions that from the outside looks like
> confidence and
> conviction and
> courage.
> Then they have the briefest encounter with Jesus himself.
> No fanfare . . .

137. Langknecht, "Easter Sermon."

No meals . . .

No cacophony of Pentecost . . .

And for just a second they have him in their hands . . .

But then he sends them on to Galilee . . .

Promising that where he sends them . . . he will meet them.

And then he does . . .

And when they gather together in Galilee,

the ground shifts under their feet again . . . figuratively this time . . .

because they are not in Galilee in order to be reconstituted . . .

they are in Galilee to be sent to the ends of the earth.

They are sent to places where there are no blueprints. No memories.
No bones.

Nothing . . . except his own promise . . .

To meet them where he sends them.

"Lo, I am with you always."

Jesus sends them to places where everything will be new.

And they go.[138]

Langknecht's sermon does an excellent job of meeting listeners where they may be—in a place of incredulity—and contextualizes the amazing call of Easter so that we can see the radical transformation to which we are invited by the risen Christ. Notice how Langknecht's language and scope avoid reducing the resurrection only to a personal experience. His pronouns and scope are broad and communal, keeping well to the tone of Matthew's gospel.

Themes for the Sundays of Easter

Here are some options for shaping sermons for Sundays in the Easter season thematically according to the assigned lectionary texts and liturgical tradition:

2nd Sunday, "Thomas Sunday": The account in which Thomas' doubt becomes faith and the generosity of the risen Christ who meets our doubts and inspires belief.[139]

---

138. Langknecht, "Easter Sermon."

139. See also Stookey, Calendar, 59.

3rd Sunday, "Meal Sunday": A good Sunday to celebrate Eucharist and do some intentional linking and teaching in the sermon about how the resurrection affects our interpretation of the sacrament.[140]

4th Sunday, "Good Shepherd Sunday": In Year C the reading from Revelation portrays Christ as the lamb, which is an interesting conundrum. How is Jesus both the shepherd and the lamb? This question flows alongside other theological conundrums in which Jesus is both crucified and risen and we are both justified by Christ and yet sinners.[141]

5th Sunday, "I Am Sunday": This Sunday highlights continuity between the God revealed in the burning bush to Moses and the God who is raised in Jesus.[142] The resurrection is something mysterious and holy, reminding us that the fullness of God is beyond our grasp. The transcendence in the texts for this Sunday can be a good balance in the sermon compared to the more immanent sense of Jesus as Good Shepherd in the previous week.[143]

6th Sunday: "Preparation for Ascension": This Sunday focuses on preparation for continuing Christ's work when he is no longer physically present among us.[144] In the face of congregations and denominations wracked by conflict and division, preachers can envision Jesus' commandment for us to love each other as a promise of the gift of the Spirit's work in us.[145]

7th Sunday, "Ascension": In most congregations who follow the Christian year, this Sunday marks a celebration of Ascension, which anticipates Pentecost. Stookey clearly names four theological themes for Ascension:

---

140. Ibid., 61.

141. Ibid., 62–63.

142. Ibid., 63–64.

143. Ibid., 64.

144. Stookey highlights that the Risen Jesus is still present with us but in a new "mode." Ibid., 64.

145. Ibid., 64–65.

1. God has completed the saving work of Christ.[146]

2. The completion of resurrection means the "raising up" of all of creation—this is what is in store for the world.[147]

3. In returning to God, Jesus takes the fullness of human life into the being of God—the human experience will always be a part of the life of God.[148]

4. Jesus Christ is unconfined by time or space—Jesus is for all times and all places.[149]

8th Sunday, "Pentecost": Pentecost can be viewed as the closing of the official season of Easter.[150] Texts may feel out of place because we move backwards to the origins of the church when our texts from Acts on prior Sundays have moved forward from this. Theologically this is meant to build the communal life of the church on the reality of the resurrection and to show continuity in Christ's body, the church.[151] In Stookey's words, "The Spirit is the One who forms the church by making the Risen Christ manifest in power."[152]

While Pentecost may end the official season of Easter, each Sunday is actually a "little Easter" as we continue to allow our worship and our lives to be shaped by the power of the Resurrection.

Sermon Forms

Finally, in sermon forms that are driven by the narrative thrust of the gospel moving from "trouble to grace" or "itch to scratch" we also see the dynamic of the cross and resurrection at play. Utilizing a narrative form, such as Gene Lowry's "Loop," Paul Wilson's "Four Page Sermon," or the traditional African American pattern "Start low. Go slow. Strike fire. Sit down," can implicitly invoke a gospel experience that moves listeners experientially through the shift from cross to resurrection.

146. Ibid., 67.
147. Ibid., 68–70.
148. Ibid., 70–71.
149. Ibid., 71–72.
150. Ibid., 73.
151. Ibid., 73–74.
152. Ibid., 74.

Lowry's Loop

Sermons built around a plot are inherently interesting and narrative preaching has gained traction in many pulpits in the past forty years, but preachers may not always be aware of the theological dynamics that link these forms to the heart of the gospel. Lowry's loop consists of five stages of the sermon plot:

1. "Upsetting the equilibrium" introduces listeners to a complication or tension. It may be the central tension or concern of the sermon or at this stage it may be a preliminary tension that opens the door to the main issue or concern of the sermon.[153] Preachers will want to avoid disclosing the resolution at this point but should certainly give a sense of direction, which can function as a promise of where the sermon is going. It is also important that any tensions that are introduced do find resolution at some point—if preachers spark the "itch" in their listeners then they should provide a means to "scratch."[154]

2. "Analyzing the discrepancy" deepens and unpacks the tension introduced in the first move while also setting the stage for how this tension or concern will relate to the gospel.[155] Richard Eslinger highlights the importance of doing real theological diagnostic work here rather than keeping the discourse on the level of description or keeping things focused only on human experiences.[156] A good example of this is in Tom Long's sermon "Troubled?," cited earlier, where Long names the trouble as both the distillation of a particular verse of Scripture out of the context of Christ's broader work and identity and the church's tendency to focus on "the positive" rather than engaging our world's troubles head-on.[157]

3. "Disclosing the clue to resolution" moves listeners into new territory—they have a new perspective where a way forward is seen where there was previously no way.[158] Eslinger notes that often the

---

153. Eslinger, *Web*, 35–36. See also Lowry, *Homiletical Plot*, 28–38.
154. Eslinger, *Web*, 35.
155. Ibid., 36–37. Lowry, *Homiletical Plot*, 39–52.
156. Eslinger, *Web*, 37.
157. Long, "Troubled?"
158. Eslinger, *Web*, 37–38. Lowry, *Homiletical Plot*, 53–73.

new way forward parallels the confounding sense of reversal that is often found in the gospel itself.[159]

4. "Experiencing the gospel" leads to God's response and an experience of the good news of how God is "scratching" the "itch."[160] A danger for preachers is not developing this page fully so that listeners move from the "answer" to "what we must do" without a sense of God's action or God's empowerment.[161] Being vivid in this stage will help listeners have an experience of the gospel.

5. "Anticipating the consequences" invites listeners to participate in envisioning a future that unfolds in light of the experience of gospel disclosure.[162]

The narrative of the cross and resurrection move through these stages as well and, because the move from cross to resurrection is paradigmatic for Christians, invoking the movement and the experience of reversal that lies at the heart of the resurrection is to invoke the cross and resurrection implicitly in the sermon even if cross and resurrection are not mentioned explicitly. Revisiting the stages of Lowry's loop and the movement from cross to resurrection:

1. "Upsetting the equilibrium" speaks to the situation of the cross and Jesus' death. Jesus' disciples did not anticipate that this is how things would unfold; they had other hopes for his ministry and the inauguration of God's Kingdom.

2. "Analyzing the discrepancy" offers an opportunity to reflect on the nuances of Jesus' death, the many ways to think about why Jesus died, and the many factors at play.

3. "Disclosing the clue to resolution" places us with the women at the tomb; we wonder what has happened and begin to sense the miraculous.

4. "Experiencing the gospel" allows the joy of the resurrection to come to bear for us. We stand with the disciples who experience Jesus' presence and experience the gift of peace and the Holy Spirit breathed in their midst.

159. Eslinger, Web, 38.

160. Ibid. Lowry, Homiletical Plot, 74–79.

161. Eslinger, Web, 38.

162. Ibid., 39. Lowry, Homiletical Plot, 80–87.

5. "Anticipating the consequences" allows us to live into Jesus' call to move into the world as agents of the resurrection. The presence of the risen Christ goes with us.

Wilson's Four-Pages

Wilson's four-page sermon method offers some of the same dynamics of Lowry's narrative form with a more explicitly theological approach. Wilson is concerned that the gospel is the content of preaching and that the sermon's movement is centered around God's activity in the particular Scripture text and in our world. For Wilson, the gospel is not identical with the content of Scripture but rather scripture is a means to get to the gospel.[163] He also sees the cross and resurrection as key to Jesus' identity and work as savior, writing, "If preachers avoid the cross and resurrection, people may find no reason to believe Jesus, for he is then just another person."[164] To insure that God is at the center of the sermon and to increase the likelihood that listeners will experience the hope of the gospel, a sermon theme sentence that engages God's action is crucial to Wilson's approach. The theme sentence needs to have one of the members of the trinity as the subject of the sentence, an active verb, be relatively short (five to six words) and be hopeful.[165] The theme sentence is not a summary of the whole sermon but instead points a way forward and serves as a guide or direction for the preacher.[166] If God's action is not immediately apparent in the scripture text, preachers may ask "what God is doing behind the text" or "what the text says about an attribute of God," such as God's love or God's power.[167]

The theme sentence serves as a lynch pin for a sermon form that is built around four discreet units in the sermon or "pages." The pages move from trouble to grace and alternate their focus on the biblical text and our world. The "classic" form proceeds:[168]

---

163. Wilson, *Practice of Preaching,* 35.

164. Ibid.

165. Wilson, *Four Pages,* 37–44.

166. Ibid., 38–39.

167. Ibid., 40.

168. Ibid., 16–18, 73–232.

1. Trouble in the text

2. Trouble in our world

3. Grace in the text

4. Grace in our world

However, the pages can be "shuffled" and remain true to the four-page form as long as the sermon maintains a general move from trouble to grace.[169] Similar to Lowry, the movement through the four pages moves us from the experience of the cross to the joy of the resurrection. The theological focus on God's action keeps the sermon centered around what God is doing in the text and in our world rather than on what we are doing or what we should be doing. Theologically this acknowledges human fallenness and our need for God in Jesus Christ—this too resonates with the reality of Christ's person and work in the cross and resurrection. The focus on God provides a strong foundation for a call to mission that grows from the joyful possibility of life in Christ, which makes faithful discipleship possible by the grace of the resurrection rather than from our own energies alone.

The concept of grace is a challenging one, one that is better communicated through image and story rather than the use of freighted theological language. Even the word "grace" can be challenging and abstract for listeners, while it may be deeply meaningful for the preacher. Preachers might want to challenge themselves to avoid using the word grace in their sermons for a couple of months to experiment with "imaging" the experience of grace in other ways.

In my Pentecost sermon on Ezek 37:1–14, I utilize a four-page sermon form to move listeners from the Valley of Dry Bones to an encounter with the Holy Spirit; the very Spirit of God blows through this valley breathing new life into dead-dry bones, creating new life from death, and bringing new hope from broken dreams. Beginning with an image of a mass grave and the agony of unfinished work and hopes, as portrayed in Michael Ondaatje's best-seller *Anil's Ghost*, I move from the literary context to the context of our world as a way to set up movement into the trouble in the text on page one of the sermon.[170]

> Anil frequently encounters family-members of victims of political violence, who have run out of options and are desperate to

169. Ibid., 246–49.
170. Ondaatje, *Anil's Ghost*.

learn the fate of their loved ones. These family members hover at the edges of mass-graves, valleys of bones. Sometimes these bones can be identified and families can find some peace. Often there is too much damage, the trail of evidence is cold, the bones are too dry. In their quest to learn Sailor's identity and to find some justice for him and his family, Anil and her partner allow these particular bones to serve as a stand-in for all the political victims whose bones cry out for justice and peace.[171]

But Anil and her partner cannot accomplish their aims.

We are left with a sense of incompleteness, unfinished business, making the best out of the worst circumstances. . . . The vision of dry bones in our text from Ezekiel today bears some similarity to this story and countless similar real-life stories of dead-ends, dry-bones, and valleys of broken dreams.

However, Ezekiel is not left alone in this dead-end valley of dry bones.[172]

On page one I describe the circumstances of Israel. The terrible events that surround Ezekiel's immediate context are only the most recent in Israel's sorted past, which includes the centuries earlier division of Israel into two kingdoms and years of unfaithful and idolatrous leadership that leads to God's judgment and the defeat and destruction of the Northern Kingdom at the hands of Assyria. A near contemporary of Jeremiah, Ezekiel was likely dragged away into exile around the same time as Je-hoi-a-kin and he prophesies from Babylonia. Jerusalem has been sieged and utterly destroyed. The temple and the palace lay in ruins. The educated, the political and religious leaders, and those with means and power have now all been taken away to Babylonia, leaving the remaining Jewish population with no leadership and no religious center.

This is the grim background for our verses today and now the Spirit his called Ezekiel out to a vast valley full of bones. These are not full skeletons lying neatly in rows, but a jumbled mass of bones picked clean of any tissue. A scapula here, a femur there . . . these bones are utterly incongruous with life. They are the broken bodies, hopes, and dreams of God's people. The Spirit leads Ezekiel all around the valley. He cannot look away. Bones and dust and broken dreams as far as his eyes can see.[173]

171. Ibid.
172. Sancken "Broken Dreams."
173. Ibid.

After a transition to page two, I recount stories of those suffering with loss and broken dreams today: a Congolese immigrant who has lost relationships and identity, a teenaged athlete on the verge of getting a scholarship to a top school who has suffered a possibly career-ending injury, a couple struggling year after year with infertility, and a wealthy heiress with a disability who suffered abuse at the hands of her father and more than one husband.[174] In retrospect, I may have included too many stories, but I included this range of stories to show that no one is exempt from experiencing the valley of dry bones and to increase the likelihood of resonating with diverse members of the congregation. The use of stories here also offers listeners a hand in the work of interpretation and in making connections between God's action in the text and in their own lives. In the transition to page three, I name my Holy Spirit-centered theme and intentionally invoke the cross to describe God's posture towards humanity in preparation for moving to the "grace" pages of the sermon. "God has promised us that the valley of dry bones and broken dreams is not our final destination—and more than that, the Holy Spirit is in the business of transforming valleys of dry bones and broken dreams into hope, new life, and new possibilities. Because our God has traveled this way himself, carrying a cross through the darkest valleys of human existence—no valley or human experience of brokenness is untouched by the hand of God."[175]

Page three follows the trajectory of the text. I add additional imagery to this already evocative text to help listeners have a more sensory encounter.

> With a rushing rattle, bone smacks against bone, sinews and ligaments, and muscles snake around the bones.
>
> Smooth skin enrobes the bones, skin of every hue, pinks and tans, deep rich bonzes, and shining ebony.
>
> But the bones do not yet live, and so God commands Ezekiel to prophesy to the Breath—to the Spirit to bring life.
>
> "Come from the four winds, Holy Spirit, come Breath of God, and breathe upon these lifeless bodies, that they may live."
>
> And the Holy Spirit blows through the whole valley and breath comes into them, and they live, and stand on their feet, a vast multitude—filling the valley with life!

174. Ibid.
175. Ibid.

Out of the valley of broken-dreams, the Holy Spirit the Breath of God brings life and hope to the people of Israel.

Thus says the Lord,

"I am going to open your graves, and bring you up from your graves, O my people; I will put *my spirit within you*, and *you shall live*, and you shall know that I, the Lord, am acting among you."

Ezekiel's vision of transformation and life for Israel is comprehensive and holistic involving not only human lives but the very transformation and healing of the land itself. All the destruction and pain, the power of human sinfulness and violence, these are no match for God.[176]

Moving to page four, I use a litany of the activity of the Holy Spirit, moving from Hebrew Scriptures through the New Testament, and up to today making explicit connection to the liturgical context of Pentecost.

God commands and Ezekiel speaks, but make no mistake, the Holy Spirit is the prime actor in this Valley of Dry Bones. The word for Breath or Spirit occurs ten times in these fourteen verses.

The same creator Spirit who moves across the primordial waters,

who engenders life in Adam in Genesis,

who empowers the servants of God, the faithful judges, kings, and prophets,

who stirs John the Baptist

and descends upon Jesus and sustains him,

who blows among the early Christian church in today's passage from Acts—removing barriers, burning in their hearts and minds, and inspiring the church from then until now.

This same spirit is also blowing through the valleys in our lives and world, bringing new life and hope where there used to be only dry bones and broken dreams.[177]

Page four returns to the stories from page three, showing how the Spirit sustains and transforms. I tried to not provide easy answers or tidy solutions. The real experience of suffering was not erased; rather the Spirit transformed the outlook and the possibilities of the figures from the earlier stories. The Congolese immigrant forges new connections and his gifts are being acknowledged by his church community, providing a

176. Ibid.
177. Ibid.

sense of identity in his new context.[178] The couple struggling with infertility stops treatment, finds a wonderful support group, and pursues adop-
tion.[179] The teenaged athlete has surgery but in the meantime pursues
other interests and focuses on his grades. He becomes a more rounded
person and, with his good grades and gifts in drama and theater, gets
numerous acceptance letters from a range of colleges and universities. He
now has more options open in his future.[180] The heiress becomes a lawyer,
only pursuing pro-bono cases. She discovers a love for music after getting
powerful hearing aids. She creates an endowment for a girl's choir at her
church.[181]

The sermon ends with joyful encouragement and moves eschatologically,

> The marvelous works of the Holy Spirit are varied and diverse!
>
> Out of the valley of broken dreams, the Spirit transforms loss and
> death into hope and new life.
>
> The Spirit brings healing.
>
> The Spirit fosters connection and relationships.
>
> The Spirit works for justice.
>
> The Spirit brings courage for change and lasting security.
>
> And just as Ezekiel is called to speak Spirit-filled words of hope and
> power to Those dry and broken bones, secure in his trust that God can
> work miracles and wonders to bring about God's good purposes for
> creation,
>
> So too we are called to testify.
>
> To testify to the valleys where dreams go to die,
>
> To the dry and broken scattered bones in our world.
>
> To say to these bones,
>
> "Hear the word of the Lord, Oh bones!
>
> "The Holy Spirit has come among us! Blowing through the deepest
> valleys in our lives!"
>
> "Listen-up Oh you bones!"
>
> We do not have to settle for making the best of a bad situation.
>
> We have a deep and holy hope!"
>
> God's promise of complete and total transformation.

178. Ibid.
179. Ibid.
180. Ibid.
181. Sancken "Broken Dreams."

Resurrected bones,

Renewed dreams,

A new heaven and a new earth where justice and peace shall reign,

Where God shall walk among us wiping the tears from our eyes . . .

Where suffering and pain and death will be no more.

"Listen Oh Bones and Live!"[182]

This sermon is informed by the cross primarily in its four-page form that moves listeners from the experience of death to resurrection. While keeping a pneumatological focus appropriate to the celebration of Pentecost, I also did explicitly name the cross and resurrection at key transitional points in the sermon in order to enhance the connections listeners might make between Ezekiel's experience in the text, the work of Christ, and the continued work of Christ in their lives today.

African American Narrative Pattern

While not always immediately recognized as a narrative-preaching model, the traditional African American peaching pattern, described with the rhyme "Start low. Go slow. Strike fire. Sit down," is narrative both in its broad movement towards a celebrative climax, while tracking the gospel experience of moving from death to resurrection or from slavery to promised land, and in its sense of situating the particular preaching text within the broader story of God's redemption of creation. Unlike Lowry and Wilson, my categorization of this traditional approach to preaching is more descriptive than offering a specific preaching method. African American preachers whose sermons follow the movement from low to high can employ a variety of forms, from more expository to points followed by brief application-focused excurses. The tone and use of distinctive rhetoric is what evokes the sense of narrative thrust and the use of celebration that may or may not explicitly mention the cross offers a sense of joyful release and resurrection hope.

CONCLUSION

The methods and examples discussed in this chapter show options for how preachers can employ the cross and resurrection in a variety of ways

182. Ibid.

including in the theologically-oriented rhetorical release of celebration, as a means of validating experiences of suffering, as a specific hermeneutical lens for exploring Scripture for preaching, as a means for teaching about church doctrine, as a means of preparation for discipleship, as a means of engaging the liturgical events of Good Friday and Easter, or through the use of narrative sermon forms. Preachers can adapt these options for a wide range of styles and approaches to preaching as appropriate for the preacher's personal gifts and context. Some practices remain helpful across all these modes, such as using details to help the sermon connect to the senses and imaginations of listeners and using examples that ring true to real life that resist easy or tidy resolution.

Bibliography

Abelard, Peter. "A Solution." In *A Scholastic Miscellany: Anselm to Ockham*, translated and edited by Eugene Rathbone Fairweather, 283–84. Philadelphia: Westminster, 1956.

Adams, Joanna. "The Only Question." In *A Chorus of Witnesses: Model Sermons for Today's Preacher*, edited by Thomas G. Long and Cornelius Plantinga, Jr., 267–70. Grand Rapids: Eerdmans, 1994.

Aden, LeRoy, and Robert G. Hughes. *Preaching God's Compassion: Comforting Those Who Suffer*. Minneapolis: Fortress, 2002.

Armstrong, Karen. *Twelve Steps to a Compassionate Life*. New York: Knopf, 2011.

Auden, W. H., and Edward Mendelson. *Collected Poems*. New York: Vintage, 1991.

Barth, Karl, and Amy Marga. *The Word of God and Theology*. London: T. & T. Clark, 2011.

Barth, Karl, and Geoffrey William Bromiley. *The Doctrine of Reconciliation: (Church Dogmatics, Volume IV, 1-3)*. Edinburgh: T. & T. Clark, 1956.

Bartlett, David Lyon. *Between the Bible and the Church: New Methods for Biblical Preaching*. Nashville: Abingdon, 1999.

Berger, Peter L., and Anton C. Zijderveld. *In Praise of Doubt: How to Have Convictions without Becoming a Fanatic*. New York: HarperOne, 2009.

Bock, Darrell L., and Mikel Del Rosario. "The Table Briefing: On the Heart of Islam." *Bibliotheca Sacra* 171 (2014) 96–103.

Bradley, Robert. "Prophetic Sermon." Sermon, Advanced Preaching Class from United Theological Seminary. Dayton, OH, March 1, 2015.

Brock, Rita Nakashima, and Rebecca Ann Parker. *Proverbs of Ashes Violence, Redemptive Suffering, and the Search for What Saves Us*. Boston: Beacon, 2002.

Brown, Brene. *Daring Greatly: How the Courage to Be Vulnerable Transforms the Way We Live, Love, Parent, and Lead*. New York: Gotham, 2012.

Brown, Joanne Carlson. "And a Little Child Will Lead Us: Christology and Child Abuse." In *Christianity, Patriarchy, and Abuse: A Feminist Critique*, edited by Joanne C. Brown and Carole R. Bohn, 1–30. New York: Pilgrim, 1989.

Brown, Sally A. *Cross Talk: Preaching Redemption Here and Now*. Louisville: Westminster, 2008.

————. "Negotiating the Shifting Semantics of Sacrifice in Preaching." Paper presented at the annual meeting for Prophetic Preaching. Memphis, TN, December 2–4, 2004.

————. "When Lament Shapes the Sermon." In *Lament: Reclaiming Practices in Pulpit, Pew, and Public Square*, edited by Sally A. Brown and Patrick D. Miller, 27–37. Louisville: Westminster, 2005.

Brueggemann, Walter. "Duty as Delight and Desire: Preaching Obedience That Is Not Legalism." *Journal for Preachers* 18.1 (1994) 2–14.

————. *Finally Comes the Poet: Daring Speech for Proclamation*. Minneapolis: Fortress, 1989.

Brunner, Emil. *Truth as Encounter*. Philadelphia: Westminster, 1964.

Buechner, Frederick. "A Sprig of Hope." In *A Chorus of Witnesses: Model Sermons for Today's Preacher*, edited by Thomas G. Long and Cornelius Plantinga, Jr., 225–33. Grand Rapids: Eerdmans, 1994.

————. "The Magnificent Defeat." In *A Chorus of Witnesses: Model Sermons for Today's Preacher*, edited by Thomas G. Long and Cornelius Plantinga, Jr., 3–11. Grand Rapids: Eerdmans, 1994.

Buttrick, David. *A Captive Voice: The Liberation of Preaching*. Louisville: Westminster, 1994.

————. *Homiletic: Moves and Structures*. Philadelphia: Fortress, 1987.

————. *Preaching Jesus Christ: An Exercise in Homiletic Theology*. Philadelphia: Fortress, 1988.

————. *Preaching the New and the Now*. Louisville: Westminster, 1998.

Campbell, Charles L. *Preaching Jesus: New Directions for Homiletics in Hans Frei's Postliberal Theology*. Grand Rapids: Eerdmans, 1997.

Capon, Robert Farrar. *The Foolishness of Preaching: Proclaiming the Gospel against the Wisdom of the World*. Grand Rapids: Eerdmans, 1998.

Chapell, Bryan. *Christ-centered Preaching: Redeeming the Expository Sermon*. Grand Rapids: Baker, 1994.

Charter for Compassion. "The Charter for Compassion." Charter for Compassion. Accessed August 29, 2015.

Colijn, Brenda B. *Images of Salvation in the New Testament*. Downer's Grove, IL: InterVarsity, 2010.

Cotten, Trystan T., and Kimberly Springer. *Stories of Oprah: The Oprahfication of American Culture*. Jackson, MI: University Press of Mississippi, 2010.

Craddock, Fred B. *As One without Authority*. 3rd ed. Nashville: Abingdon, 1979.

————. *Overhearing the Gospel*. Nashville: Abingdon, 1978.

Crawford, Evans E., and Thomas H. Troeger. *The Hum: Call and Response in African American Preaching*. Nashville: Abingdon, 1995.

Davies, Alan T. "Jews and the Death of Jesus: Theological Reflections." *Interpretation* 23.2 (1969) 207–17.

Dean, Kenda Creasy. *Almost Christian: What the Faith of Our Teenagers Is Telling the American Church*. Oxford: Oxford University Press, 2010.

————. "Review of Souls in Transition." *The Christian Century* 127.3 (2010) 34–35.

Drash, Wayne. "When Kin of Slaves and Owner Meet." *CNN*. May 20, 2010. Online: http://www.cnn.com/2010/LIVING/05/20/slavery.descendants.meet/

Dykstra, Robert C. *Discovering a Sermon: Personal Pastoral Preaching*. St. Louis, MO: Chalice, 2001.

Ebeling, Gerhard. *God and Word*. Philadelphia: Fortress, 1967.

———. *Word and Faith*. Philadelphia: Fortress, 1963.

Ernst Fuchs. "The New Testament and the Hermeneutical Problem." In *The New Hermeneutic. Vol. 2 of New Frontiers in Theology*, edited by James M. Robinson and John B. Cobb Jr., 111–45. New York: Harper and Row, 1964.

Eslinger, Richard L. *The Web of Preaching: New Options in Homiletical Method*. Nashville: Abingdon, 2002.

Fitzmyer, Joseph A. "Reconciliation in Pauline Theology." In *To Advance the Gospel: New Testament Studies*, 162–85. New York: Crossroad, 1981.

Forde, Gerhard O. *Theology Is for Proclamation*. Minneapolis: Fortress, 1990.

Fox, Emily Jane. "Enter through the 'Poor Door': Income 'Segregation' in NY." *CNNMoney*. July 28, 2014. http://money.cnn.com/2014/07/28/luxury/housing-inequality-poor-door/?iid=EL.

Galli, Mark, and Craig Brian Larson. *Preaching That Connects: Using the Techniques of Journalists to Add Impact to Your Sermons*. Grand Rapids: Zondervan, 1994.

Geertz, Clifford. *The Interpretation of Cultures: Selected Essays*. New York: Basic, 1973.

Gibson, Scott M. *Preaching for Special Services*. Grand Rapids: Baker, 2001.

The Globe and Mail. "Taking Christ out of Christianity." *The Globe and Mail*. March 22, 2008. Online: http://www.theglobeandmail.com/news/national/taking-christ-out-of-christianity/article674573/.

González, Justo. *The Story of Christianity*. 2nd ed. Vol. 1. New York: HarperOne, 2010.

Grand Avenue Temple. "Making a Difference in Downtown KCMO." Grand Avenue Temple, United Methodist Church. Online: http://grandavenuetempleumc.org/

Greenhaw, David M. "As One with Authority: Rehabilitating Concepts for Preaching." In *Intersections: Post-critical Studies in Preaching*, edited by Richard L. Eslinger, 105–122. Grand Rapids: Eerdmans, 1994.

Gross, Nancy Lammers. *If You Cannot Preach like Paul*. Grand Rapids: Eerdmans, 2002.

Hall, Douglas John. "Confessing Christ in the Religiously Pluralistic Context." In *Many Voices, One God: Being Faithful in a Pluralistic World*, edited by Walter Brueggemann and George W. Stroup, 65–77. Louisville: Westminster, 1998.

———. *The Cross in Our Context: Jesus and the Suffering World*. Minneapolis: Fortress, 2003.

Harader, Joanna. "On Sacrifice and Suffering." *The Christian Century*. March 17, 2015. Online: http://www.christiancentury.org/blogs/archive/2015-03/sacrifice-and-suffering.

Harris, James H. *Preaching Liberation*. Minneapolis: Fortress, 1995.

———. *The Word Made Plain: The Power and Promise of Preaching*. Minneapolis: Fortress, 2004.

Hays, Richard B. *First Corinthians*. Louisville: Westminster, 1997.

Hick, John. *An Interpretation of Religion: Human Responses to the Transcendent*. New Haven: Yale University Press, 1989.

Hilkert, Mary Catherine. *Naming Grace: Preaching and the Sacramental Imagination*. New York: Continuum, 1997.

———. "Preaching the Folly of the Cross." *Word and World* 19.1 (1999) 39–48.

Hoffman, Elisha. "Leaning on the Everlasting Lord." In *Sing to the Lord: Hymnal, Number 596*. Kansas City: Lillenas, 1993.

Howard, Robert. "Gone Baby Gone!." Sermon, Disciples Christ Church from First Christian Church. Globe, AZ, March 29, 2015.

———. "Risen Lord Spotted in Neighborhood Near You!." Sermon, Disciples Christ Church from First Christian Church. Globe, AZ, April 5, 2015.

Howell, Ryan T. "How Do People Define the 'Good Life?'" *Psychology Today*. August 1, 2013. Accessed August 29, 2015.

Hughes, Robert G. *A Trumpet in Darkness: Preaching to Mourners*. Philadelphia: Fortress, 1985.

Inbody, Tyron. *The Many Faces of Christology*. Nashville: Abingdon, 2002.

Ireland, William J. Jr., "When the Wine Gives Out." In *The Library of Distinctive Sermons*, edited by Gary W. Klingsporn, 280–84. Vol. 6. Sisters, OR: Multnomah, 1996.

Irwin, Rose. "Crossroads at the Cross." Sermon, Advanced Preaching Class from United Theological Seminary. Dayton, OH, March 1, 2015.

Jensen, David Hadley. *In the Company of Others: A Dialogical Christology*. Cleveland: Pilgrim, 2001.

Jervis, L. Ann. *At the Heart of the Gospel: Suffering in the Earliest Christian Message*. Grand Rapids: Eerdmans, 2007.

Jeter, Joseph R., and Ronald J. Allen. *One Gospel, Many Ears: Preaching for Different Listeners in the Congregation*. St. Louis: Chalice, 2002.

Jones, L. Gregory. *Embodying Forgiveness: A Theological Analysis*. Grand Rapids: Eerdmans, 1995.

Kay, James F. *Preaching and Theology*. St. Louis: Chalice, 2007.

———. "The Word of the Cross at the Turn of the Ages." *Interpretation* 53.1 (1999) 44–56.

Kepnes, Steven. "A Handbook for Scriptural Reasoning." *Modern Theology* 23.3 (2006) 367–83.

Kilby, Phoebe. "Crossing the Line: Racial Healing in a Family and Community." *Peacebuilder Online*. June 15, 2011. Online: http://emu.edu/now/peacebuilder/2011/06/crossing-the-line-racial-healing-in-a-family-and-community/.

Killinger, John. *Preaching to a Church in Crisis: A Homiletic for the Last Days of the Mainline Church*. Lima, OH: CSS, 1995.

Knitter, Paul F. *Introducing Theologies of Religions*. Maryknoll, NY: Orbis, 2002.

Kohn, Sally. "Is It Enough To Be Politically Correct?" *NPR*. December 19, 2014. Online: http://www.npr.org/2014/12/19/371277215/is-it-enough-to-be-politically-correct.

Kramer, Lindsay. "Super Bowl 2015: How Much Does a 30-second Television Commercial Cost?" *Syracuse*. January 28, 2015. Online: http://www.syracuse.com/superbowl/index.ssf/2015/01/super_bowl_2015_how_much_does_commercial_cost_tv_ad_30_second_spot.html.

LaFountain, Philip N. "Theology and Social Psychology: Pluralism and 'Evangel' in the Thought of Peter Berger and John Howard Yoder." *Theology Today* 69 (2012) 18–33.

Langknecht, Hank. "Easter Sermon." Sermon, Trinity Lutheran Seminary Chapel. Bexley, OH, April 27, 2011.

———. "Easter Vigil Homily on Luke 24:1–12." Homily, Trinity Lutheran Seminary Chapel. Bexley, OH, April 22, 2000.

Lathrop, Gordon. *The Pastor: A Spirituality*. Minneapolis: Fortress, 2006.

Lee, Jung Young. *Korean Preaching: An Interpretation*. Nashville: Abingdon, 1997.

Lindbeck, George A. *The Nature of Doctrine: Religion and Theology in a Postliberal Age*. Philadelphia: Westminster, 1984.

Lindsay, Mark R. Barth, *Israel, and Jesus Karl Barth's Theology of Israel*. Hampshire: Ashgate, 2007.

Lischer, Richard. *The End of Words: The Language of Reconciliation in a Culture of Violence*. Grand Rapids: Eerdmans, 2005.

———. *A Theology of Preaching: The Dynamics of the Gospel*. Nashville: Abingdon, 1981.

Long, Thomas G. "Bold in the Presence of God: Atonement in Hebrews." *Interpretation* 52.1 (1998) 53–69.

———. "Troubled?" Calvin Theological Seminary: Center for Excellence in Preaching. May 22, 2006. Online: http://cep.calvinseminary.edu/audio-sermon-archives/#ss.

———. *What Shall We Say?: Evil, Suffering, and the Crisis of Faith*. Grand Rapids: Eerdmans, 2011.

———. *The Witness of Preaching*. 2nd ed. Louisville: Westminster, 2005.

Loscalzo, Craig A. *Evangelistic Preaching That Connects: Guidance in Shaping Fresh & Appealing Sermons*. Downers Grove, IL: InterVarsity, 1995.

Lose, David J. *Confessing Jesus Christ: Preaching in a Postmodern World*. Grand Rapids: Eerdmans, 2003.

Lowry, Eugene L. *The Homiletical Plot: The Sermon as Narrative Art Form*. Expanded ed. Louisville: Westminster, 2001.

———. *The Sermon: Dancing the Edge of Mystery*. Nashville: Abingdon, 1997.

Making Caring Common Project. "MCCP Report: The Children We Mean to Raise." *Harvard Graduate School of Education*. June 25, 2014. Online: http://www.gse.harvard.edu/news-impact/2014/06/making-caring-common-report-the-children-we-mean-to-raise/.

Marano, Hara Estroff. "The Dangers of Loneliness." *Psychology Today*. July 1, 2003. Online:https://www.psychologytoday.com/articles/200307/the-dangers-loneliness.

McClain, William B. *Come Sunday: The Liturgy of Zion*. Nashville: Abingdon, 1990.

McClure, John S. *Other-wise Preaching: A Postmodern Ethic for Homiletics*. St. Louis: Chalice, 2001.

McDill, Wayne. *The Moment of Truth a Guide to Effective Sermon Delivery*. Nashville: Broadman and Holman, 1999.

McGrath, Alistar. "Cross, Theology of the." In *Dictionary of Paul and His Letters*, edited by Gerald F. Hawthorne and Ralph P. Martin, 192–97. Downers Grove, IL: InterVarsity, 1993.

McKenzie, Alyce M. *Preaching Biblical Wisdom in a Self-help Society*. Nashville: Abingdon, 2002.

Mitchell, Henry H. *Black Preaching: The Recovery of a Powerful Art*. Nashville: Abingdon, 1990.

———. *Celebration and Experience in Preaching*. Nashville: Abingdon, 1990.

Moltmann, Jürgen. *The Crucified God: The Cross of Christ as the Foundation and Criticism of Christian Theology*. New York: Harper & Row, 1974.

Moltmann, Jürgen. *Theology of Hope; on the Ground and the Implications of a Christian Eschatology.* New York: Harper and Row, 1967.

Murphy, Debra Dean. *Teaching That Transforms: Worship as the Heart of Christian Education.* Grand Rapids: Brazos, 2004.

Nelson, Douglas E. "Raging Faith." In *A Chorus of Witnesses: Model Sermons for Today's Preacher,* edited by Thomas G. Long and Cornelius Plantinga, Jr., 44–47. Grand Rapids: Eerdmans, 1994.

Niebuhr, H. Richard. *Christ and Culture.* New York: Harper and Row, 1951.

————. *The Kingdom of God in America.* New York: Harper and Row, 1959.

Nieman, James R., and Thomas G. Rogers. *Preaching to Every Pew: Cross-cultural Strategies.* Minneapolis: Fortress, 2001.

Ondaatje, Michael. *Anil's Ghost.* New York: Alfred A. Knopf, 2000.

Orwin, Clifford. "All Quiet on the (Post) Western Front?" *The Public Interest* 123 (1996) 3–21.

Pacatte, Sr. Rose. "A Decade Later, 'The Passion' Still Raises Questions of Anti-Semitism." *National Catholic Reporter.* February 22, 2014. Online: http://ncronline.org/news/art-media/decade-later-passion-still-raises-questions-anti-semitism.

Pelikan, Jaroslav, and Walter A. Hanson, eds. *Luther's Works: Lectures on Galatians 1535 Chapters 1–4.* Vol. 26. Saint Louis: Concordia, 1963.

Petre, Jonathan. "One Third of Clergy Do Not Believe in the Resurrection." *The Daily Telegraph.* July 31, 2002. Online: http://www.telegraph.co.uk/news/uknews/1403106/One-third-of-clergy-do-not-believe-in-the-Resurrection.html.

Plantinga, Cornelius, and Sue A. Rozeboom. *Discerning the Spirits: A Guide to Thinking about Christian Worship Today.* Grand Rapids: Eerdmans, 2003.

Powery, Luke A. *Dem Dry Bones: Preaching, Death, and Hope.* Minneapolis: Fortress, 2012.

————. *Spirit Speech: Lament and Celebration in Preaching.* Nashville: Abingdon, 2009.

Randolph, David James. *The Renewal of Preaching: A New Homiletic Based on the New Hermeneutic.* Philadelphia: Fortress, 1969.

Rice, Charles Lynvel. *Interpretation and Imagination: The Preacher and Contemporary Literature.* Philadelphia: Fortress, 1970.

Rose, Lucy Atkinson. *Sharing the Word: Preaching in the Roundtable Church.* Louisville: Westminster, 1997.

Samovar, Larry A., and Richard E. Porter. *Communication between Cultures.* Belmont: Wadsworth, 1991.

Sampson II, Frederick G. "The Death of Hope." In *Preaching with Sacred Fire: An Anthology of African American Sermons, 1750 to the Present,* edited by Martha J. Simmons and Frank A. Thomas, 818–22. New York: Norton, 2010.

Sancken, Joni. "Out of the Valley of Broken Dreams." Sermon, Parkview Mennonite Church. Harrisonburg, VA, May 27, 2012.

Schweitzer, Don. *Contemporary Christologies: A Fortress Introduction,* Minneapolis: Fortress, 2010.

Shenk, David W. "Muslims and Christians: Eschatology and Mission." *The International Bulletin of Missionary Research* 33.3 (2009) 120–23.

Singh, David Emmanuel. "Rethinking Jesus and the Cross in Islam." *Mission Studies* 23.2 (2006) 239–60.

Smedes, Lewis B. "Stations on the Journey from Forgiveness to Hope." In *Dimensions of Forgiveness Psychological Research & Theological Perspectives*, edited by Everett L. Worthington, 341–54. Philadelphia: Templeton Foundation, 1998.

Smith, Christian, and Melinda Lundquist Denton. *Soul Searching: The Religious and Spiritual Lives of American Teenagers*. New York: Oxford University Press, 2005.

Smith, Christian, and Patricia Snell. *Souls in Transition: The Religious and Spiritual Lives of Emerging Adults*. Oxford: Oxford University Press, 2009.

Smith, James K. A. *Desiring the Kingdom: Worship, Worldview, and Cultural Formation*. Grand Rapids: Baker, 2009.

Smith, Tovia. "For Most Kids, Nice Finishes Last." *Harvard Graduate School of Education*. July 15, 2014. Online: http://www.npr.org/sections/ed/2014/07/14/331346884/for-most-kids-nice-finishes-last.

Spong, John Shelby. "An Open Letter To the Moderator of the United Church of Canada: The Rt. Rev. Jordan Cantwell." Personal Blog. October 1, 2015. Online: http://johnshelbyspong.com/2015/10/01/an-open-letter-to-the-moderator-of-the-united-church-of-canada-the-rt-rev-jordan-cantwell.

Stendahl, Krister. *Paul among Jews and Gentiles, and Other Essays*. Philadelphia: Fortress, 1976.

Stookey, Laurence Hull. *Calendar: Christ's Time for the Church*. Nashville: Abingdon, 1996.

Stuempfle, Herman G. *Preaching Law and Gospel*. Philadelphia: Fortress, 1978.

Suchocki, Marjorie. *The Whispered Word: A Theology of Preaching*. St. Louis: Chalice, 1999.

Swartley, Willard M. *Covenant of Peace: The Missing Peace in New Testament Theology and Ethics*. Grand Rapids: Eerdmans, 2006.

Taylor, Barbara Brown. "The Silence of God." In *God in Pain: Teaching Sermons on Suffering*, 110–14. Nashville: Abingdon, 1998.

———. "The Will of God." In *God in Pain: Teaching Sermons on Suffering*, 115–19. Nashville: Abingdon, 1998.

———. "Beginning at the End" in *A Chorus of Witnesses: Model Sermons for Today's Preacher* edited by Thomas G. Long and Cornelius Plantinga, Jr., 12–20. Grand Rapids: Eerdmans, 1994.

Thomas, Frank A. *They like to Never Quit Praisin' God: The Role of Celebration in Preaching*. Cleveland, OH: United Church, 1997.

Tillich, Paul. "Communicating the Christian Message: A Question to Christian Ministers and Teachers." In *Theology of Culture*, edited by Robert C. Kimball, 201–13. New York: Oxford University Press, 1959.

Tomson, Peter J. *Presumed Guilty: How the Jews Were Blamed for the Death of Jesus*. Minneapolis: Fortress, 2005.

Trelstad, Marit. "Introduction." In *Cross Examinations: Readings on the Meaning of the Cross*, edited by Marit Trelstad, 1–16. Minneapolis: Fortress, 2006.

"U.S. Religious Landscape Survey: Summary of Key Findings." *Pew Research Forum on Religion & Public Life*. June 1, 2008. Online: http://www.pewforum.org/files/2008/06/report2religious-landscape-study-key-findings.pdf.

Volf, Miroslav. *Exclusion and Embrace: A Theological Exploration of Identity, Otherness, and Reconciliation*. Nashville: Abingdon, 1996.

Watts, Isaac. "Alas and Did My Savior Bleed." *Chalice Hymnal*. St. Louis: Chalice, 1995.

Weaver, J. Denny. "Violence in Christian Theology." In *Cross Examinations: Readings on the Meaning of the Cross*, edited by Marit Trelstad, 225–40. Minneapolis: Fortress, 2006.

Webb, Joseph M. Old *Texts, New Sermons: The Quiet Revolution in Biblical Preaching*. St. Louis: Chalice, 2000.

Webber, Robert. *Ancient-future Time: Forming Spirituality through the Christian Year*. Grand Rapids: Baker, 2004.

———. *The Services of the Christian Year*, Vol. 1. The Complete Library of Christian Worship. Nashville: Hendrickson, 1994.

Williams, Delores. "Black Women's Surrogacy Experiences and the Christian Notion of Redemption." In *Cross Examinations: Readings on the Meaning of the Cross*, edited by Marit Trelstad, 19–32. Minneapolis: Fortress, 2006.

Wilson, Paul Scott. "Beyond Narrative: Imagination in the Sermon." In *Listening to the Word: Studies in Honor of Fred B. Craddock*, edited by Gail R. O'Day and Thomas G. Long, 131–46. Nashville: Abingdon, 1993.

———. *Broken Words: Reflections on the Craft of Preaching*. Nashville: Abingdon, 2004.

———. *The Four Pages of the Sermon: A Guide to Biblical Preaching*. Nashville: Abingdon, 1999.

———. *The Practice of Preaching*. 2nd ed. Nashville: Abingdon, 2007.

———. *Setting Words on Fire: Putting God at the Center of the Sermon*. Nashville: Abingdon, 2008.

Wink, Walter. *The Powers That Be: Theology for a New Millennium*. New York: Doubleday, 1998.

Wynne-Jones, Jonathan. "Two Percent of Anglican Priests Don't Believe in God, Survey Finds." *Independent*. October 27, 2014. Online: http://www.independent.co.uk/news/uk/home-news/survey-finds-2-of-anglican-priests-are-not-believers-9821899.html.